"Captain Bolger has presented the now and future Army a superb treatise on how to train mounted troops in tactics and fieldcraft. As a handbook for young leaders, I consider it superior.... As a text for senior officers on the taxonomy of well-conducted field exercise, it has no peer.

I personally believe, on the evidence of Bolger's account, that the soldiers of Task Force 2-34 Infantry (the Dragons) individually and collectively learned more at Fort Irwin than they might have learned in two weeks of war. And all emerged alive. Those Dragons may no longer serve together, but infantry and armored units in which they will train or fight in years to come will profit from what they learned. The NTC breeds battle-wise soldiers bloodlessly.

That says it all."

Paul F. Gorman
General, U.S. Army (Retired)

Also by Daniel P. Bolger:

AMERICANS AT WAR, 1975–1986
  An Era of Violent Peace

FEAST OF BONES*

Coming from Ivy Books

DRAGONS
AT WAR

LAND BATTLE IN THE DESERT

Daniel P. Bolger

IVY BOOKS • NEW YORK

Ivy Books
Published by Ballantine Books
Copyright © 1986 by Daniel P. Bolger

Library of Congress Catalog Card Number: 86-5018

ISBN 0-8041-0899-4

This edition published by arrangement with Presidio Press

Manufactured in the United States of America

First Ballantine Books Edition: April 1991

For four soldiers:
John W. Bolger, Col. Walter B. Clark,
the late Capt. Kyle L. Edmonds, and the late
Capt. R. Keith Norman

Contents

Preface

The United States Army came up with a winner in the National Training Center (NTC), at Fort Irwin, California. Intensive, realistic operations against determined opposing forces allow visiting units a unique opportunity to hone combat skills and learn about their own organizations. Probably the most important lesson learned at Irwin is that leadership provides the critical variable, despite the wealth of sophisticated, lethal weaponry that surrounds the modern soldier. The nature of battle has changed so much, yet the nature of man has altered so little. The NTC proves time and again that one man can make a difference and that a few trained men can sway an engagement.

The author had the good luck to participate in NTC Rotation 1-83 with Task Force 2-34 Infantry (the Dragons). The battalion task force was led by a cadre of committed, hard-working soldiers, most of them well known to this writer. This chronicle of the battalion's missions offers an insight into how a military unit functions under stress, and it gives a few examples of what soldiers do when they train together for war. There were mistakes and accidents, and they were recorded and analyzed. These are part of the nature of the difficult NTC scenario. There were also small victories and good fortune, duly noted.

Field operations always seem to consist of an attempt to impose order upon confusion, and the challenging Fort Irwin rotation pushed the men of 2-34 Infantry to their limits of skill and endurance. Being there with a cohesive, proud unit such as 2-34 Infantry made it a lot easier for all of us. There was strength in the battalion. Certainly, there were no harder-working officers in the Army than the Dragon leadership. Embarrassing errors occurred, and the author contributed more than his share as the commander of Bravo Company. But, as the NTC observer controllers say, "Don't be thin-skinned." Officers need training too.

Glossary

A-7—USAF Corsair II attack jet; it plays on the OPFOR side at NTC.
AAR—After Action Review.
ADA—Air defense artillery; antiaircraft guns and missiles.
ADC-T—Assistant division commander for training; a full colonel.
ADM—Atomic demolition mine.
Air assault—A tactical movement of a ground unit by helicopter as part of an ongoing combat operation. This normally implies combat at the landing zone.
ALOC—Administration-Logistics Operations Center. This is where supply, maintenance, and personnel actions are designed and coordinated. The logistics officer (S-4) and adjutant (S-1) share the ALOC, with the S-4 in charge.
APC—Armored personnel carrier.
ARTEP—Army Training and Evaluation Program; a list of tasks, conditions, and standards for unit training in the performance of combat missions. ARTEPs exist for all units from squad/crew to battalion task force, to include combat support and combat service support elements. Often, the ARTEP is considered as a "test," especially when evaluators are supplied by external units.
AT—Antitank.
Attachment—Temporary assignment of a force to another higher headquarters. Along with tactical control, the new commander must insure full logistic support for the attachment.
AVLB—Armored vehicle launched bridge.

BMP (*Boyevaya mashina pekhoty*)—Armored infantry vehicle used by the Soviet army. It carries a 73-mm gun and an AT-3 Sagger antitank missile. The Fort Irwin OPFOR reproduce this particular type.
BRDM—A small, lightly armored, wheeled Soviet armored vehicle. It is used for reconnaissance, antitank, air defense, and command and control tasks. The OPFOR at Fort Irwin recreate this vehicle.
Button up—Close up vehicle hatches. Vision is greatly limited with hatches shut.

CALFEX—Combined Arms Live Fire Exercise; a training mission involving the integration of all direct fire, indirect fire, Army aviation, and Air Force close air support.
CEV—Combat engineer vehicle, M728. An engineer version of the M-60 tank, the CEV features a short-barrelled 165-mm demolition gun, a dozer blade, and a heavy-duty A-frame to assist in movement of barriers.
Chaparral—U.S. air defense missile, based on the Sidewinder air-to-air missile.
Company team—A combined-arms organization of tank and mechanized infantry platoons under a tank or mechanized infantry headquarters.
Counterbattery—Indirect fires delivered on enemy indirect fire means.

Cross-attachment—The exchange of one or more mechanized infantry platoons from a mechanized infantry company for one or more tank platoons from a tank company.

CSC—Combat support company.

CS irritant gas—A riot-control chemical agent whose acrid fumes affect the respiratory tract and exposed skin surfaces. CS causes tears, skin irritation, and possibly nausea. It is used as a chemical warfare training aid by U.S. forces.

CSS—Combat service support; supply, personnel administration, maintenance, and medical services.

Dragon—The U.S. M-47 medium antitank guided missile with 1,000-meter range; or a member of 2-34 Infantry.

DS—Direct support. This command relation requires one support unit (engineers, field artillery, or air defense, for example) to furnish priority support to a designated unit. A DS unit responds to the needs of this single element, rather than to the force as a whole.

EA—Engagement area. In the defense, a means of controlling fires.

FA—Field artillery.

FASCAM—Field artillery scatterable mines.

FFT—Force-on-force training; U.S. against the live OPFOR, using MILES and training ammunition.

FIST—Fire support team; the artillery forward observers/fire planners sent over to direct artillery, mortars, and close air support for infantry and armored companies.

FO—Forward observer.

FORSCOM—United States Army Forces Command, with headquarters at Fort McPherson, Georgia. Forces Command supervises active Army and Army Reserve units in the continental United States. FORSCOM insures those elements are prepared for combat deployment.

FRAGORD—Fragmentary order; an abbreviated operation order.

FSO—Fire support officer.

GS—General Support. This command relation requires one support unit (engineers, field artillery, or air defense, for example) to respond to the force as a whole. A GS unit has the flexibility to provide support to several units' needs or the requests of the supported commander.

GSR—Ground surveillance radar.

HHC—Headquarters and Headquarters Company.

ITV—The U.S. M901 Improved TOW Vehicle. This M113 variant has a cantilever double-tube launcher/sight turret that can be lifted hydraulically from behind cover.

LAW/Viper—U.S. unguided light antitank rocket. The Viper was never produced, though the name survives in the MILES simulator for the LAW (which has been in production since Vietnam).

LD—Line of departure; it must be crossed exactly on time to permit a coordinated attack.

LFT—Live-fire training; U.S. against automated targets, using actual ammunition.

LP—Listening post, usually used at night.

M60—A U.S. main battle tank; also the model number of a U.S. 7.62-mm infantry machine gun.

M113—The U.S. armored personnel carrier.

Mechanized—With reference to U.S. Infantry, these troops make use of armored personnel carriers.

Medevac—Medical evacuation, usually by helicopter for training accidents.

MILES—Multiple Integrated Laser Engagement System. This training device allows U.S. soldiers to "shoot" and "get shot," using eye-safe lasers.

MOPP—Mission oriented protective posture. This refers to the use of chemical suits, boots, gloves, and masks in various combinations, as determined by the U.S. mission, enemy threat, and weather situation.

MOPP suit—Chemical protection suit.

MRB—Motorized rifle battalion.

MRR—Motorized rifle regiment.

MTLB—A Soviet lightly armored, tracked personnel carrier. The Soviets use this track to carry artillery ammunition, for command and control, and other utility tasks. At Fort Irwin, the OPFOR mechanized infantry ride in actual MTLBs captured by Israel in Middle East combat.

NBC—Nuclear/biological/chemical.

OCs—Observer controllers.

OER—Officer Evaluation Report; this document is prepared by an officer's superiors and reports his performance to Department of the Army.

OP—Observation post.

OPCON—Operational control. This command relation places a subordinate unit under a headquarters for tactical orders only. The parent formation retains supply and administrative responsibilities.

OPFOR—Opposing Forces, especially those of the Warsaw Pact armies and their allies. Specifically, OPFOR are the Soviet-model unit portrayed by specially trained U.S. battalions at the National Training Center.

OPORD—Operation order.

Parrumphs—Irregular light infantry guerrilla units employed in support of Fort Irwin OPFOR operations.

"Pull" Logistics—The use of requests to supply centers, followed by pickup by the requesting unit.

"Push" Logistics—Sometimes called "log packs"; the assembly of ready-made collections of food, fuel, and ammunition brought up to fighting units in escorted convoy under battalion task force supervision.

RDF—Rapid Deployment Force.

Redeye—Short-range surface-to-air heat-seeking missile, carried by two-man air defense teams.

RPG—Rocket-propelled grenade; Soviet light antitank weapon.

S-1—Adjutant, personnel officer.

S-2—Intelligence officer.

S-3—Operations officer.

S-4—Logistics officer.

SA-9—Soviet surface-to-air missile, carried aboard the BRDM.

Sagger—This Soviet antitank guided missile has a 3,000-meter range. It is slower and less accurate than the U.S. TOW.

SAU-122—A Soviet self-propelled, tracked 122-mm howitzer. Fort Irwin's OPFOR have created a replica of this model.

Stand-to—The time, usually prior to dawn, when all men must be awake, cleaned up, in position, and with weapons ready. Wake-up must be well prior to stand-to.

T-72—A Soviet tank, with a 125-mm cannon. The OPFOR at Fort Irwin reproduce this particular model.

Task Force—Battalion-sized combined arms organization built around tanks and mechanized infantry.

Team—A portion of an infantry squad; or a company-sized combined arms organization.

TOC—Tactical Operations Center. This is where combat operations are planned and controlled. Operations, intelligence, and fire support sections make up the TOC, along with affiliated communications and security. The operations officer (S-3) is responsible for internal TOC structure and function. The headquarters company commander moves and secures the TOC.

TOW—Tube-launched, optically tracked, wire-guided heavy antitank guided missile. With its 3,000-meter range, good accuracy, and powerful warhead, the TOW is a principal antiarmor weapon in mechanized infantry units.

Trains—Logistics facilities. Those at higher level are progressively less mobile.

VTR—Vehicle tracked recovery; a maintenance tracked vehicle that tows and helps repair damaged and inoperative vehicles.

Vulcan—U.S. air defense cannon.

Wheels—The U.S. jeeps and supply/maintenance trucks that support each tank and infantry company.

XO—Executive officer.

ZSU-23-4—Self-propelled, light-armored, quad-barrel 23-mm Soviet air defense gun track. The Fort Irwin OPFOR deploy a re-creation of this type of vehicle.

Guide to Military Map Symbols

Units:

```
                          ┌──── UNIT SIZE
                          │
UNIT ──── 2 ⊠ B ──── SUPERIOR UNIT DESIGNATION
DESIGNATION   └──────── BRANCH/FUNCTION
```

Unit Sizes: ## US/ OPFOR Units:

- · SQUAD
- ·· SECTION   US   OPFOR
- ··· PLATOON   ☐   ⬚
- · COMPANY ⊓ TEAM
- " BATTALION ⊓ TASK FORCE
- ''' REGIMENT

Unit Types:

⊠ MECHANIZED INFANTRY	◸ AIR DEFENSE	⊞ MEDICAL
⊠ INFANTRY	⊠ MECHANIZED ARTILLERY	⊠ GROUND RADAR
⊘ ARMORED CAVALRY SCOUT/RECON	△ ANTITANK	⌁ SIGNAL
⬭ ARMOR	⊓ ENGINEER	⊠ MAINTENANCE
☐ SUPPLY	● TRANSPORT	⌧ CHEMICAL
☐ TRAINS	☐ COMMAND POST	△ OBSERVATION POST

Tactical Symbols:

US	OPFOR			
⊟	⊟	TANK	▭ MINEFIELD	⬤ ARTILLERY DELIVERED MINES
◇	◆	APC	▲▲▲ ANTITANK DITCH	
(NONSTANDARD)			>──< LANE	XXXXX BARBED WIRE
⊷	☐ TANK		TANK TRAIL	HARD-TOP ROAD
⬭ ☐	☐ APC			
⬫ ☐		ITV		

Chapter One

A Desert Area As Big As Rhode Island

"It's the most stressful environment I've ever been in, including the war in Vietnam. The pace is tremendous. There is no time to stop and regroup or reorganize."[1]
A battalion commander after an NTC rotation

The sun is still just a rosy hint in the east, and the star sprinkle is fading into the vast blue vault of the departing night. The torn, jagged edge of the Soda Mountains etches a dark silhouette against the brightening sky. The desert floor is in deep shadow, and the western mountains' dawn-side facings are beginning to lighten, along their jumbled peaks. The desert appears silent, empty, and pristine. Not even the slightest breeze touches the tough little creosote bushes that carpet the sand and rocks. Appearances, however, are deceiving. Tired eyes strain in dusty binoculars, and dirty hands shield nervous faces, eyes gazing to the east. They have waited all night, shivering through the black hours in scooped-out foxholes and road-weary tanks, waiting and watching, looking toward the coming dawn. Many are nodding in fits and starts or rubbing stubbled chins and red eyes, trying hard to pay attention. The men crouch and stretch, their thin lines of weapons and vehicles strung across the forward edge of low ridges in disconnected clusters. Hidden in the shadows below and before them are a long, zigzag, antiarmor ditch, wire rolls and fences, and a deep minefield. The men feel ready.

There! There they are! Plumes of white dust rise and glisten miles away. It is the sign of the enemy, the rolling collection of "rooster tails" kicked up by their massed T-72 tank and BMP infantry fighting vehicle formations. They are still a good five miles out, their squat green vehicles indistinguishable in the shadows. But the dust clouds, tenuous harbingers of battle, move relentlessly closer.

Field phones buzz and radios crackle as vigilant outposts

report the activity. Airwaves and landline wires fill with inquiries and messages. Calls go out to the artillery, but, despite repeated requests, the big guns do not answer. A frantic scout tries to raise the heavy mortar; there is no reply. Could the wire be cut? Were the mortar crews still sleeping? The shift sergeant at the battalion Tactical Operations Center (TOC) had not told anyone that the mortars have been off the radio net all night, so the unanswered pleas continue.

A few explosions of enemy artillery indicate that opposing communications are indeed intact. More ominously, smoke begins to build from several locations about a mile and a half in front of the battalion's positions. Weather conditions have created a temperature inversion that allows the smoke to settle and develop into a thick, maddeningly impenetrable blanket. The defending American battalion commander, departing the battalion TOC, knows that the smoke will blind his long-range tank gun and antitank missile sights. If only the battalion had been issued the new thermal sights before deploying! But they had not. Behind the smokescreen, the enemy rolls on.

As if losing visual contact were not bad enough, the lieutenant colonel commanding the American battalion soon discovers serious problems in directing his companies and platoons. The radios whine and warble with enemy jamming, broken only by chopped bits and pieces of reports from the scouts and company forward positions. Rushing over the granite rocks and creosote scrub in his dirty brown armored personnel carrier, the commander vainly tries to call brigade headquarters for assistance. Artillery frequencies hum with silence and the Air Force liaison officer is broken down somewhere and out of touch. A momentary lapse in the heavy radio interference reveals a vehicle count by a scout sergeant—thirty T-72 tanks or more, at least eighty infantry carriers. It is a full-scale regimental attack, and the battalion will have to try to handle it alone. The enemy is but three miles away, advancing unmolested.

Smoke lies like thick cotton across the battalion front. It hangs there, filling TOW missile sights and tank reticles with nothingness. The colonel orders his infantry to get down to the antitank ditch with hand-held armor-defeating weapons. B Company responds through the barrage jamming and sends its foot soldiers into the thick white clouds to defend the battalion's obstacle system and minefields. A Company and the attached tank company cannot be raised. The colonel calls his

TOC and tells them to call those units on the field wire, but the communications officer discloses that the wire to the tank company never went in and that A Company's line rings repeatedly without an answer. The colonel, who had only three hours of broken sleep in the past seventy-two, curses impotently across the radio. Nobody hears him through the jamming.

Enemy shells are exploding across the frontline positions, driving gunners into their tanks and fighting positions. A Company and the tank company do not consider sending anyone into the clouds of smoke to protect the mines and wire and the critical, snaking antitank ditch. The battalion mortars remain off the net. Only the scouts, the TOW platoon, and B Company are in communications. It is the TOWs who first report the chemical attack.

"Gas!" is the cry across the cluttered, rasping, half-jammed battalion radio net. The busting artillery spreads the chemical attack in the still dawn air. Like the smokescreen, the gas does not dissipate. Everyone does not get the word, and in this moment of choking and struggling into greasy, sweaty rubber masks, the enemy's tanks break out of the smoke.

The TOC officer, muffled by the stifling protective mask, calls the colonel to say that the enemy has breached the mines, torn out the wire, and caved in the ditch in multiple places. The colonel's APC is still bouncing forward to a vantage point, but he knows the smell of things already. They breached too easily, he thought. They must have cut gaps the night before. It was too late now. His APC grinds to a halt, and he leans out of the cargo hatch.

Below and to the right his tank guns and infantrymen bark fire at the enemy tanks and infantry vehicles wriggling through the obstacle lanes and out of the smoke. Opposing artillery blasts regularly surround the battalion's beleaguered gunners. Gas drifts lazily into the low spots as his masked soldiers labor over their weapons.

The enemy return fire is accurate as tanks and BMP infantry carriers halt briefly to shoot at their tormenters. The colonel could see it was about an even tradeoff as vehicles slow to a halt and quit firing on both sides. The enemy outnumbers him three to one and can afford to take some hits. Could he reposition anyone to the next battle position? He calls B Company. Nothing. A Company and the tank company are also silent. The TOC elbows through the jamming to announce that scouts observed the tank company being overrun and that B Company's commander had dropped off the net shortly after heading down to the tank ditch. The battalion commander stares down, watching the clouds of smoke beginning to separate as enemy BMPs flood through the barrier's many holes. They were through; they were going for the trucks and supplies parked in the nearly defenseless combat trains. The TOC hears the TOWs go under, buried by more than a company of determined BMPs and T-72s. Then the enemy rolls into the TOC itself, destroying the command post by fire before charging on.

The colonel watches the enemy's trail elements clear the gaps, under desultory fire from the stunned survivors of the battalion. The sun is still not even above the horizon. It has taken the colonel only seventeen minutes to lose his entire command. Another day at the Fort Irwin National Training Center is under way.

The United States Army National Training Center at Fort Irwin, California, is a unique place. It is a one-thousand-square-mile classroom without walls, a 642,820-acre playing field complete with a very determined, wily "home team" unaccustomed to losing. Fort Irwin, known as the NTC in Army circles, is both an education and a test. Unlike many large-scale military operations, the pressures of political scrutiny and public revelations do not play a major part. A cadre of skilled, pitiless evaluators investigate and assess every action in the cold light of published Army doctrine and meticulously arrive at realistic combat results. Like all good military training, the NTC experience is extremely demanding. It is training that, to quote the United States Army Forces Command (FOR-SCOM) "comes as close to the reality of combat as is possible within the constraints of safety and resources."

There were several reasons why Fort Irwin became the site of the Army's most grueling stateside training. For one thing the post is gigantic, with over half a million acres of usable training land. It is bordered by the Death Valley National Monument to the north and the China Lake Naval Weapons Center (home of the Sidewinder air-to-air missile and other high-technology implements of destruction) to the west and northwest. Other neighbors in the California desert include Edwards Air Force Base sixty miles or so southwest and Twenty-nine Palms Marine Corps Base sixty miles or so southeast. Barstow is the nearest town of any size, and even it is thirty-five miles to the southwest of the grim little Fort Irwin cantonment.

Barstow, for the record, is more than one hundred twenty miles northeast of Los Angeles, well beyond the San Gabriel Mountains. Also, Barstow is more than one hundred fifty miles from that desert rhinestone, Las Vegas. Irwin would mean utter isolation and boredom to the average American. To the Army, it means unlimited space for maneuvers, no upset civilians nearby, and plenty of landscape in which to shoot everything from pistols to heavy artillery.

And what a savage, unusual landscape it is! The area was formed at the close of the last glacial period when several nearby volcanoes were still active. The action of vulcanism and scouring glaciers provided a mix of rocky mountain peaks, lava fields, and wide, rolling valley floors. Fort Irwin is a high desert, with an average elevation well over 1,000 feet. It is littered with igneous rock, and it has three small mountain ranges—Tiefort to the south; Granite in the western central region; and the Avawatz, straddling the northeast boundary of the post, the southern wall of Death Valley. The mountain ranges have many spurs and outcroppings, usually sloping gently to the valley floor, but in spots they rise as sheer cliffs.

Irwin's climate is typical of high desert. Summer temperatures usually exceed 100 degrees Fahrenheit in the daytime, dropping into the 70s at night. In the winter months, days range into the low 80s, and nights are often near freezing. The prevailing west winds rise as the day heats up. Gusts over sixty-five miles per hour can occur, especially in the winter.

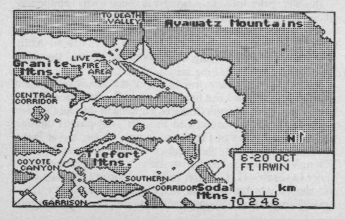

The relative humidity is low, around 25 to 35 percent in the hot
season and only about 40 to 65 percent in the cold periods.
Precipitation is minimal, but when it does rain, the effect is
dramatic. Most rain occurs in the winter time, though even July
and August have an occasional shower. The rainfall often cre-
ates flash floods, which move rapidly through canyons and
washes, seeking the low ground. These floods travel long distances in the scrabbly gullies, producing a loud, rumbling
noise. Naturally, these ''gully washers'' have a pronounced
effect on the terrain. The lower slopes of all hills and mountains are laced with ditches and steambeds, and many valleys
are as wrinkled as washboards from this effect. In deference to
similar landforms in the Sahara, these washes also are called
wadis. They range from shallow trenches to wide, high-walled
cuts that are almost canyons. To soldiers, this broken terrain is
a defender's delight. It offers cover from direct-fire weapons.

Plant life is very much in evidence, although the bushes and
shrubs are stunted and average only three to four feet in height.
Every valley and rolling slope is carpeted with yellow-green
creosote bushes, the main form of vegetation at Irwin, although
the shadscale scrub, alkali sink, Joshua tree, Mojave yucca,
and blackbush juniper can also be found. Only a botanist can
tell the difference. The plants have thick stems that can easily
puncture a wandering jeep tire. At night creosote looks dis-
tressingly akin to the basaltic rock lumps that share the land
with the bushes. Dismounted troops can hide in the shrubs.
Vehicles cannot find such concealment.

Besides rocky hillsides, sandy water-cut wadis, and valley
floors dotted with creosote, Irwin also has seven dry lake beds,
called *playas*. Each bed is the low end of a particular valley
drainage system. One of them (Bicycle Lake) is an Army
airfield. Archaeologists dig routinely at the playas, searching
for primitive artifacts.

Before the Army came to Fort Irwin, the area was inhabited
by the Pinta Indians. The Spaniard priest Fr. Francisco Garces
passed just south of Irwin in 1769, en route to present-day San
Bernardino. The so-called Old Spanish Trail passed through
the southeast corner of Fort Irwin, with a major stop at Bitter
Spring. John Fremont, the Pathfinder, passed that way in 1844.
The Army established a small garrison at Bitter Spring in 1860
under Lt. James H. Carleton (later a major general). In 1885
the discovery of borax in the area established the Borax Trail,
running from Death Valley south past Bicycle Lake, roughly

paralleling the modern route of the Irwin-Barstow Road, the path of the famous twenty-mule teams.

Modern Fort Irwin became a military reservation in 1940, when it was used to train antiaircraft units, taking advantage of the clear skies and remote location. In 1942 the desert reserve was named Camp Irwin, after Maj. Gen. G. Leroy Irwin, who commanded the 57th Field Artillery Brigade in World War I. The camp was deactivated in 1951. Reopened in August 1961 as Fort Irwin, the post remained in use by the regular Army until 1971. In September 1972 Irwin was turned over to the California National Guard for reserve-unit training.

The development of a National Training Center at Fort Irwin was a response to several interrelated military conditions that arose in the 1970s. Foremost among those was the poor state of the U.S. Army at the end of the Vietnam War.

Vietnam hurt the Army more than it did most American institutions. The American military had been unable to accomplish its mission, despite a lot of expensive, high-technology gear and a sincere effort by most of the uniformed professionals. Leaving aside political restrictions on Army actions and sidestepping for the moment the cultural damage done by a cruelly unfair draft system and the strident, sadly misinformed young agitators, the Army recognized early that much of the disaster was traceable to self-inflicted damage. After all, the Army had designed the bizarre, 365-day "unvacation" plan for troop rotation. The Army had installed air-conditioned officers' clubs and pizza huts, swimming pools and golf courses in vulnerable rear-base areas. Commanders led from a thousand feet up in command and control helicopters on too many occasions, in accord with Army doctrine.[2] And in an ill-considered decision guaranteed to have a deleterious effect on morale, most commanders led for six months only, then rotated to staff and safety. The justification was "seasoning" as many leaders as possible. The results were contempt among the year-tour infantrymen for their constantly changing leaders, an insatiable demand for junior officers (resulting in the likes of Rusty Calley), and units where the command was changed more frequently than the GIs' rotting jungle fatigues. It was all conscious, Army-derived policy. The Army had given itself a series of debilitating headshots.

The Army's ability to fight "two and a half" wars (the McNamara theory) was proven sadly hollow. Korea, the continental United States, Hawaii, Alaska, and especially Ger-

many were stripped to the bone to feed Vietnam. Basic
training, NCO schools, and officer instruction were geared to
the Southeast Asian world of helicopters, fire bases, patrols,
ambushes, cordon and search, and the wiles of the Vietnamese
enemy. It could be validly argued that the Army got so busy
worrying about the proxies of Moscow in Indochina that it
damn near forgot about the real things squatting across the
border in Europe. This argument prevailed in the Army as
disengagement from Vietnam concluded. The U.S. Army,
bleeding from multiple organizational cuts and shots, its im-
potence alleged worldwide, needed a mission.

The Russians obliged. After the Cuban missile crisis of
1962, which resulted in Moscow's humiliation, the Russians
began arming at a tremendous rate, lavishly rebuilding their
vast tank fleets, producing nuclear-tipped ICBMs, churning out
fighter planes and submarines, building every weapon imagin-
able from bayonets to ballistic missiles. It seemed Russia had
suddenly decided to become *the* military power on the globe.
It certainly did not bode well for the Americans with their
ill-trained, gutted Seventh Army in West Germany.

The 1973 Arab-Israeli War was viewed in the U.S. Army as
a small-scale rehearsal of what it would be like to tangle with
the Russians in "conventional" (versus nuclear or guerrilla)
warfare. Many "lessons" were perceived, and to a few not
much argument was offered. First, armored warfare was still
viable and could be effective. Third, Israeli initiative, training,
and tactical doctrine, coupled with somewhat better equipment, allowed Israel, outnumbered, to fight and win. The Syr-
ians and Egyptians fought pretty much by the Warsaw Pact
book, with first-rate Soviet tanks and missiles and a big advantage in numbers. They surprised Israel, but the Israeli army
fought them to a halt and counterattacked successfully. American military men hoped that this presaged an American response in case of Soviet aggression in Europe.

Either way, the Americans had to get their heads out of the
jungle and back into the big leagues of Europe. Doctrine,
weapons, and training all needed revision. The draft was gone,
so previously accepted truisms such as unlimited manpower
were over. Equipment would be less than desirable. The reserves, the unholy mess of the National Guard with its old M1
rifles, had to be refitted and, for a change, seriously trained and
evaluated. Training had to get back to basics. U.S. forces
overseas in Germany and, to a lesser extent, Korea, became

high priorities. When a new idea or item of gear came out, it went overseas first. Slowly, imperceptibly at first, then more quickly, improvement came.

Army units in Germany could maneuver on the ground they would operate on if "the balloon went up." The Seventh Army had fine, well-established ranges and exercises at major training areas such as Grafenwoehr and Hohenfels. It had the mighty autumnal REFORGER war games every year. It had first call on training bullets and fuel and money, and it became pretty adept.

Units in the United States did not fare as well in the 1970s era of limited Army budgets. In effect, they were levied and stripped as needed to fill Europe and Korea. They were last in line for money and facilities, making do rather than training. It was tough on units such as the 1st Division at Fort Riley, which had a brigade in West Germany and equipment stockpiled there for its other men to fly to in event of war (the REinFORcement of GERmany—hence REFORGER). Army leaders began to pre-position more equipment in the Federal Republic of Germany by the late seventies, and pretty soon almost every mechanized and armored unit in the lower forty-eight had a mission in Germany. By 1979 equipment was concentrated overseas for the 1st Infantry Cavalry Division, 4th Infantry Division, 2d Armored Division, and 1st Cavalry Division (an armored unit).[3] Reserve units were also given missions in NATO, and everyone had to learn how to fight the Soviets. Digging huge ditches, blowing up demolitions, tearing new tank trails, firing heavy artillery, coordinating attack helicopters, and close air support—it all took space and money not readily available on most American posts. And that was why Fort Irwin became important.

Irwin was seen as the place where U.S.-based units could go to exercise the way their counterparts in Germany did. It would be better than Germany—no burgermeisters complaining about artillery rocking the rathaus or Polizei chasing tanks down the autobahn. It was available immediately, and the only real problem was that it was a high rocky desert, more like central Iran than like central Europe.

Enter the Ayatollah Khomeini, who trashed ten years of American cooperation with the fickle Shah of Iran in a tumultuous religious upheaval in February 1979. The high-priced but available Persian Gulf crude oil flow seemed in jeopardy, especially once the Ayatollah's thugs outdid even Shah Reza

Pahlavi's hated SAVAK by seizing the American embassy on 4 November 1979. As if this were not enough trouble, in December 1979 the Soviet Union elected to intervene with ground troops in Iran's backward, oil-poor neighbor, Afghanistan. With the rapid, unexpected collapse of the Shah, the U.S. Army was caught watching the front porch of Europe while the back door at the Straits of Hormuz swung open. There was a real joker in the deck, all right.

President Jimmy Carter, convinced at last that the Russians were really bent on mayhem, announced in January 1980 that the United States could not and would not tolerate foreign hands on the Persian Gulf petroleum jugular. This was the formal, public birth of the Rapid Deployment Force (RDF),[4] the American units oriented to securing United States interests in the Persian Gulf. The RDF had a broad charter on a place half a world away. It would counter threats of internal instability (as in the Ayatollah's Iran), regional conflict (the festering Iran-Iraq war, for example), and, most especially, any Soviet move into the oil states. In summary, the RDF would go in if the oil stopped coming out.

Irwin/Iran was a convenient connection, to be sure. Irwin's high desert was eerily similar to that of Iran. There was only so much Army, and many REFORGER units and other divisions committed to Germany also drew RDF missions. The Russians would be about the same wherever they reared their heads, and the idea of the Central Front in Germany now had a validly disturbing competitor in the Persian Gulf. Irwin became really vital, as there were no (nor diplomatically could there be) U.S. forces already in place in the Persian Gulf. The Army's RDF needed a training area.

The Army's RDF units were all based in the continental United States, so Irwin was accessible to them. Its wide valleys and remote location would allow free use of heavy weapons, air power, and large maneuver units. Those units not designated for RDF contingencies would still learn the principles of full-scale combined-arms warfare in a gigantic natural arena uninhibited by safety constraints or range limits. The Soviet threat was real enough and Congress would furnish the money needed to create the National Training Center at Fort Irwin.

Still, other good training areas were possibilities, especially Fort Hood, Texas. Even the excellent, varied challenge of the Irwin terrain would serve to allow men to experience only the desert. Units that might fight in Europe needed more than that.

What was necessary to make the NTC unique was an application of a technique developed as a result of aerial combat over North Vietnam. What the Army wanted was a real, live enemy.

Notes

1. Maj. Charles R. Steiner, "Thunder in the Desert," *Armor*, May/June 1982, 12.

2. Lt. Gen. John H. Hay, Jr., *Vietnam Studies: Tactical and Material Innovations* (Washington, D.C.: U S. Government Printing Office, 1973), 82. See also Michael Maclear, *The Ten Thousand Day War* (New York: St. Martin's Press, 1981), 324–25.

3. The 1st Infantry Division of Fort Riley, Kansas, tested the RE-FORGER concept in the early 1970s. Currently, there are four prepositioned equipment sites in West Germany, three in the south and one in the north. Two more such sets will be finished by late 1986 in the Netherlands. In the present interim plan the 2d Armored Division will use the single northern base, with the 1st Infantry, 4th Infantry, and 1st Cavalry divisions to the south. The eventual plan allocates the northern sites to the III Corps (2d Armored, 1st Cavalry, and 5th Infantry divisions) and the southern locations to the 1st Infantry, 4th Infantry, and 24th Infantry divisions.

4. The Rapid Deployment Force, officially activated in 1980 as the Rapid Deployment Joint Task Force (RDJTF), is now under the United States Central Command (CENTCOM), activated at MacDill Air Force Base, Florida, on 1 January 1983. Army RDF units serve under Third Army, Fort McPherson, Georgia.

Note: Other sources for material in this chapter include: Col. Taft C. Ring, "The Evolution of Training Strategy in the 24th Mech" (Fort Stewart, Ga.: 24th Infantry Division Mechanized, 27 May 1983); 7th Infantry Division, "Terrain Analysis: Fort Irwin, Brave Shield XVII" (Fort Ord, Calif.: 7th Infantry Division, 1 January 1978); Col. E. S. Leland, Jr. "Mojave Victory Dependent Information" (Fort Stewart, Ga.: 1st Brigade, 24th Infantry Division [Mechanized], October 1980); Gen. William C. Westmoreland, *A Soldier Reports* (Garden City, N.Y.: Doubleday, 1976); Gen. Glenn K. Otis, "The Enormous Responsibility of Preventing World War III," *Army*, October 1983; President James Earl Carter, "The State of the Union Address," 20 January 1980; Gen. Richard E. Cavazos, "Readiness Goal Is Ability to Deploy on Short Notice," *Army*, October 1983.

Chapter Two

The OPFOR

"When I lecture to Western officers on tactics in the Soviet Army, I often close my talk by putting a question to them—always the same one—in order to be sure that they have understood me correctly. The question is trivial and elementary. Three Soviet motor-rifle companies are on the move in the same sector. The first has come under murderous fire, and its attack has crumbled; the second is advancing slowly, with heavy losses; the third has suffered an enemy counterattack and, having lost all of its command personnel, is retreating. The commander of the regiment to which these companies belong has three tank companies and three artillery batteries in reserve. Try and guess, I say, how this regimental commander uses his reserves to support his three companies. 'You are to guess,' I say, 'what steps a Soviet regimental commander would take, not a Western one but a Soviet, a Soviet, a Soviet one.'

"I have never yet received the correct reply.

"Yet in this situation there is only one possible answer. From the platoon level to that of the Supreme Commander all would agree that there is only one possible decision: all three tank companies and all three artillery batteries must be used to strengthen the company that is moving ahead, however slowly. The others, which are suffering losses, certainly do not qualify for help. If the regimental commander, in a state of drunkenness or from sheer stupidity, were to make any other decision he would, of course, be immediately relieved of command, reduced to the ranks, and sent to pay for his mistake with his own blood, in a penal battalion.

"My audiences ask, with surprise, how it can be that two company commanders, whose men are suffering heavy casualties, can ask for help without receiving any? 'That's the way it is,' I reply, calmly. 'How can there be any doubt about it?'

" 'What happens,' ask the Western officers, 'if a Soviet platoon or company commander asks for artillery support? Does he get it?'

" 'He has no right to ask for it,' I say.

" 'And if a company commander asks for air support—does he get it?'

" 'He has no right to ask for support of any sort, let alone air support.'

"My audience smiles—they believe they have found the Achilles heel of Soviet tactics. But I am always irritated—for this is not a weakness, but strength."

Viktor Suvorov, Inside the Soviet Army[1]

The Vietnam War was not much like the one in Korea, especially in the air battles over the north. America's civilian and military leadership evolved a tortuous, straight-jacketed set of rules of engagement for those flying into North Vietnam. Aside from using fighter bombers (B-52s were thought too provocative in the minds of those who hoped the North Vietnamese were playing incremental escalation), following flight paths that zigzagged like the path of SAM-sucking pinballs, and bombing targets selected by high-level civilians over working breakfasts, the air war by 1968 was looking bad for the visiting team from across the Pacific. The incredibly high kill ratios of "MiG Alley" over Korea were not to be found in the scudding clouds and heavy flak over Haiphong. Two enemy jets to one Yankee plane was the usual exchange, a far cry from the 13:1 ratio of the Yalu in 1950–53. American pilots from the Air Force and aviators from the Navy started to wonder what had gone wrong. There they were with hotshot Century Series fighter-bombers such as the F-105 and multipurpose, carrier-launched F-4 Phantom jets, hung all over with powerful radars and death-dealing, long-range radar missiles. And, damn, the stuff just wasn't doing the deed.

The Navy got the message first. Captain Frank W. Ault, former commander of the aircraft carrier USS *Coral Sea*, directed a study entitled, innocuously enough, "Air-to-Air Systems Capability Review of 1968" for U.S. Naval Air Systems Command. Captain Ault's report gave the bottom line that everyone in the fighter community had suspected—poor dogfighting skills, over-reliance on "wonder weapons" like the disappointing Sparrow missile, and insufficient training on the air-to-air combat mission. Somehow, in between taking out bridges in Route Pack Four and practicing to lob the Big One on Vladivostok, the nuts and bolts of aerial fighting had been glossed over. The Navy acted on the report. VF-121, which trained replacement aviators for Vietnam, instituted a special course devoted to close combat between jets. It was nicknamed Top Gun, and it worked. From 1969 to 1972, naval fliers dropped thirteen Vietnamese jets for every one they lost.

But that was only half the solution. Top Gun pitted F-4s against F-4s, both pilots hot and heavy but flying in a style and an aircraft made in the United States. The Air Force took things one step beyond. Its Red Baron study confirmed the results of the Ault Report and stated that pilots had the best chance of surviving after they had completed their first ten missions. The USAF decided to provide those first ten missions in training. In 1972 it established the 64th Fighter Weapons Squadron at Nellis Air Force Base, Nevada, near Las Vegas and just across Death Valley from Fort Irwin. The 64th was organized as an "Aggressor" squadron, flying little T-38 Talon trainers, then the similar F-5E Freedom Fighter. The Aggressors were trained from the start to fly and fight the way the Russians do. They shook up and "shot down" a lot of hot pilots. In 1975 the 64th

Aggressor Squadron became the core of Nellis AFB's Red Flag program, a giant air exercise that tested bombing, air combat, ground support, electronic warfare, and even cargo missions in the face of an elaborate Soviet-style air defense array, mock industrial targets, a motorized rifle division in column, and live, television-tracking "surface-to-air" guns and missiles. The USAF flight community not only fought, it analyzed and evaluated the "battles," searching for lessons; and as the Aggressors got better, so did the visiting units. The key was that the "enemy" must fight like the Soviets. The Russians do things differently in the air. To beat them, one must understand their methods.

They do things differently on the ground too. Up until the mid-seventies, the American Army never talked about fighting the Soviets. If not engaging actual or make-believe Viet Cong or NVA regulars, the Army's *FM 105-5 Maneuver Control* and Army regulations specified an enemy of "non-definitive nationality depicted as 'Aggressor.' " The Aggressors were marked by a green triangle in a white circle (the Circle Trigon), supposedly spoke Esperanto, and used strange weapons known as the INTERA tank and the Ripsnorter antitank missile.[2] They had Ming-the-Merciless crested helmets. It must be assumed that these Aggressors were designed to be inoffensive to real American enemies. They tended not to be employed in accord with the original program's intent—nobody really read the dull reams of Aggressor tactics and doctrine dutifully cranked out by the Army's intelligence community. Aggressors fought like Americans with crested helmets. That is, if they fought at all. *Aggressors* began to connote people who were role-players more than enemies. They lighted fires so they could be found by night patrols and died willingly so they could be searched. And Aggressors were usually far outnumbered by the Americans. It smacked a lot of cowboys and Indians, with very stupid, indolent Indians.

The return from Vietnam and the focus on Europe doomed the bumbling, play-dead Aggressors. The term would survive to designate any enemy force (as in the 64th Aggressor Squadron at Nellis), but the program died in 1975–76 when the Army's how-to-fight manual, *FM 100-5 Operations*, made it to the field. The enemy was boldly spelled out as "the forces of the Warsaw Pact." The floodgates opened, and information about the Soviets' equipment, tactics, and organization began to get out to units. The INTERA and Ripsnorter gave way to the T-62 and the Sagger, and the armies of the Warsaw Pact and their many imitators and assistants worldwide were given the name Opposing Forces, or OPFOR, for short.

The original NTC concept always included an active OPFOR, like that of the Air Force's Red Flag program at nearby Nellis. The idea was similar to that used by the Air Force—the NTC OPFOR would use Soviet-type equipment and organize as a motorized rifle regiment. Most important of all, Fort Irwin's OPFOR would not be a play-dead training aid. They would be meticulously schooled in Warsaw Pact tactics and doctrine by the Army's premier experts on opposing force training, the Fort Hood Red Thrust Detachment. The OPFOR would not be a scratch force but permanent units that worked on their Russian methods. Significantly, the Irwin OPFOR would be taught to play to win, to be resourceful and confident. In some ways NTC's Soviets would be better than the real ones.

Actual Soviet soldiers serve in the largest armed force on this planet. Depending on whose figures are used, the Soviet Union has about 50 tank divisions, about 134 motorized infantry divisions, 7 divisions of paratroopers, 8 air assault (helicopter-landed) brigades, and 15 artillery divisions. There are also 5 naval infantry brigades.[3] The Soviet "Army," a unified command of all services, has five components: the Strategic Rocket Forces, the Land Forces, the Air Defense Forces, the Air Forces, and the Navy.[4] Including command, general support, internal security, construction, railroad, and border guard units, the Soviet Union deploys over 5 million uniformed servicemen. About 2 million serve in the land forces (including the Red "marines," a navy element, and the airborne and air assault units, which work directly for the supreme command). The land forces have, in the latest estimates, over 50,000 tanks, 62,000 armored reconnaissance and infantry carriers, 24,000 artillery pieces and multiple rocket launchers, and almost 3,500 helicopters.[5] Military conscription is universal for all Soviet male citizens. Even without conjuring up the nightmare statistics for ICBMs, ballistic missile submarines, chemical warheads, and long-range bombers, these numbers are very impressive. They impressed the United States Army.

Still, there are lies, damn lies, and statistics. Behind the hordes, one can see a few facts of life beyond argument. First, American units fighting Russians in Europe or in the Persian Gulf can expect to be outnumbered. Since America usually counters the Red hordes with her seventeen regular Army divisions, things look very bad. Doctrine says three attackers and one defender should battle to a standstill. But this Red array looks like ten to one, just for openers.

Things aren't quite that bad, however. Two-thirds of the Russian units are at half strength or less, expecting a fill of reservists in case of war. But Soviet reserve soldiers *never* train, not even a weekend a month. The understrength divisions tend to have older, even obsolescent, equipment.[6] There are stories of rifle divisions "motorized" in civilian trucks in the August 1968 callup.[7] The performance of the reserve divisions initially deployed to Afghanistan in 1979 was not very good.[8] Every callup has a drastic effect on the Soviet economy, so they are never done "for practice," unless one considers Czechoslovakia-1968 and Afghanistan-1979 to be warmups for World War III.

The Americans are not so bad off as common knowledge has it. The seventeen active divisions can count on three large United States Marine Corps divisions. Reserves, who do train regularly and habitually associate with active units in their exercises, are in excellent shape, the best since the Second World War. American Army doctrine allows for armored cavalry regiments, independent infantry, mechanized infantry, and armored brigades, each a self-contained force equal to one-third of a division. Counting reserves, who are much closer to full strength than Soviet low-category units and routinely exercised, the Americans actually deploy eleven infantry divisions, sixteen infantry brigades (equal to five divisions), four Marine divisions, one airborne division, one air assault division, one air cavalry combat brigade (a unique attack helicopter unit), eight mechanized infantry divisions, six mechanized brigades (the equivalent of two divisions), six armored divisions, four armored brigades, seven armored cavalry regiments, and thirty-two artillery brigades. About half the American ground units are reserve components.[9] The Russians labor under the above view of American ground power.

Russian numerical strength is further diluted by America's allies. These include some of the most formidable military establishments in the modern world. The British and French have sizable ground forces. The Canadians are respected. The West Germans are particularly feared and have a large, capable standing army. The Australians, the Japanese, the South Koreans, and especially the People's Republic of China are causes for concern in the Kremlin. In the Middle East, the Americans have the good fortune to have as allies the redoubtable Israelis and the Egyptians, the best of the Arab powers. Of these, the Chinese alone could swallow whole the Soviet ground force.

Moscow is bedeviled by its own allies. The Warsaw Pact nations with large armies are Poland, East Germany, Czechoslovakia, and Hungary. These four are also the most politically restive. They are as much a worry to the Soviets as they are to NATO. Rumania and Bulgaria are hardly the leading lights of the European military tradition. Libya, Cuba, Angola, and Syria are bush leaguers and drains on Russian resources. The North Koreans and North Vietnamese are capable but have local axes to grind. All in all, the Russians probably would be better off if they had never bothered to arm their socialist brothers. The east Europeans require heavy concentrations of Soviets all across their homelands to insure they remain locked in the Communist orbit. Indeed, a case can be made that the many contentious minorities of the Soviet Union also soak up their share of the Red ground forces, typical in a garrison state.

The net result of all of this is that American military planners think the Russians may achieve a two- or three-to-one local advantage in Europe (more at the point of attack, of course) and a bit less in southwest Asia. So American battalions would have to handle Russian regiments. The Irwin OPFOR were structured on this assumption.

A real Soviet motorized rifle regiment has some pronounced strengths and weaknesses. First of all, there are many of them, no matter how one divines the stats. Secondly, the Russians have passable equipment, and a lot of it. Admittedly, a T-72 may not be a match for an M60A3 tank, but how fast can one M60A3 shoot? Third, the Soviet regiment has a doctrine stressing mass, offensive action, and ruthless speed. Fourth, the regiment is organized with its own organic tanks, engineers, reconnaissance, and air defense. It is a mobile, hard-hitting, combined arms organization. [10]

Inevitably, there are soft spots. Logistics are primitive by Western standards—this unit does not sustain, it burns up and is discarded. It is a non-refillable, no-deposit model. Command and control is inflexible by Western standards. Initiative is not a natural tendency in the Soviet society, and adhering to orders is more critical than success. There are no noncommissioned officers in the American sense. There are ''sergeants,'' but they are just two-year conscripts with a little extra schooling.

They do not read maps, talk on radios, or give orders. They provide discipline and execute orders. Hardly any enlisted men reenlist in the Soviet units.[11]

Russian companies fight in accord with set battle drills. In a Soviet motor rifle battalion, there is one radio net. The company commanders may transmit; mainly, however, they receive then execute the drills. Platoon commanders may also transmit but rarely do so. Section sergeants do not even have transmitters.[12] In a battlefield rife with electronic warfare, this is not all bad, that is, unless things go wrong. Only the leaders have the maps and plans.[13] Everyone else has his orders. The concept of adhering to orders regardless of circumstances is the insurance against failure, although that policy can be expensive in terms of casualties. The Russians have the needed numbers, however.

If there can be said to be a typical Soviet army unit, it would be the 2,400-man motorized rifle regiment. Referred to in Soviet military literature as an "all arms" organization, this regiment is found in every motorized rifle division and tank division, as well as in a few specialized nondivisional units. Tank divisions include one motorized rifle regiment. Three are found in a motorized rifle division.[14] A motorized rifle regiment (MRR) comes in two varieties. The really first-rate, elite kind are built around the BMP, a little fighting vehicle that resembles a tank but carries eight infantrymen in the rear. It has a three-man crew of its own. The BMP is low to the ground and has a small turret just behind the front-mounted engine. The BMP is fast (traveling at more than forty miles per hour), it can swim rivers, and it is equipped with an overpressure system to allow it to run through chemical or radiological contamination with its passengers in shirtsleeves. The vehicle is a true fighting machine, not just a track-laying taxi. It has a 73-mm smoothbore cannon and an AT-3 Sagger antitank missile in the squat turret. The BMP also has firing ports that permit its squad to shoot out of the hull while buttoned up inside.[15] The BMP-equipped motorized rifle regiment appears to be a potent organization.

But, like the Russian army in general, the BMP looks better than it is. The vehicle is very cramped: it is less than eighty-six inches high at the turret. It has large fuel pods placed inconveniently on the armored back doors. The armor is a magnesium alloy that burns nicely when brought to a high-temperature, like that produced by an impacting tank round.

The diesel in the back doors helps turn the whole thing into a *flambé*. Aside from flammability, the gun is more like a big, low-velocity grenade launcher (and not a very good one), and the Sagger missile is slow and inaccurate. The NBC overpressure system leaks, and the eight troops in the back hardly ever get out anymore, even under close ambush by determined Afghan rebels. The worst thing about the BMP is that it is expensive. Only one-third of all the motorized regiments have authorized BMPs on their establishments.[16]

The Russians have introduced a BMP-2 model with a 30-mm automatic cannon and an advanced antitank missile (either the AT-4 Spigot or the longer-ranged AT-5 Spandrel). The dimensions are still far too tight, the magnesium alloy armor still burns, and the fuel pods are still on the outer surface of the rear troop doors.[17] Worst of all, the Soviet soldiers continue to get into the thing and do not like to get back out, greatly reducing their fighting power and their security. These BMP-2s are just coming into the units.

The other two-thirds of the motorized rifle regiments are organized around the BTR-60PB, a wheeled armored personnel carrier. This vehicle has a passing resemblance to the old Oscar Mayer "Wiener Wagon," complete with eight big rubber tires. It is long and boat-hulled, with a little turret near the front. It is powered by two gasoline engines in the back and can go over fifty miles per hour on roads. The carrier can swim rivers. The BTR-60PB transports an eight-man squad and a three-man crew. It mounts a 14.5-mm heavy machine gun and

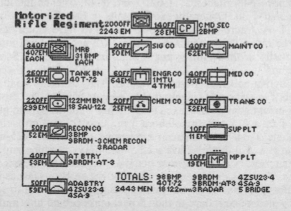

a coaxial 7.62-mm machine gun in the small cupola. This is the standard Soviet armored personnel carrier.[18]

The BTR-60PB has a few problems. First, its two gasoline engines and weak drive train are very unreliable, with one of the two usually disconnected. Second, the infantry aboard must dismount through side hatches, a move not conducive to long life under fire. Third, its wheels degrade rough-terrain performance. Last, its gasoline fuel is highly explosive. The Russians are currently producing a BTR-70, with a millimeter of extra armor and a few modifications to the balky twin power plants.[19] Like the BMP-2, it is just reaching the line units.

Motorized rifle regiments are built around these infantry vehicles. Both varieties have three motorized rifle battalions (MRBs). A motorized rifle battalion is an austere unit, with three motorized rifle companies (MRCs) of ten vehicles apiece. Three BMPs or BTRs make up a platoon; and three platoons, plus one command track, compose a company. All MRBs have a one-vehicle battalion headquarters and six excellent Soviet 120-mm mortars. A BTR-equipped battalion also has an anti-tank missile/gun platoon assigned.[20] There are no mechanics, fuel trucks, scouts, or medics. It is strictly a fighting unit.

The other maneuver force in the motorized rifle regiment is the tank battalion. Every Soviet MRR has its own tank battalion, composed of three companies of thirteen tanks each. Every tank company has three four-tank platoons and a single commander's tank. The battalion totals forty armored vehicles, as its commander also has a tank. The battalion may be equipped with the T-55, T-62, T-64, T-72, or even the long-rumored T-80. Generally, Soviet units in East Germany have the T-64. Cadre-strength units in the USSR have motor pools of the older T-55s and T-62s. The T-72 and T-80 are found primarily in those full-strength units based inside the Soviet Union.[21]

Russian tanks are no-frills models. They are very small by American standards (ninety inches average height at the turret) and mount heavy cannons. The T-55 has a 100-mm rifled gun; the T-62 a 115-mm smoothbore firing fin-stabilized projectile, and the T-64/72/80 share a monstrous smoothbore 125-mm main gun. All models have a 12.7-mm heavy machine gun on their turrets and a 7.62-mm coaxial weapon aside their cannons. The tanks are maneuverable but not nearly so fast as the BMPs or BTRs. Their low silhouettes make them hard to see. They also make it hard to hide Soviet tanks behind hills and in holes and still allow the tankers to peek over to shoot. The T-64/72/80 models have laser range finders.[22]

Like the infantry vehicles, the tanks have their problems. They are also very cramped and uncomfortable inside. They carry about thirty to forty main gun rounds (a third less than most comparable Western tanks). All are diesels, a plus for fire suppression.[23] The T-64, however, has a "revolutionary" opposed piston diesel engine that has turned out to be afflicted with numerous problems, resulting in a very underpowered tank. All of these armored craft have manual transmissions (hammers for beating them into range are standard driver issue), and getting the power plants out for routine service requires removal of the whole turret. The T-64/72/80 series has only three crewmen because of provisions for an automatic loader. These autoloaders are notorious for either loading the gunner's arm (unpleasant) or loading propellant before projectile (with spectacular and terminal results). They are often disconnected, which results in an even slower rate of fire as the smaller crew tries to work around the bulky autoloader mechanism in the squeezed turret space. Finally, for all the efforts to enlarge the main guns, the crude Soviet ammunition technology still means that the NATO/Israeli 105-mm gun (standard since the 1950s) outperforms their big 125-mm cannons in terms of armor penetration.[24]

Besides tanks and infantry, the commander of an MRR has other units at his disposal. He controls a battalion of 122-mm cannon artillery. In frontline units, this is the SAU-122 self-propelled gun. Lower-priority units have to make do with the D-30 towed pieces. Some units have only a six-gun battery. The majority have three six-gun batteries, a total of eighteen guns to fire in support of the motorized rifle regiment.[25] Additional artillery, "the God of Battles" to the Red Army, is often attached.

Unlike American artillerists, Russian gunners accept calls for fire only from their battery commanders, who are forward in observation posts. They also have no qualms about rolling along with the advance and firing directly at targets, which avoids messy radio jabber and confusing calculations.[26] For the Soviets, massing fires means massing guns in one location under one command. The Americans leave the weapons dispersed and rely on radio and technique to mass the effects. Soviet artillery tends to be preplanned, firing off elaborate, First World War–style schedules. The Russians have so many guns, mortars, and rocket launchers that they can afford to dispense with sophistication and still get solid, massive fire support, albeit inflexible.

Another form of artillery is the regimental antitank battery, which is under the Soviet artillery branch and is likely to be employed en masse. It has nine wheeled BRDM-2 missile carriers, mounting AT-3 Saggers or AT-5 Spandrels.[27] These missiles are wire guided. The Russians trained the Egyptians to use them in concentrated barrages in the 1973 war with Israel, where they were somewhat effective. The BMP, it should be recalled, has its own missile capability, though it is time consuming to stop and fire in the assault.

The last type of artillery available in the MRR is the air defense battery, also under the ground forces artillery branch, and not to be confused with the national forces of air defense, which defend the Soviet Union against American strategic strikes. The regimental antiair battery has four ZSU-23-4 self-propelled guns and four SA-9 short-range air defense missile carriers. The ZSU, nicknamed the Shilka, is particularly capable of putting up a lot of flak, although typically it is on a weak-engined chassis. The guns and missiles provide coverage to the regiment as a whole.[28]

The motorized rifle regiment also has an engineer company, with a platoon of sappers for clearing/laying mines and barriers, a platoon of bridging elements, and a technical platoon for surveying and route reconnaissance. The regiment can cross small rivers and clear tank ditches and mines without external support.[29]

Rounding out the fighting elements is a reconnaissance company. This multicapable unit has a carrier platoon (three BMPs or BTRs), a radar platoon (three BRDM-2s with ground radar that can scan over six miles out), a scout-car platoon (three more BRDMs and five motorcycles), and a chemical recon platoon (three specially designed BRDM-2s with chemical "sniffers" and radiological detectors). This gives the MRR commander an ability to look deep into the enemy's rear, clear his route of march, gather intelligence, frustrate enemy scouts, or guard a flank.[30]

The regiment's service units include a chemical defense company (for decontamination), a medical evacuation company, an ammunition/fuel transport company, a signal company, and a maintenance company (rudimentary repairs and recovery to clear routes). These outfits are all there to provide supply and services to the regiment's three MRBs and tank battalion.[31] In general, the Soviets load up with food, fuel, and ammunition and intend to go until depleted resources or casualties render the command ineffective. This is one of the reasons the Russian armed forces must be so large.

The final piece of the regiment is the regimental headquarters. It has two armored infantry vehicles (BMPs or BTRs, depending on the type of regiment) and a few trucks. Its total strength is fourteen officers and twenty-eight enlisted men. By comparison, the command and control element of an American battalion has thirteen officers and thirty enlisted men.[32] The regimental commander controls his combined arms unit with careful, detailed plans and well-known march and combat drills. His force has ninety-eight infantry vehicles, forty tanks, and eighteen artillery guns. It has air defense, engineers, reconnaissance capability, and a strong complement of antiarmor missilery independent of the battalions. The regiment is built for speed and fights in massive, linear formations, supported by screaming rocket launchers and pounding 122-mm cannons. Its goal is swift, crushing, overwhelming assault.

After all the tanks are added up and all the guns are enumerated, the regiment will be only as good as its riflemen, the monosyllabic, largely non-Russian ethnic conscripts. These are the glum rankers who will have to fire the rocket-propelled grenades, clear the mines, fire the assault rifle bursts, throw the grenades, and fix the bayonets. Their training is stultifying, endless repetition. They rarely use their vehicles—the BMPs are kept like new cars, too good to be driven.[33] The Soviet infantry conscript is taught tactics in simulation and in massive, showpiece exercises that would seem more like staged displays than war games to Western soldiers. The Red Army private does as he is told and waits until his two years are up. He is underpaid, underfed, used as a common laborer, and hardly ever allowed to go on leave or pass. His leaders do not trust him. To them, he is just another number, one who needs to be watched.

The Russian army comes down to that, in the end. It is massive and powerful, but it is like an avalanche, fixed in its path, inflexible, inexorable. It is an army where initiative is rare, an army of good socialist science that fights by formula. The Soviet army is an army of attack, of numbers, of imposing appearance. It is an army with laser range finders on its tanks and armored Hind attack helicopters that still refuses to issue socks to its troops, preferring leg wrappings because they are not so expensive. It is more scared of America than the Americans can know. The Russians, you see, have to live on their side of the great facade.

The United States Army's version of a motorized rifle regiment (MRR) at Fort Irwin is the heart of the National Training Center, much as the Air Force's Red Flag is built around its Aggressor Squadron. The Opposing Forces (OPFOR) at the NTC are made up of tankers from the 1st Battalion, 73d Armor, and infantrymen of the 6th battalion (Mechanized), 31st Infantry. Permanently stationed at Irwin, these two battalions combine to replicate a full-strength, first-line Russian regiment. Interestingly enough, both units retain full sets of United States equipment and are required to maintain proficiency in American tactics.

The units were trained initially in late 1981 by the Army's Opposing Forces Training Detachment (Red Thrust) from Fort Hood, Texas. The regiment is equipped with T-72 tanks, BMPs (the 73-mm gun model), ZSU-23-4s, SAU-122-mm self-propelled artillery, MTLB all-purpose tracked carriers, and the usual BRDM-2s and motorcycles. This is the type of MRR the Soviets wish they had more of—full-strength, modern equipment and highly trained personnel.

The T-72s, BMPs, ZSUs, and SAUs are visually modified (VISMOD) versions of the Vietnam-era M551 Sheridan Armored Reconnaissance Airborne Assault Vehicles, a variety of light tank. The little Sheridans never panned out in combat— their 152-mm gun/missile weapon was so big that every time the cannon fired, it lifted the tank off the ground and screwed up the missile electronics in the bargain. The chassis is reliable enough, and its small size and agility make it a good substitute for Soviet vehicles. The NTC fitted rounded, Soviet-style false turrets over the actual ones, added built-up fenders and searchlights and a big, simulated 125-mm cannon to create the appearance of real T-72s. A smaller gun and a missile rail and other body fixtures make a BMP. The ZSU's radar dish and quad 23-mm guns are emplaced on a built-up turret to suggest that air defense vehicle. The SAU's stubby howitzer and blocky turret are faithfully duplicated. All of these tracked vehicles are painted Soviet-style forest green and have big, bold turret numbers in the Russian mode.

The BRDM-2s are created from M880 trucks, the Army

model of a Dodge pickup truck. Slab sides and missile, chemical, or air defense simulation accessories are added to create these vehicles. Like real Russian BRDM-2s, they are wheeled vehicles.

The soldiers of the OPFOR wear unique dark green uniforms, complete with rakish black berets or U.S. helmets without camouflage covers, to simulate Russian-style helmets. These soldiers are trained to fight out of the Russian army's tactics manuals, respond to Russian flag signals, and often carry actual Soviet weapons for added realism. They are cocky and capable, and right from the first rotation in January of 1982, they established an elite reputation.

The OPFOR re-create a Soviet motor rifle regiment capable of fighting to its full "on-paper" capability. The T-72 tanks never eat the gunner's arm or suffer attentuation at long range because of poor ammunition. The BMPs really can fire the 73-mm gun (treated as a cannon, not the weak "grenade lobber" it truly is) and the Sagger, which is accepted as equal to the American TOW in range and accuracy, though the actual AT-3 is not at that standard. There is no provision for BMP's flaming up when hit by incendiary bullets, and all the antichemical overpressure systems are assumed to work perfectly. In other words, these vehicles and weapons perform according to their technical specifications. The deck is stacked in favor of the Russians on purpose. It is an old intelligence maxim to assume the enemy is at peak capability. This theory of crediting the possible is called "worst-case" analysis.

"Worst-casing it" is true across the board. The Russian logistic system (or lack thereof) is not duplicated. One of the reasons the Soviet units have so many weapons is that they intend to discard, not restore, any wastage. The OPFOR maintain like American units everywhere. They fix at the lowest level possible. More critically, they exercise the vehicles regularly and learn their ins and outs. There are no Saran-wrapped motor parks here.

Soviets have a notoriously regimented command and control system, which NTC really does not address. OPFOR commanders and troops quickly showed the rest of the Army a degree of initiative that was truly outstanding. All OPFOR elements call for artillery and mortar fire, something only Russian battery commanders do routinely. Everyone gets the plan, via American-style operations orders. Maps and maneuver graphics, state secrets in Mother Russia, are disseminated to the lowest level in United States Army fashion. Radio traffic is intentionally limited but is a lot closer to American practice than to Russian technique.

The OPFOR know Fort Irwin terrain very well, and most leaders (and more than a few troops) read maps tolerably well. This terrain knowledge would certainly not typify a Soviet force, unless for some reason America invaded the USSR or eastern Europe. The OPFOR understand and employ Russian tactics with decisiveness. If leaders "die," subordinates assume control and finish the mission. In brief, the OPFOR are the Russians as *they* wish they were.

Like the Air Force, with its Aggressor Squadron, the Army consciously advertised the OPFOR as a unique, career-enhancing assignment. In order to fulfill the dual mission of OPFOR missions and American tactical proficiency, the two battalions switch off in their portrayal of the Soviets. The battalion commander of the "base" battalion (say, the infantry) becomes the regimental commander. His three rifle companies each become motorized rifle battalion commanders. Platoon leaders lead motorized rifle companies; squad leaders head BMP platoons. The base battalion's combat support company supplies the artillery, air defense, and antitank units. The Headquarters and Headquarters Company plays its normal service and support roles, and supplies the command post. Normally, the tank battalion plays the Soviet tankers and both battalions share responsibility for the reconnaissance units.[34] The busy line companies train on U.S. tactics when the full OPFOR regiment is not required.

The good thing that comes out of this is that everyone functions at a higher echelon than normal, and the opportunity to show up the visiting Americans is great. Captains play at being lieutenant colonels and do well at it. Junior sergeants see what it is like to push platoons. These Americans rise to the occasion.

The bad thing about the OPFOR is that there is not much infantry to put on the ground. All those BMP VISMODs are, after all, dressed-up tanks with engines where the soldiers should ride. It takes only two men to operate a VISMOD, and men in the U.S. battalion are not taught to play riflemen when it is their turn to be the MRR. To get men on the ground, OPFOR leaders have to drop out platoons and MRCs if the mission calls for it. As a result, the OPFOR fight mounted nine times out of ten. It is true that the actual Russians prefer not to dismount as well, although they certainly have the capability. This is a violation of the usual rule of worst-casing things.

The OPFOR certainly get a lot of mileage out of their few foot soldiers and their probing reconnaissance troops. They quickly developed a pervasive surveillance capability through aggressive patrolling. To even up the infantry deficiency, the OPFOR are given a force of guerrilla "irregulars" called Parrumph tribesmen who roam the visiting unit's rear areas, wreaking havoc and gathering information.[35] It is suspected that the Fort Irwin observer controller personnel (the graders and referees for the force-on-force battle) assist on occasion by passing American unit locations to the OPFOR. Either way, the OPFOR usually collect a lot more information than the opponents would want them to know.

The Irwin OPFOR are good at their assignments. Their characteristic regimental-level array is awesome, a fast-moving fleet of determined enemy soldiers who shoot with deadly aim and press onward in a great, disciplined mass. These soldiers deploy with assurance from march columns into battle lines. They infiltrate with skill, breach obstacles with ease, and win time and time again. They are a very tough home team to beat. More than one army commander has remarked that, compared to the OPFOR, the real Soviets will seem like the second-string.

Notes

1. Viktor Suvorov (pseud.), *Inside the Soviet Army* (New York: Macmillan Co., 1982), 170–71.

2. Department of the Army, *FM 105-5 Maneuver Control* (Washington, D.C.: Department of the Army, December 1967), Appendices E, F, and G.

3. International Institute for Strategic Studies, "The Military Balance 1983/84," *Air Force*, December 1983, 76–78. These figures are as authoritative as any.

4. Suvorov, *Inside the Soviet Army*, 51.

5. "Military Balance," 76–78.

6. Andrew Cockburn, *The Threat Inside the Soviet Military Machine* (New York: Random House, 1983), 129–30.

7. Viktor Suvorov (pseud.), *The Liberators* (New York: W. W. Norton, 1981), 140–42.

8. *The Threat*, 132–33.

9. "Military Balance," 72–74; Department of the Army, "Command

and Staff," *Army*, October 1985, 329–42. The American figures are al-most as "soft" as those for the USSR, as the U.S. Army is forever reorganizing, reforming, and redesignating its many commands and units.

10. *Inside the Soviet Army*, 70–71, 111.

11. *The Threat*, 143, 188–89, 194–204.

12. Frank A. Chadwick, "Designer's Notes," *Assault* (Bloomington, Ill.: Game Designers' Workshop, 1983), 2.

13. *Inside the Soviet Army*, 232–33.

14. Department of the Army, *Soviet Army Operations* (Arlington Hall Station: U.S. Army Intelligence Threat Analysis Center, April 1978), 2-11, 2-12, 2-13.

15. Department of the Army, *FM 23-1 (Test) Bradley Infantry Fighting Vehicle Gunnery* (Washington, D.C.: Department of the Army, 8 December 1983), 2-7 to 2-23. See also *The Threat*, 151–52; Capt. Scott R. Gourley and Capt. David F. McDermott, "Evolution of the BMP," *Infantry*, November/December, 1983, 19–22.

16. *Inside the Soviet Army*, Brig. Richard E. Simpkin, "When the Squad Dismounts," *Infantry*, November/December 1983, 16–17; "Evolution of the BMP," 10–22.

17. Frank Chadwick, "Soviet Organization," *Assault* (Bloomington, Ill.: Game Designers' Workshop, 1983), 3; "When the Squad Dismounts," 15–16; "Evolution of the BMP," 19–22.

18. *Bradley Gunnery*, 2-25 to 2-26. See also *The Threat*, 150–51.

19. *The Threat*, 150–51; *The Liberators*, 137–38; "Soviet Organization," 3.

20. *Soviet Army Operations*, 2-19.

21. *Soviet Army Operations*, 2-10; "Soviet Organization," 3.

22. *Bradley Gunnery*, 2-3 to 2-6, 2-7; "Soviet Organization," 3.

23. *Bradley Gunnery*, 2-7; *The Threat*, 140; Defense Intelligence Agency, *Warsaw Pact Ground Forces Equipment Identification Guide: Armored Fighting Vehicles* (Washington, D.C.: Defense Intelligence Agency, August 1980), 15, 19, 23, 27.

24. *The Threat*, 141, 144–45, 146–48; "Soviet Organization," 3.

25. *Soviet Army Operations*, 2-10, 2-31.

26. Department of the Army, *ST 7-170 Fire Support Handbook, United States Army Infantry School* (Fort Benning, GA.: U.S. Army Infantry School, 1983), B-7, B-13; "Soviet Organization," 1–2.

27. *Soviet Army Operations*, 2-10.

28. *Soviet Army Operations*, 2-10, 2-45; *The Threat*, 156–57.

29. *Soviet Army Operations*, 2-46.

30. *Soviet Army Operations*, 2-42.

31. *Soviet Army Operations*, 2-42, 2-43, 2-44.

32. *Soviet Army Operations*, 2-11; Department of the Army, *Army Reference Data, Vol. I* (Fort Knox, Ky.: U.S. Army Armor School, 1979), 302.

33. *The Threat*, 190; *The Liberators*, 151–52.

34. Interview with 1st Lt. Kenneth Schwendeman, 13 February 1984.

35. Interview with Capt. Jack Finley, 20 October 1982.

Chapter Three

Enter the Dragons

"But just as herdsmen easily divide their goats when herds have mingled in a pasture, so these were marshaled by their officers to one side and the other, forming companies for combat."

Homer, **The Iliad**[1]

"There never were such men in an Army before. They will go anywhere and do anything if properly led. But there is the difficulty—proper commanders—where can they be obtained?"

Robert E. Lee[2]

National Training Center rotation 1-83 was the eighth unit exercise conducted since the formal opening of the Fort Irwin NTC in January 1982. The 1st Brigade, 24th Infantry Division (Mechanized), from Fort Stewart, Georgia, would move men by air and some machines by rail to the California desert, drawing out the balance of their combat equipment from depot stockages at Irwin. The battles would commence on 7 October 1982 and run through 21 October 1982. The OPFOR, primed for almost a year, had displayed their professionalism over and over in the seven previous rotations, so the job for the Stewart troops would not be an easy one.

NTC rotations are built around a brigade headquarters controlling a tank battalion and a mechanized infantry battalion. In the American Army, brigades come in two main types: separate and divisional. Separate brigades have their own artillery, supply, engineer, cavalry, aviation, and service units assigned. Divisional brigades, three to a division, have a headquarters and two to five fighting battalions. All of the other combat power and support elements are assigned from divisional assets based on the brigade's mission. The 1st Brigade was a typical divisional brigade.

In 1982 1st Brigade consisted of two mechanized infantry battalions and a tank battalion. The NTC forces were designated as the 2d Battalion, 70th Armor, and the 2d Battalion (Mechanized), 34th Infantry, leaving the 2d Battalion (Mechanized), 21st Infantry, behind. Admittedly, this created a pretty thin brigade (since a brigade can handle up to five maneuver battalions), but Irwin was and is a battalion exercise. The brigade would move the units and issue orders, but the tunes would be called by the Fort Irwin observer controllers of the Fort Irwin Operations Group. The 24th Infantry Division (Mechanized) gave 1st Brigade a hefty slice of the division's artillery, engineers, and support command to help the brigade in its mission. Some of those units would be split out to aid the fighting battalions.

Just as the OPFOR's (and Soviet's) motorized rifle regiment is the lowest combined echelon, so the American battalion *task force* offers the normal fighting element of the U.S. Army. The task force is built around either a tank battalion or a mechanized infantry battalion. Whereas the Soviets and their allies add tanks to beef up their motorized rifle battalions, American mechanized infantry units trade infantry companies for tank companies with sister armor battalions to create task forces of two mechanized companies and one tank company, or vice versa. This is part of a procedure called *task organizing,* and it is based on the mission (task) to be accomplished, the enemy forces, the terrain and weather, the troops on hand, and the time available. The brigade plays a major role in organizing such task forces, and also dips into its stock of engineers, ground radar squads, air defense platoons, and other special troops to reinforce these combined arms battalion task forces.

One of the task forces deploying to Fort Irwin in October 1982 was structured around the 2d Battalion (Mechanized), 34th Infantry. This example, typical of an Army line infantry battalion, offers an excellent vehicle to examine the nature of training at the National Training Center and, more important, to examine the methods soldiers use in training to prepare for the methods used in war. The men of Task Force 2-34 Infantry were organized, equipped, and led the same way as most other mechanized units in the American Army in 1982. They are the part that gives a clue to the whole.

Since the formation of armies in earliest historical times, the infantry has always been a part of warmaking on the ground. An infantryman is a soldier who fights on foot. At times and places (during the era of the tough Roman legions or in the time of the Swiss pikemen in the early Renaissance, for example) the infantry was capable of deciding battles singlehandedly. More typically, the foot soldier has needed the help of a mounted shock force (horse cavalry became main battle tanks) and projectile firing elements (archers and siege engines, now field howitzers and antitank guided missiles). Infantrymen also need constructors and destructors (engineers), messengers and signalers, commissaries and armorers, scouting troops, spies, and clerks in ever-growing numbers. New weapons create new specialists as vital as the old, so that a modern infantryman finds air defense missilemen and ground sensor troops marching along with the old reliable sappers and cavalry. Throughout the long march of time, the infantry and its fellow arms have always been as good, or as bad, as the men who led them.

American infantrymen still fight on foot, though they may reach that fight by helicopters, parachutes, or armored personnel carriers. In 1982 most American infantry was known as "mechanized," that is, mounted in armored personnel carriers (APCs). The Russians, as seen earlier, field a fully mechanized army. American Army leaders still have plenty of foot infantry and probably will keep them for a long time. APCs just do not fit too well in Central American jungles or in Air Force cargo jets bound for a suddenly "hot" war far overseas. Still, mechanized infantry is the main force of the United States Army.

In 1982 the 2d Battalion (Mechanized), 34th Infantry, was part of the 1st Brigade, 24th Infantry Division (Mechanized), stationed in southeast Georgia at Fort Stewart. The battalion's name, 2d Battalion, 34th Infantry, was a throwback to the old days when three-battalion regiments of infantry staffed the Army's divisions. There are no more infantry "regiments" in the sense of tactical units, though the lineage of the most famous of America's regimental units lives on in the two-part names of the battalions. The 2d Battalion, 34th Infantry, had a history stretching back to July 1916, when it formed at El Paso, Texas. The unit arrived in Lorraine Province, France, in November 1918, just in time to see the end of the Great War. The brief stay in Lorraine gave the regiment its motto: *Toujours En Avant* (Always Forward), and the unit adopted the Lorraine cross into its blue, gold, and white heraldic crest. In World War II the 34th was sent to New Guinea in 1944 as part of the 24th Infantry Division, though its performance was less than adequate.

The core of the battalion's heritage resided in the memory of the 34th Infantry's finest hours. In October 1944, as the regiment fought ashore at Leyte Island in the Philippines, savage

Japanese artillery and machine-gun fire stalled the infantry on the beach. In a moment commemorated on a poster (one of the most popular paintings in the U.S. Army in Action series decorating some offices on every Army installation worldwide), Col. (now Maj. Gen., Ret'd.) Aubrey S. "Red" Newman stood up in the brutal hail of bullets and fragments and bellowed, "Get the hell off the beach! Follow me!" Electrified by his example and enraged by the pent-up frustration of being pinned down, the 34th's 3d Battalion stormed off the beach. The regiment received a Presidential Unit Citation for its defense of Kilay Ridge the following night, when the 1st Battalion of the 34th stood off repetitive, violent Japanese banzai surges. A Company, 1st Battalion, and the entire 3d Battalion, 34th Infantry, was cited in 1945 in a Presidential Unit Citation issued for aiding in the reconquest of Corregidor, that fortified spit of island in Manila Bay in the Philippines. The 34th Infantry Regiment's reputation was based on the Leyte battles, where it gave the American infantry its motto: Follow Me! Leyte gave the regiment its unofficial (until 1981) nickname: Dragons, its radio call sign for the Philippines operation.

The 34th's battle record since the Philippines is brief and tragic. Committed in July 1950 in Korea, understrength and ill trained, the 34th paid the price for its life of ease in occupied Japan. By August 1950 the regiment had been decimated in a series of humiliating routs all too typical of the early American performance in Korea. A somewhat gratuitous Presidential Unit Citation was awarded for this depressing interlude. The survivors of the 34th were withdrawn to Japan in August 1950 for reconstitution, though the regiment did not return to the Korean peninsula until the war had ended. The 34th was sent to Germany in 1958 and converted to a mechanized unit. It spent the Vietnam War in West Germany, finally "disbanding" in 1971 through the old Army trick of switching flags with a unit from the heavily decorated 1st Infantry Division upon that force's withdrawal from Southeast Asia. There was no element of the 34th Infantry on active duty until 1975.[3]

In June 1975 the 2d Battalion, 34th Infantry, was reactivated at Fort Stewart, Georgia. It was and is the only active battalion of the 34th. It was a standard, foot-mobile unit at the time, part of the 24th Infantry Division. The battalion (along with the 24th Division) began to mechanize in the summer of 1979, receiving armored personnel carriers. The Dragons and the other battalions at Stewart were declared fully mechanized in

October 1979. The bottom fell out in Iran in November 1979, and by the fall of 1980, the 34th and its parent division were firmly locked into most Rapid Deployment Force contingency plans.

In the fall of 1982, the 2d Battalion (Mechanized), 34th Infantry, was organized under MTOE 0745HFC1060 (H Series), a modified table of organization and equipment used by most stateside mechanized infantry outfits.[4] The battalion proper consisted of five companies: A, B, C, Combat Support, and Headquarters. The lettered "line," or rifle companies, were organized identically with a company headquarters section (command section, maintenance, supply, and administrative elements), a weapons platoon (three 81-mm mortars mounted in armored personnel carriers and two TOW antitank missile launchers in M901 Improved TOW Vehicles), and three rifle platoons (three rifle squads in M113A1 or M113A2 armored personnel carriers and one platoon headquarters track as well). The Combat Support Company (CSC) contained a headquarters section similar to the line companies' section, the Scout Platoon (three M113A1/A2s and three M901 ITVs), the Heavy Mortar Platoon (four self-propelled 107-mm mortars in armored personnel carriers), and the Antitank Platoon (twelve more M901 Improved TOW Vehicles). The Headquarters and Headquarters Company (HHC) consisted of the battalion command section and the staff sections, the company headquarters, the medical platoon (aid station and three M113A2 armored ambulances), the maintenance platoon (two M88 tank recovery

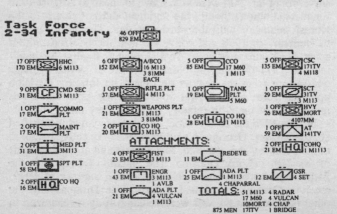

vehicles and the battalion mechanics and parts supply), the communications platoon (radio repairs, wire laying and switchboards, and the powerful radio-teletype link to brigade), and the ubiquitous support platoon (fuel, food, and ammunition trucks).

Just as Soviet motor rifle units are built around the BMP or BTR vehicles, so the American mechanized infantry battalions are built around the M113 series armored personnel carriers. The M113, normally called a *track* by American soldiers, is a fully tracked, diesel-powered personnel carrier with aluminum armor capable of stopping small arms and most artillery fragments. It looks like a sixteen-foot-long shoebox on treads, with a sloped front. The M113 is just over seven feet in height. Its standard weapon is a pedestal-mounted MS(HB) .50-caliber heavy machine gun. The *HB* stands for "heavy barrel," and the inch-long slugs fired by this powerful automatic weapon can punch holes in Soviet BMPs. The M113's "50" takes a lot of criticism, since it is hand fired from a one-man cupola. It does not have any destruction capability against tanks. It is an old (World War I era) design, but it is reliable and has a range of more than 1,500 meters against infantry, as well as antiaircraft utility.

The M113 is a very sound vehicle in a mechanical sense, capable of forty miles an hour on a paved road and fifteen to twenty miles an hour cross-country. Its slablike backside is a ramp for troop exit, and it has a rectangular cargo hatch on top for soldiers to fire from as the carrier moves along, a circular track gunner's cupola centered just behind the front-mounted engine, and another circular hatch (for the driver) on the left front. It can carry up to eleven men in the back. The M113 is a rifle squad *carrier* and was not designed as a fighting vehicle per se. It is used as one anyway.[5]

The M113 comes in two basic varieties—the M113A1 and M113A2. The A2 has an improved suspension system for better cross-country performance, as well as modifications to the vehicle's engine-cooling system. Both models could be found in the Dragons' inventory in 1982. Bravo Company, for example, had nine M113A2s and seven M113A1s.

Besides the squad carrier, the M113 series includes many variants, most in service in the 1982 mechanized infantry organizations. Adding another radio converted the squad carrier to a platoon or company headquarters, marked by dual antennas. Even more radios, some very high powered, were added to create fire support team tracks for artillery fire observation and control (one per rifle company) and the air liaison officer (ALO) vehicle (one, in the battalion headquarters). The battalion commander and his operations officer (S-3) each had tracks with multiple radios as well. The medical platoon added heaters and stretchers and deleted the .50-caliber to create three armored ambulances, one per line company.

Other M113 variants were more unusual, different enough to merit separate model numbers. The mortar platoons (81-mm, three tubes per company and 107-mm, four in CSC) had tracked M113-type mortar carriers with wide circular cargo hatches and mortar mounts in their rear areas. The line companies had old M125A1s, transferred from Fort Hood in 1980.[6] The battalion heavy mortars had relatively new M106A2 vehicles. Mortar carriers permitted fire from the vehicle, ease of ammunition transport, and speedy setup. The Soviets still ground-mount their mortars, a capability that both American types also retain. The mortar tracks mounted the .50-caliber machine gun as well as their tubes.

The most unusual fighting machine in the Dragons' arsenal was the M901 Improved TOW Vehicle, or ITV. The ITV is built on a standard M113A2 hull. It has an electric/hydraulic Emerson Electric turret erector mounted on top, straddling a modified track gunner's cupola. The turret has the optical tracking unit for the TOW guided missile and two launch tubes. Most intriguing of all, the entire turret can be lifted a few feet above the hull, allowing the ITV to hide in a defilade position behind a hill and still see and fire, periscope-style. The TOW is deadly accurate from 65 to 3,000 meters (more with later missile models, though the 34th had the original version) and is designed to kill tanks with one shot. This heavy antitank guided missile can track vehicles moving up to twenty miles an hour with little trouble. The TOW's large, shaped charge warhead can penetrate tank armor by burning its way through, rather than punching in, as a tank sabot round does. The ITV weds that powerful missile to a very survivable carrier, making it the single most potent vehicle in the mechanized battalion. Other ITV capabilities include a heat-sensitive thermal sight that reveals enemies in bad visibility and even sees through smoke. The ITV can fire its own smokescreen from bow-mounted grenade launchers or kill enemy foot troops with a 7.62-mm M60 machine gun included in the turret system, though not part of the erection unit.[7] There were twenty-one

ITVs in the Dragon battalion. On paper each letter company had a section of two, with twelve in the CSC Antitank Platoon and three in the Scout Platoon. In reality the 34th's commander (like most mechanized battalion commanders) had centralized all but the scout ITVs in CSC's Antitank Platoon to improve training and maintenance. Such powerful weapons needed special attention.

The ITV has been a bit of a disappointment, though not exactly a failure. It requires a great deal of special maintenance, both from the crews and from the battalion's two authorized (and overextended) turret mechanics. The hydraulic electric turret develops malfunctions now and then, and though the vehicle can fire its weapons nine days out of ten, it often operates with some degree of degradation. In a battlefield sense the ITV's unusual silhouette instantly identifies it for special enemy attention. It may prove too complicated for actual day-to-day war, with its nest of fluid tubes, cables, its unusual requirements of nitrogen bottles and special batteries for thermal capability, and its ammunition load of only twelve rounds. Later ITV versions project fixes for the thermal system, but the 34th had the first type.

The last M113 family track in the battalion, like the ITV, had a distinctive silhouette, marking it also as a key target. This was the M577 Command Post Carrier, which has a double-decker cargo area to allow soldiers to operate comfortably inside. The battalion had six of these ungainly, unarmed tracks. The operations (S-3) and intelligence (S-2) sections each had one. The supply and personnel (S-4/S-1) operated their Administration-Logistics Operations Center (ALOC) from a command post carrier. The heavy mortars used an M577 for their fire direction center. Communications platoon's radio-teletype system had its own M577. Finally, the medics operated their aid station out of the sixth double-size track.

Summarizing all of this, the 2d Battalion (Mechanized), 34th Infantry, disposed ninety-eight M113-type vehicles (fifty-eight M113A1/A2s, twenty-one M901 ITVs, nine M125A1s, six M577s, and four M106A2s) in its complete organization. The similar M113 chassis types eased servicing and repairs, and it created a common thread throughout most of the unit for training and operations. The Dragons had six other armored vehicles (the two M88 tank recovery vehicles in HHC and the one M578 light recovery vehicle in A, B, C, and CSC). Additionally, the battalion had over sixty wheeled tactical jeeps and trucks for administration, command and control, and logistics.

Operating by itself, or "pure," the 34th was capable of sustained combat operations, especially in restrictive terrain such as woods or towns. The unit could take on and destroy tanks with its ITVs. It was deployable on all USAF airlifters, either with or without its APCs. Of course, the light armor of the M113s and the nonarmor of fatigue shirts made the mechanized infantry a vulnerable organization under artillery barrages. In addition, the weight and bulk of its aluminum combat vehicles, though limited, insured that the battalion's tracks would probably move by sea. In brief, the battalion was a powerful, mobile force that was optimized for midintensity warfare.

Pure operations were the exception, not the rule, in the 1st Brigade, 24th Infantry Division (Mechanized). For the National Training Center, the Dragons became Task Force 2-34 Infantry (TF 2-34), undergoing "task organization." The brigade commander detached C Company from the 2d Battalion, 70th Armor, and sent it to TF 2-34. TF 2-34 gave up its C Company to the tank battalion. This made TF 2-34 "mech heavy" and TF 2-70 "tank heavy," which is a typical alignment in the U.S. Army. Additionally, brigade attached engineers, air defense troops, ground surveillance radars, and motorcycle scouts from the 101st Airborne Division (Air Assault), Fort Campbell, Kentucky, another Rapid Deployment Force unit. Each of these elements increased the capabilities of the Dragons.

The tankers of Company C, 2d Battalion, 70th Armor, operated seventeen M60A3 main battle tanks, five in each of three platoons and two in the company headquarters. The fifty-three-ton tanks are armed with the well-proven 105-mm main cannon, as well as a coaxial 7.62-mm machine gun and a .50-caliber weapon for the tank commander. Carrying four men, the M60A3 could go more than twenty miles per hour cross-country. The M60A3 has full thermal imaging sights that can see enemy vehicles and men by their heat signatures. Its XM21 solid state computer and laser range finder make it a formidable tank killer out to 2,200 meters, even on the move. It is rumored that the M60A3 can hit out to 5,000 meters against stationary targets.

The M60 series of tanks, tested in battle by the Israelis, has several pronounced advantages over comparable Soviet tanks.

The high silhouette and big turret (the M60's main disadvantage) allow it to store one-third more ammunition than a Soviet T-72, and also allow it five degrees more main gun depression. These five degrees permit the M60 to hide "hull down" behind slopes and still poke its tube over the ground to destroy enemy vehicles. The Russian tanks have to expose themselves in similar situations. The M60 has better armor protection, but after all, it is a bigger target too. The other principal advantage of the M60 is its maintainability. Like most American equipment, it is built to be fixed, capable of numerous "field rigs," and allows relatively easy power pack and suspension maintenance.[8] This is a far cry from Soviet tanks, where one must often pull off the turret to fix the motor.

When mixed with mechanized infantry, tanks offer a rapid-fire, hard-target killing ability not available with TOW missiles. Tanks shoot and move quickly, carry a large load of main-gun and machine-gun rounds, are not greatly affected by artillery fragments, and can cross or crush improperly built obstacles and rough terrain. TF 2-34's tanks would be its main antitank weapon because of these factors. There is another element to tanks, called "shock action," which relates to the innate uneasiness most foot troops display when firing hand-held weapons at a charging, firing, fifty-three-ton metal monster. This shock effect can only be created when tanks roll in numbers, under firm command, at the decisive time and place. As TF 2-34 would find, shock action is easier to define than to accomplish.

C Company, 3d Engineer Battalion, would provide combat engineering for the Dragons. Its direct support (DS) platoon had three engineer squads with hand implements (shovels, axes, picks, chain saws), mounted in M113A1/A2s. These troops could lay and clear mines, install barbed wire, assist in building log obstacles, and emplace and fire heavy demolitions. The DS platoon headquarters included a five-ton dump truck and a 1¼-ton Gamma Goat light truck.

C Company provided some other assets that greatly augmented that DS platoon. The engineer company provided a versatile, powerful M728 Combat Engineer Vehicle (CEV), a 57.5-ton tanklike engineer system. The CEV is based on a main battle tank design, complete with turret. The M728 has a 165-mm demolition gun, a squat explosive projector capable of blowing open walls or bunkers. The CEV has a blade in front for dozing vehicle positions and clearing rubble. It also carries a heavy-duty A-frame to assist in moving heavy barrier materials or clearing wreckage. Besides the CEV, the DS platoon also received a D7F bulldozer, a green version of a standard civilian earthmover. The D7F moved about on a huge tractor trailer to save wear and tear on the dozer. The bulldozer was the piece of choice for digging tank positions and antitank ditches.

The company also provided an ungainly AVLB, a turretless tank chassis carrying a gigantic scissors bridge. The AVLB (armored vehicle launched bridge) can be erected in two to five minutes, spanning ditches up to eighteen meters in width. The bridge can carry M60A3 tanks with ease. Company C also had a "swing" capability, in that it was built to support three battalions (tank or infantry), and 1st Brigade had only two en route to NTC. This third platoon became a general support (GS) unit, moving between task forces as missions demanded. Usually, a task force in defense needed more engineer support than in the attack.

Air defense was provided to the Dragons by the antiaircraft platoons of A Battery, 5th Battalion, 52d Air Defense Artillery. One platoon of four M163 Vulcan self-propelled guns was allocated to TF 2-34. The M163 is yet another M113 version, mounting a six-barreled 20-mm Gatling-style cannon device. The Vulcan has a firing rate of up to 3,000 rounds per minute and a range of 1,200 meters. It is limited by its range-only radar to fair-weather engagements and carries less than a minute's worth of ammunition at maximum expenditure rate. The Vulcans work together in two-gun sections to protect moving tanks and tracks at the frontline. Their ground-firing role is definitely something to consider.

Five Redeye short-range surface-to-air shoulder-fired missile teams were also provided to TF 2-34. These two-man teams were attached to infantry platoons, since their jeeps would not last long in combat. The Redeye is a heat seeker with about a two-kilometer range, severely limited by its huge backblast and inability to shoot at anything but the rear end of a jet or the side of a helicopter.[9] It is better than nothing.

On occasion the task force received another sort of air defense platoon. This platoon was armed with four M730 Chaparral self-propelled surface-to-air missile carriers. Once again the M113 family of vehicles is the basis for the carrier. The Chaparral launcher carries four ready missiles and eight reloads. The missiles cannot be fired on the move. Chaparral is nothing more than the green version of the USAF/USN AIM-9 Sidewinder, a heat-seeking, up-the-tailpipe guided missile. It has a range of about 5,000 meters and is best employed to guard fixed or rarely moved installations, such as supply dumps or brigade-level command posts. Chaparral was really not suited for frontline use, but TF 2-34 had enough logistics activities and slow-moving administrative units to get some mileage out of the Chaparral platoon.

Other attached support elements were the ground surveillance radar teams from B Company, 124th Military Intelligence Battalion. These radars, mounted (naturally) in M113A2s, are the AN/PPS-5. They can detect enemy vehicles out to ten kilometers and enemy men out to five kilometers, in all weather, and even through light vegetation. Unfortunately, the radars emit an electronic blare so obvious to enemy collectors that their life in real combat may be painfully short.

Four motorcycle scouts from the 101st Airborne Division were given to the TF 2-34 operations officer to use as he saw fit. Trained as reconnaissance soldiers, they could also act as messengers. Nobody in the Dragons knew quite what to use them for, but they seemed like a good idea.

A tremendous amount of other combat power was readily available to the Dragons with a radio call or a ring of the wireline. The eighteen M109A2 155-mm self-propelled howitzers (SP) of 1st Battalion, 35th Field Artillery, were in direct support of 1st Brigade, providing responsive artillery fires on call and as planned in advance. These big guns could shoot a bewildering array of ammunition: nuclear (government-classified high explosives), chemical (nerve gas, no less), scatterable mines (remote antiarmor and antipersonnel instant minefields), improved conventional munitions (several tank-busting bomblets that rained from single shells), Copperhead (laser-guided homing round for destroying single tanks), and white phosphorus (good for screening smoke and inextinguishable fires). Of course, HC (gray) smoke, illuminating flares, and destructive high explosive rounds (set to burst in the air, on the ground, or after digging into trenches or bunkers) were also available, as they had been since the Great War.[10]

Observing and planning for these mighty weapons was a full-time job. The Dragons, like all maneuver battalions, were given a fire support team (FIST). The FIST came with an M577 for the battalion fire support officer (FSO) and one M113A2 for each line company. Rifle companies had a lieutenant and forward observers for every platoon to control artillery, mortar fire, and even air support. The tank company had only the lieutenant and his planning cell, as tank platoons called for their own fires. The FIST was there to observe, employ, and plan all indirect fires for the Dragons.

Indirect fire is a concept in which guns are aligned on targets they cannot see by use of trigonometry and mathematical relations. The FISTs send map locations back to the firing batteries or mortar platoons, who plot these targets, turn their gun tubes to face the unseen spots, adjust elevation and powder charges for the range, then fire. Adjustments are made by radio or field telephone (if a wireline is laid). The heart of the system is in the battery fire direction centers, where the forward observer's map coordinates are converted into firing data. It is not an easy method; the American Army has refined it to the point where one target can be passed to many scattered batteries for massive simultaneous firing. The batteries will take calls for fire from anyone with a radio who can give the authentic code sign. American privates in the infantry and tanks are taught to call for and adjust artillery and mortar fire. The Soviets have opted for more guns, calls only from the battery commanders, and direct fire, substituting military muscle for brainpower.

Help from the skies was also available. The United States Air Force Tactical Air Control Party (TACP) provided a ground forward air controller (FAC) to the Dragons. In his M113 with special radios, the FAC planned and used all manner of jets, to include the mighty A-10 with its huge 30-mm antiarmor gun and the flashing F-16. The FAC was able to coordinate Air Force and Army aviation in joint air attack teams, using agile AH-1S Cobras and swooping A-10s to destroy massed enemy formations. The FAC worked closely with the FSO to allow continuous artillery fire support even as jets rolled in.

Brigade also controlled other important units, including signal, supply, maintenance, chemical, military police, and electronic warfare (collection and jamming) outfits. It operated a medical clearing station and a huge cache of ammunition and barrier material. All of these gave support to the 34th and to the brigade in general. Additionally, like aces up its organizational sleeve, brigade had speedy UH-60 Blackhawk troop and cargo helicopters and deadly Cobras at its disposal. These helicopters could ferry in quick resupply or reinforcement or, in the case of the Cobras, roar to the front to restore a penetration with TOWs and cannon fire.

In summary TF 2-34 was a whole that could become stronger than the sum of its parts. Unlike their opponents, whose organization was fixed, the Dragons would regroup forces in accord with changing missions. They would get help from brigade as their tasks required, and they had to be ready to fight a combined arms battle. The National Training Center would test TF 2-34's abilities in every operational and logistic area. Without doubt the most critical, and most stressed, would be command and control. The heart of the American tactical system was its flexibility, as long as the leaders could rise to the challenge. If they did, the Americans would outperform the stylized, by-the-numbers Soviets (or the Irwin OPFOR), even though outgunned. But if the Dragons' leadership faltered, the results would not be pretty. In the final analysis it would be men, not machines, that would make the difference.

Leaders

To understand how American combat units are led, one must first understand the two clashing concepts that influence the peacetime officer corps. The first, which is obvious and is shared by officers in every army not at war, is to prepare men and units for combat by building competent, cohesive units. This is done through arduous, realistic training; firm, fair discipline; and leadership by example. The National Training Center experience is designed to aid this process and to provide a close-to-war environment for rotating units.

The other idea extant in the American Army's officer corps is pernicious and it also is shared by other armies, though some United States Army policies abet this thought to a dangerous degree. This is the theory that an officer's success and reason to exist is to get promoted: mind you, not to discharge great responsibility, nor to command large units, but strictly to achieve the highest rank possible.[11] Command, staff, schools, professional writing, awards, and publicity in and out of the Army are but means to this end. Unit success is important inasmuch as it contributes to one's individual career success. Most dangerous of all, since it is easier to simulate a fine unit or good training than it is actually to create either, image becomes more important than substance.

The interest in promotion is not universal, but officers quickly find themselves immersed in its effects. Like it or not, all officers become players in this Great Game of self-advancement. When taken at face value, the Army promotion and personnel policies seem fair and reasonable, and they were no doubt intended to supply the best leaders possible for Army units. This does occur to a large extent, but there is a cost affiliated with the current system. When taken to extremes, interest in personal promotions can cloud military judgments. Superiors may be fooled; subordinates are not.

There is not one written source for this promotion fixation. It is found, if one looks for it, in numerous Army regulations concerning promotions, assignments, awards, schooling, and evaluations. It is buried in lectures at West Point and in OCS and ROTC lesson plans. It can be heard constantly in any officers' club after duty hours, marked by the buzz words *career-enhancing, the boss says, OER, primary zone, year group,* and always, *my career.* The path to the top is assumed to be the goal of all—the American Army manages officers as individuals, unaffiliated with regiments (as in Commonwealth countries), and officers are unable to stay in uniform unless promoted.[12] There are no career lieutenants or captains. It is move up or move out.

The system pervades everything, and an officer is in it before he knows it. The basic pattern for a combat arms stairway to the stars is well known. Many American 2d lieutenants have mapped out their careers the way one would an AAA trip plan to Oregon, and most senior officers know "where they stand" down to the micromillimeter. The path begins as a new lieutenant. Real movers still go to the Military Academy at West Point, hold high cadet rank, and graduate near the top of their class. They go into combat arms (technical branches have few generals) or the engineers and try mightily to be honor graduates at their basic courses, Airborne School (parachutist's course), and Ranger School (a patrolling-based leadership and stress course). The good lieutenant leads a platoon, serves as an executive officer or a scout or mortar platoon leader, and tries to get selected for primary battalion staff duty or, best of all, company command. He avoids training units and brigade and higher staffs. If not selected for a company—or after his command—he attends an advanced course at his branch school or another combat arm's branch school. Again, he must strive to achieve the highest possible grade.

After the advanced course, the officer usually makes captain and goes to command. He wants a line unit, not a headquarters or a combat support company or some training unit. He also tries to pick up some staff experience, sticking to S-3 or G-3 (operations), which is the route of commanders. Once command is finished, the captain does not stay around with troops—no, he competes for Army-funded graduate schooling and an instructor slot at West Point or in an ROTC unit. He knows that assignment to recruiting, reserves, or training units at this point might be the bureaucratic equivalent of the old Mafia kiss of death. The captain gets an advanced degree. It does not matter in what, though a name school does help. A degree in underwear folding from Yale outranks a degree in modern Soviet history from University of North Carolina.

The man on the move gets picked to attend the Command and General Staff College at Fort Leavenworth, the big hurdle to be a top dog. At CGSC, captains should be on the major's promotion list or already majors. It is there that one finds the most intense competition in the Army, because one tenth of a point here or there may make or break the rest of a promising career. Heart attacks from stress are not unusual. Top men in each class become known, especially helpful when the knowers sit on promotion and command boards. CGSC majors must get to troop units and serve as S-3s at brigade or battalion. Being an executive officer is also good, but one must be an S-3. The old rules apply—no training units, headquarters commands, or high-level staffs.

Good reports as an S-3 and a "name" help when selection for lieutenant colonel and a battalion roll around. One gets a battalion as a lieutenant colonel and competes to be known in the division. Successful battalion command merits one the Army War College, an ungraded gentleman's course at Carlisle Barracks, Pennsylvania, where the future leaders of the Army size up each other. The "best" full colonels are selected to command brigades, and two out of three of those earn the star of a brigadier general. The best brigadiers go to be assistant division commanders, then earn their second stars and command those divisions. Three-star lieutenant generals and four-star generals round off the pyramid.

The rules of this road are simple: be known, hit all the stations, get the highest possible OERs (officer efficiency reports), amass every award possible, and, always, cultivate powerful superiors. Dissent is not usually a good idea, though it can work if one is shrewd. Ingratiation can help, but it must not be too obvious. An American battalion or brigade commander enjoys perquisites normally associated with nobility. A general is a demigod on earth, whose merest vocalized whim can be translated into instant action. The bottom line is always the same, from lieutenant to lieutenant general—be known, be known, be known.

The path described above is under fire presently in the Army, which is just as well. A true regimental system (in the British sense) seems to be on the horizon. Command tours have been lengthened from a head-spinning six months to two years at battalion and brigade. Efforts to rotate units, not men, are already under way. Many senior Army leaders see the evils in the present promotion ethic, which sacrifices substance for image. In the officer corps, also, one can hear disgust and dismay with the current system and a yearning for a more unit-oriented career plan.[13]

Still, in 1982, the Great Game was alive and well, both in the Army as a whole and in TF 2-34 in particular. The National Training Center, after all, could be viewed as a battalion commander's comparative examination, with results going straight to the four-star general at Forces Command and all levels in between.[14] One can read statements to the contrary, but reality seems to confirm that it is better to do well at NTC than not, in a career sense. The Great Game was the shadow behind the officers of the Dragons at Irwin.

The 2d Battalion (Mechanized), 34th Infantry, did not exist in a vacuum at Fort Irwin. The 24th Infantry Division (Mechanized), the "Victory" Division, heavy division of the Rapid Deployment Force, was well represented by its highest command element. The division commander, a respected, soft-spoken old soldier whose concern for men and mission was evident to all, was on hand for most of the rotation.[15] He was a stabilizing influence. His two assistant division commanders were also on hand. The assistant division commander for support helped in the equipment draw and turn-in. The assistant division commander for training (ADC-T), a highly intelligent, almost eccentric colonel, was present for most of the exercise. He meant well, but now and then he let his enthusiasm for the latest combat equipment influence his judgment. The ADC-T would have an effect on the mock battles, though not the one he expected. Overall these senior officers were supportive and had a positive or neutral influence on matters. After all, NTC was well below this level of command. With a few notable exceptions, it offered encouragement mainly, not directives or pointed advice, allowing TF 2-34 to do its own work.

The officers of 1st Brigade headquarters were also bystanders more than actual participants because of the nature of the Irwin scenario. The commander was relatively new to the brigade, having arrived unexpectedly when the old commander made brigadier general. The brigade commander had a background in armored cavalry operations, and his ways were still a mystery to his subordinates. Coming on the heels of a very dynamic colonel, the new brigade commander found a unit where close supervision and inspection of all operations by brigade were the norm. The old commander had seemed a "micro manager," though he really was not. The new colonel would first become known when he allowed the battalions to fight their own battles, as was intended at NTC. But the 2-34 was not used to that sort of brigade headquarters.

The brigade staff also was in flux. The executive officer was leaving within weeks to take command of a new battalion. Honed in the old colonel's methods of cramming support down the battalions' throats (that is, having equipment or supplies led directly to the subordinate unit under brigade staff control rather than sent off into the night to a map location), the staff was changing gears to a less-centralized planning system. Unfortunately, the gears were shifting in the middle of the NTC rotation.

The simulated battles would be won or lost by the Dragons, with the brigade and division leadership along as supporters, critics, and supervisors. The 2d Battalion (Mechanized), 34th Infantry, was under the command of a lieutenant colonel who had served two tours in Vietnam, one as a mechanized platoon leader and executive officer in the 25th Infantry Division and one as an airmobile infantry company commander in the famous 1st Cavalry Division. The battalion commander had taken over in November 1980, when the old commander "resigned" after only six months, rather than be relieved for numerous failures. The Dragons had been in bad shape at the time, though probably not as bad as the new commander was told.

The lieutenant colonel was a strange figure, simultaneously loved and hated. He played the Great Game like a virtuoso. Yet he had definite standards of tactical proficiency, discipline, and training organization that contributed to unit cohesion. He became known as the man whose unit never left the field. He was pushing his new battalion from one exercise to the next with little time off, working weekend after weekend, relentlessly training. He himself often seemed on a different regimen, and some said he stressed doing as he said rather than as he did. The battalion performed well indeed on a February 1981 Army Training Evaluation Program (ARTEP) exercise and was a star participant in the October 1981 BOLD EAGLE joint exercise at Eglin Air Force Base, Florida. At BOLD EAGLE the 34th was everywhere, changing missions with aplomb and assuredness, penetrating deep into the rear of the "enemy" 101st Airborne. In the Great Game the battalion commander was known. Also, the Dragons were better—the system did work, it seemed.

Before the NTC rotation, the 2d Battalion, 34th Infantry's crowning achievement under the battalion commander was its February 1982 exercise in DRAGON TEAM 3-82. This was a no-notice air deployment to (and field operation at) Fort Bragg, North Carolina. Conducted under the auspices of XVIII Airborne Corps and the Rapid Deployment Force, DRAGON TEAM loaded and moved TF 2-34 to Fort Bragg in less than thirty-six hours, subjected the unit to a fast-paced maneuver with battalions of the 82d Airborne Division in freezing rain and sticking mud, then returned the unit to Fort Stewart.[16] This particular training mission was tough and realistic, and the battalion commander justly made an Army-wide reputation for his men's efforts. Combined with his other achievements, the lieutenant colonel became known as a tactical expert and a trainer without peer.

The battalion commander looked at NTC as a personal challenge, both to maintain his career momentum and to establish himself with the new brigade commander. The Dragons had ignored a July 1982 Annual General Inspection by the post inspector general—the old brigade commander had told them to concentrate on the upcoming Fort Irwin operations. But the new brigade commander was shocked to find an IG report that his 2-34 Infantry was unsatisfactory in all aspects of equipment maintenance. As a result, the battalion commander felt extra pressure to excel, as the new brigade colonel's first impression was not good.

August 1982 brought additional pressures to the lieutenant colonel. The 2d Brigade of the 24th Infantry Division had deployed to Fort Irwin on NTC rotation 6-82 (1–15 August 1982). The 5th Battalion, 32d Armor, task force had done satisfactorily, but the task force based on 3d Battalion (Mech-

PREPARATION FOR FORT IRWIN: EXERCISES
2d Battalion (Mechanized), 34th Infantry

Unit	Exercise Title	Date	Location
TF 2-34 INF	Battalion ARTEP*	Feb/Mar 81	Fort Stewart, GA
Company B, 2-34 INF	U.S./Canadian Exchange	Feb/Mar 81	CFB Gagetown, NB
TF 2-34 INF	BOLD EAGLE 82	Oct 81	Eglin AFB, FL
Company A, 2-34 INF	Terrain Reinforcement	Dec 81	Fort Stewart, GA
Command/ Staff	CATTS**	Dec 81	Fort Leavenworth, KS
TF 2-34 INF	DRAGON TEAM 3-82	Feb 82	Fort Bragg, NC
Selected Men	GALLANT EAGLE 82***	Apr 82	Fort Irwin, CA
Company C, 2-34 INF	IRON COUGAR	June 82	Fort Campbell, KY
Company A, 2-34 INF	NORTHERN VICTORY II	June 82	Fort Drum, NY
Command/ Staff	Irwin Terrain Recon	July 82	Fort Irwin, CA
TF 2-34 INF	DESERT FORGE	Aug/Sep 82	Fort Stewart, GA

* Forces included J Company, 2d Battalion, The Royal Canadian Regiment.
** CATTS stands for Combined Arms Tactical Training Simulation. It is a moderated, evaluated war game to train battalion commanders, staffs, and company commanders in operational procedures.
*** Company A commander, CSC commander, future Company C commander, and future Company B commander participated.

anized), 19th Infantry, had undergone a two-week nightmare of embarrassing defeats and evident disorganization. After several other major difficulties the commander of that unit eventually paid the price of relief. Other divisions' mechanized battalions had not done very well either, and the after action reports from Fort Irwin stressed deficiencies in training and leadership. The division commanding general expected TF 2-34's commander to reverse that trend.

Personally the battalion commander was friendly and had a great sense of humor. He loved a good party and a stiff drink, and he was an able host and conversationalist. Some subordinates wondered how much of it was genuine and how much was reveling in the power of battalion command. Either way, the lieutenant colonel was approachable and open-minded, both on duty and off, though the battalion still usually did it his way.

Militarily the battalion commander truly was a competent tactician, having served in Germany as a brigade S-3 and having paid attention in CGSC. He was not a tactical *genius*, though one heard the word used by officers outside of the battalion. He did know the rudiments of combined arms operations and, most important, how to plan and direct simple, workable operations. This battalion commander would never win through daring innovation, but he would not lose through ignorant bumbling, either.

Another major trait was his uncanny acumen for picking staff, company commanders, and key subordinate leaders. Since he "commanded," and rarely did tasks by himself, he had to find the right horses to put his money on. This battalion commander could separate good workers from place fillers with dispassionate skill, and he was smart enough to let his better assistants do their jobs with minimal interference. He provided clear guidance and some supervision, drawing on his fundamental knowledge base of tactics and weapons.

The lieutenant colonel, in fact, typified the friction between building combat readiness and personal advancement. Like most American Army officers, he believed in both goals and thought them compatible. Because he innately favored training over self-aggrandizement (perhaps a throwback to Vietnam days, where he endured career building at his physical expense), the Dragons really were a decent unit. Still, the Great Game was around, likely to rear its head at the oddest moments, and the battalion commander was a high-stakes player.

The battalion commander's planning and routine thinking was done by the staff, his eyes and ears, specialists in the major functional areas. At the head of the staff was the battalion executive officer, an extremely bright (brighter than the lieutenant colonel in many respects), dignified, compassionate major who was unshakable in troubled situations. A Special Forces (Green Beret) officer in Vietnam, the battalion executive officer exuded confidence and knowledge and was extremely popular on the staff and in the battalion. He was imaginative, highly organized, and widely respected. The major handled logistics and administration, areas the battalion commander preferred not to bother himself about. The battalion executive officer could get an immense amount of work out of limited helpers and an impossible amount from competent deputies. The major had been around since the summer of 1981, so he was a veteran. He was a man everyone listened to and followed willingly. He routinely set a fine personal example.

On the staff the basic split in field operations is between those who work around the Tactical Operations Center (TOC) and those who work in the Administration-Logistics Operations Center (ALOC). The ALOC is the purview of the battalion XO, as long as the battalion commander is functional. The TOC is the realm of the other major on a battalion staff, the S-3 (operations) officer. The Dragons had inherited an S-3 in July 1982 who was a bona fide tactical expert in anyone's book. The S-3 was friendly, open-minded, quick of wit, and continually encouraging his subordinates. Also a Vietnam veteran (1st Cavalry Division), the operations officer fit in as if he had always been a Dragon. He had commanded five different companies, an unusually high number, and habitually led by personal example. His presence bordered on charismatic, and he was well suited to carry out the lieutenant colonel's sound concepts.

These two fine majors were a powerful advantage to the battalion commander, and they were the men who kept things running through their tireless commitment to excellence. The XO was the second in command, the S-3 third, but at times they would seem equal in influence. Together they controlled the battalion staff, the brain tissue of the task force.

The TOC crew included the S-2 (intelligence) officers and NCOs. The S-2 himself was an infantry lieutenant without any formal training. A brilliant, eccentric officer who had a master's degree from Temple in psychology, the S-2 was the sort of fellow who under pressure worked harder than usual. His laissez-faire attitude in garrison, however, belied his serious devotion and knowledge when his skills were needed. He was most reliable in the clutch and least capable in day-to-day situations. His Battlefield Intelligence Coordination Center (BICC) officer was a trained military intelligence lieutenant who did the drudgery and legwork while the S-2 stored up flashes of brilliance.

In the S-3 section the institutional memory resided in the agile mind of the S-3-Air, a captain who was "the voice of Dragon radio," stretching back to the pre–BOLD EAGLE summer training of 1981. This captain, powered only by coffee and cigarettes, could handle a dozen simultaneous crises with logic and common sense. He seemed never to sleep. He took immediately to the new S-3 and administered a Tactical Operations Center that was highly competent, speedy to react, and efficiently organized.

Besides the S-3-Air, two other fine lieutenants also served in the operations section.' The first lieutenant, in training to replace the captain after NTC, was a former company executive officer and Scout Platoon leader. He was aggressive and very intelligent. The second lieutenant was recuperating from a terrible automobile accident, and though new to the Army, lacked nothing in common sense. The other mainstay in the TOC was the operations senior NCO, a master sergeant who had trained his men to a high degree of excellence. The battalion commander had always insisted on a good TOC, and as the task force prepared for NTC, it had a great one.

The administration and logistics side of the house seemed shaky by comparison, although compared to other units, it was adequate. The S-1 (adjutant/personnel) was a decent, hardworking captain who had just arrived from brigade staff. He had worked mainly in operations up until this point, though his diligence went a long way to remedy lack of school training. Personnel actions are always in an endless snarl of missed suspense dates and regulations, and those in the 34th were no exception. The new adjutant had just begun hacking at this Gordian knot.

S-4 (logistics) was also in flux. The old S-4 had left to take a company. The new S-4 would have his troubles. This was one of the rare cases in which the battalion commander failed to notice a problem in his headquarters. The lieutenant's errors were masked at first by the battalion XO's hard work and tolerant attitude. The price paid for miscasting this officer would be substantial.

The artillery fire support officer, a sincere soul who worked in the TOC, typified one of the potential problems with the FIST concept. This FSO tried quite hard, but he arrived a bit short of doctrinal knowledge because of his inexperience. Unfortunately, FIST elements tended to be filled with the less able, the new, or those between "real" jobs in the gun batteries. As a result, the S-3 would need to keep a careful eye on this motivated but unseasoned captain.

Outside the staff were the companies. Service support was

provided by the large specialist platoons of Headquarters and Headquarters Company (Headhunters). The HHC commander was an old hand in the unit, having arrived in May 1979. In the field he moved the TOC and secured it. A free-wheeling individual, he often itched to go forward to get into the fight. Occasionally this worked to the detriment of his primary duties.

The four headquarters platoons were a strangely mixed bag. The medics had the best-trained platoon and the newest, least able lieutenant. Support platoon, which resupplied the battalion, had the best platoon leader, an experienced, hard-working first lieutenant. Unfortunately its sergeants were adequate but not outstanding, and the lieutenant had a long-standing personality clash with the new S-4, his superior in the field. Communications platoon was adequate but in decline following the departure of an outstanding (and poorly replaced) platoon sergeant, though the platoon leader was an experienced officer. The maintenance platoon was present for duty but only occasionally effective, and the battalion motor officer who led it was still relatively new to his job, though he was school trained.

Combat Support Company (the Cobras) was the other non-maneuver company. Its commander was the senior company CO in the battalion, and he normally manned the alternate command post. The executive officer was very diligent, but the first sergeant was average. The platoons here, as in HHC, normally operated separately. Scout Platoon was under a slow-talking, methodical lieutenant. Heavy mortars was under a competent platoon leader, though the loss of a particularly fine platoon sergeant hurt the mortarmen. The Antitank Platoon was led by a talented, thoughtful lieutenant who had his work cut out for him, with more than seventy men and eighteen of the complex Improved TOW Vehicles. In general, these critical platoons were carefully watched and their leaders chosen with special care.

The first of the line companies, in reputation and command experience, was Company A (Attack). Under a feisty little captain who had learned his trade in Panama's 193d Infantry Brigade, Alpha Company's leadership had been in the 34th for some time. The company seemed pretty able, but the captain was a hard taskmaster, and his relationship to his men was often adversarial. A Company was the battalion commander's most trusted rifle company; it had done well in BOLD EAGLE and DRAGON TEAM. The NTC would be the captain's last exercise before changing over his command. His executive officer and platoon leaders were good but tired of being verbally skewered, as was his first sergeant. A Company was not always a happy company.

B Company was under a new captain, the most senior officer (by time in the 34th) in the battalion, having arrived as a second lieutenant in January 1979. Blessed with a tremendous first sergeant and a spirited, intelligent executive officer, B Company was the most reliable unit in the battalion. Three of its four platoons were led by sergeants, and they were good ones. The lone officer platoon leader was the best rifle platoon leader in the battalion. The commander had served in B Company just a year earlier and was respected in the company. He led by example and related positively to his men. Because he was new, Bravo could not be counted on just yet.

C Company of the tanks was under a new commander, though the company was well used to working with the 34th (BOLD EAGLE, DRAGON TEAM). The new captain was an enigmatic figure, and he displayed some inexperience in tactical matters. His platoon leaders ranged from excellent and veteran (1st Platoon) to brand new (2d Platoon). From their first meeting the tank captain worried the battalion commander.

Of the other attachments the air defenders seemed able and useful, but the engineers were a known horror story. The DS platoon leader was brand new, and like the tanks, he had replaced an old familiar officer who was very competent. The engineer lieutenant appeared overwhelmed by his responsibilities, and his platoon sergeant was content to pilot a dump truck. This soft spot would really hurt the task force at Irwin.

Command, staff, companies, and attachments: these were the prime movers as the Dragons prepared to face the OPFOR.

Notes

1. Homer, *The Iliad*, Book 2, translated by Robert Fitzgerald (Garden City, N.Y.: Anchor Press/Doubleday, 1975), 50–51.

2. Edwin B. Coddington, *The Gettysburg Campaign: A Study in Command* (1979; reprint, New York: Charles Scribner's Sons, 1984), 12. Robert E. Lee penned these thoughts just prior to the fateful 1863 summer campaigns.

3. James A. Sawicki, *Infantry Regiments of the U.S. Army* (Dumfries, Va.: Wyvern Publications, 1981), 116–117. The Sawicki reference offers a basic record, and the author has filled in further background from notes

made while serving in the battalion from January 1979 to December 1983. The author experienced the unique privilege of hearing Maj. Gen. Aubrey S. "Red" Newman recount his recollections of commanding the 34th in World War II. General Newman visited the battalion in the summers of 1981, 1982, and 1983. His arrival was always a great day in the Dragon battalion.

4. Department of the Army, *Armor Reference Data, Volume I* (Fort Knox, Ky.: U.S. Army Armor School, 1979), 298–313. All further organizational data come from this manual. The H Series table of organization is now being superseded by the J Series structure. J Series provides for four rifle companies, an antitank company, and a headquarters company with its usual units, plus the scouts and heavy mortars. The author never could discover what became of the I Series.

5. Department of the Army, *TC 7-1 The Rifle Squads (Mechanized and Light Infantry)* (Fort Benning, Ga.: U.S. Army Infantry School, 31 December 1976), vi. This fat little manual was the first of the "how-to-fight" series to reach most field units, and it states ". . . if the situation permits, the squad will fight mounted from its APC." This was a major switch from previous doctrine, such as that found in the April 1970 *FM 7-10 The Rifle Company, Platoons, and Squads*. On page 3-16 that manual notes that "mechanized troops must immediately dismount and employ the normal tactics of any other type infantry unit" in the face of strong enemy resistance. Fighting mounted was an option only in the face of "sporadic" enemy fires. The M113's designation as a "carrier, personnel, full tracked" identifies its original role. The new M2 Bradley is designated an "infantry fighting vehicle." So the M113's new role may be a way of getting ready for a true fighting vehicle, the powerful Bradley.

6. The M125A1s had been through hell, especially at Fort Stewart. B-43 had been sunk in a 1980 swimming exercise at Fort Stewart. C-43 had crashed through a bridge and sunk in the Chattahoochee River, Fort Stewart, in May 1982. Both tracks had been pulled up, refitted, and sent back to their platoons. Because of available M125A1s in the Boeing yard inventory, the veteran mortar tracks did not participate at Fort Irwin.

7. Department of the Army, *ST 7-176 Infantry Reference Tactics Data Book* (Fort Benning, Ga.: U.S. Army Infantry School, 1983), A-2 to A-4. All equipment data that follow come from this manual.

8. Andrew Cockburn, *The Threat: Inside the Soviet Military Machine* (New York: Random House, 1983), 140–42. This summarizes Cockburn's interviews and experiences with Fort Hood troops trained by the Red Thrust detachment. The GI comparison of Soviet and American equipment is quite favorable to the big M60 tanks.

9. Department of the Army, *FM 71-2 The Tank and Mechanized Infantry Battalion Task Force* (Washington, D.C.: Headquarters, Department of the Army, 30 June 1977), I-2 to I-3. This manual has been

replaced by a series of draft manuals for both H and J Series Tables of Organization. The Redeye has been replaced by the far more lethal Stinger.

10. Department of the Army, *FM 71-100 Brigade and Division Operations (Armored/Mechanized)* (Fort Leavenworth, Kans.: Combined Arms Center, May 1977), 2-51.

11. James Fallows, *National Defense* (New York: Random House, 1981), 114–119. The Fallows book is not very popular in the Army. See also Maj. Gen. Richard L. Prillaman, "Career Development, or Stairway to the Stars," Ford Ord, Calif., 1972; reissued Fort Hood, Tex., 1980. This paper, circulated within the Army, is a literal blueprint of the "careerist" mentality. The author encountered it in an officer professional development class in December 1982. The circular is General Prillaman's opinion, but it is also one of the few succinct in-house guides to how the system really works. One excerpt will do: "The final point, be visible and widely known, is closely related to the requirement that you hold the right jobs, because you won't be able to favorably impress the fast movers if you have no contact with them. The future generals are not to be found in low-pressure, out-of-the-way places. You must be known to the right people." It might be mentioned that General Prillaman is a respected senior officer who has commanded at divisional level. Most of this author's remarks on Army careerism (the Great Game) are derived from the Fallows book and the Prillaman circular, not to mention personal experience.

12. *National Defense*, 115. This is called "up or out."

13. Gen. Edward C. Meyer, "Time of Transition; Focus on Quality," *Army*, October 1982, 21–22. "One of the key findings—which should not have been a surprise—is that the Army's current management system has buried within it all varieties of obstacles which prevent us from keeping a unit together. These obstacles are being identified, and will be rooted out because the results thus far leave little doubt that a unit-based system is the correct way to go. The Army is now committed to the adoption of a new manning system based on units." General Meyer was Chief of Staff of the Army at the time he wrote those words.

14. *FORSCOM Circular 350-83-10*, 1. The philosophy paragraph notes: "The thorough and comprehensive evaluations provided by the staff of the NTC will be used as tools by the chain of command."

15. The comments on individual officers and leaders that close this chapter are the opinions of the author. They are intended solely to provide a personal background to the NTC operations and to give an inkling of whom the commander of 2-34 Infantry had at his disposal.

16. Daniel P. Bolger, "Dragon Team 3-82: Trial Swing of the RDF's Heavy Punch," *Army*, September 1982, 14–20.

Chapter Four

Call to Arms

"Everything is very simple in War, but the simplest thing is difficult. These diffi-culties accumulate and produce a friction which no man can imagine exactly who has not seen War."

Carl Von Clausewitz, *On War*[1]

Having looked briefly at the Fort Irwin terrain, the real and OPFOR motorized rifle regiments, and the organization and leadership of the Dragons, it is time to address the way the mock engagements at the National Training Center are de-signed and resolved. The NTC experience is based on two basic types of operational training; force-on-force training (FFT) against the redoubtable OPFOR, and live-fire training (LFT) against computer-controlled mechanical targets.

Peacetime army maneuvers have traditionally depended on arbitrary rules of engagement and flocks of umpires to resolve war-game "battles." The REFORGER series in NATO is typ-ical of umpired training exercises. Officers and senior ser-geants, equipped with probability tables, radio links to "control headquarters," and a double basic load of patience, move along with participating units. These soldiers referee each "battle," using table modifiers for such items as surprise, use of artillery, visibility, and tactical deployment. This resolution results in simulated vehicle losses and troop casualties and the advance or repulse of the attacker. The control headquarters adds en-tertaining wild cards such as nuclear explosions, chemical strikes, air attacks, and refugees (all imitated by delays in movement and force attrition). In theory this replicates the mobile battle of battalions and brigades.

In practice it does depict combat, after a fashion, just as an early spring intrasquad football scrimmage bears a faint rela-tionship to the final playoff game. The umpires quickly dis-cover that tanks and APCs can easily drive past any defending enemy (or through them) unless actual physical obstacles are emplaced, since nobody dies when blank rounds are fired in their direction. The war-game officials soon learn that participating unit commanders, eager to reach their objectives (and to get a few kudos in the Great Game), are unwilling to slow down, deploy, or even wait for battle resolution in many cases. To the players, umpires are sources of nagging slowdowns, capricious simulated death ("you have just been struck by an enemy nerve gas barrage"), and frustrating "administrative halts," as exasperated control headquarters attempts to restore order to the units racing around the battlefield. Umpires and unit commanders are often seen trading harsh words near a crossroads or bridge amid a jumble of trucks, tanks, engineers, and bored infantrymen. To the average mechanized infantryman, such an operation is typified by endless hours of driving around in columns on roads, half-hearted dismounts (which soon peter out as the troops realize that the umpires count vehicles and weapons, not tactics), and missed or ice-cold meals. At corps and division, and especially at battalion and brigade, everyone on the staff gets a workout just keeping up with the frantic scramble of units and ever-changing orders. At squad and platoon, it is like a badly managed game of cops and robbers, complete with violent arguments about who shot whom. It hardly matters—even if "killed," one reliably resurrects a few hours later to continue the problem.[2]

The Army leadership was aware of this unreality factor in large unit training maneuvers, and its decision to open the National Training Center was based on the development of an ingenious solution to the endless question of who's dead. Force-on-force engagements at Fort Irwin utilize laser firings to simulate direct-fire weapons, and all men and equipment are decked out in laser detector arrays that register these low-intensity, eye-safe bursts. This concept is the heart of the training program and equipment known as MILES (Multiple Integrated Laser Engagement System).

With MILES, infantry weaponry can be "fired" against soldiers wearing receptor gear on torso and helmet. Tiny microphones on the small arms "listen" for the noise of a blank round and will not fire laser bullets without that blank. MILES firing devices look like small black boxes on the barrels of rifles and machine guns and emit a tight pulse of light energy that must strike a detector on the target. One "hit" may or may not kill the enemy—a microchip in the detector system fills in for the umpire's probability tables and decides how many machine-gun hits will be needed to kill a soldier. A man knows he is being "near-missed" as he hears intermittent beeping from his detection harness; he is dead when the beeping becomes continuous. Dead men must disarm their weapons to turn off the beeping, taking them out of the mock war. The soldier's MILES logic chip also disregards weapons that cannot damage the target; in other words, one cannot kill tanks with a rifle, though a bored missile gunner could shoot soldiers with a TOW if he had the desire.[3]

Tanks and armored personnel carriers have similar receptor devices, and like soldiers' detection harnesses, the vehicle systems have microchips that decide whether firing weapons that hit can kill the vehicle. Sometimes the tanks or tracks shrug off hits and near-misses. Vehicles with MILES sport a yellow, police-style dome light that spins once or twice for a near-miss and constantly for a destructive hit. The intercoms in a dead track fill with a shrieking beep. Like the troops, tracks and tanks that are killed have their weaponry rendered inoperative. Like the foot troops, these mobile firing platforms must fire a blank round to activate their lasers.

Antitank missiles such as TOWs and Dragons are included as well. Special, MILES-only versions of each tracker/sight have tiny "brains" that calculate the slow missile flight times that characterize these potent rounds. Another antitank weapon is the Viper (the name is a nod to a light armor-killing rocket that never made it to production), which is a very short-range simulator for the M72A2 Light Antitank Weapon (LAW). Real LAWs are one-shot throwaway tubes issued as ammunition, like grenades. Vipers for MILES are reusable, in the mold of the World War II bazooka, though they replicate a weapon that is not.

MILES runs on regular batteries, and it is designed to take a beating in the field. "Dead" men and equipment can be turned on only with a little green key, and green keys are reserved for those who control MILES exercises. It is possible to cheat by rigging dummy green keys and the like, but such cheating is usually reason for punishment under the Uniform Code of Military Justice. Soldiers in general are very happy to finally have a quick, realistic way to decide training battles.

At Fort Irwin MILES made a few rather significant alterations in the relative combat power of the Dragons and the OPFOR. First of all, TOWs were limited to twelve rounds, Dragons and Vipers to four, before rekeying was required. This was regardless of how many missile simulation rounds (the blanks for these weapons) had been stockpiled. Second,

MILES "worst-cased" the OPFOR, giving every BMP a 3,000-meter Sagger ATGM, a heavy machine gun, and an 800-meter range 73-mm gun, all of which were figured for peak performance rarely seen in the real BMP. In a strange converse, the MILES equipment on tanks and TOWs did not allow for use of the thermal imaging sights, trimming a major American strength. Third, NTC rules said that a vehicle with nonworking MILES was not part of the problem, so that this was added to an already troublesome burden of motor maintenance. Finally, MILES itself required battery replacement, laser lens cleaning, and boresight calibration (alignment with the actual weapons' sighting devices) on a regular basis. OPFOR units worked with MILES daily and knew these techniques. The 34th would have to learn about them.

Although MILES solved the direct-fire engagements of AT missiles, tanks, and infantrymen, it did not address such potent weapons as artillery, mortars, aircraft, helicopters, and air-defense guns. For this there was a network of observer controllers (OCs), members of the Fort Irwin Operations Group. In their controller role they marked indirect fires and assessed air-to-ground and ground-to-air kills. Controllers determined chemical casualties. They also decided who lived and died in minefields. These OCs carried a pistol-size controller gun capable of killing any man or vehicle. They also carried the famous green key to reset resupplied AT weapons or revive "dead" troops as replacements were processed. Unlike normal umpired exercises, Irwin's controllers "reconstituted" the dead only upon notification that proper casualty and vehicle evacuation and requisitions had been completed. Failure to send in a report or pull the "dead" men and equipment back to the battalion rear meant that the controllers left the unit in a weakened state. There were no instant revivals.

MILES allowed great, sweeping battles to occur in much more realistic style. Poor tactics or firing would result in losses. Vehicle MILES control boxes even recorded what killed them, using code numbers that designate which American or OPFOR round got them. The effects of friendly fire are often evident. MILES at NTC is a way of life, and it surely limits arguments and displays maneuver errors in larger-than-life reality. Of course, despite the refinements of the NTC and the simple beauty of MILES, there is no fear of death or maiming in these training firefights. Aside from that major omission and the lack of bursting artillery shells and aerial bombing, it would seem real enough.

With that explosive void in mind, the powers of NTC provided for an awesome live-fire training operation as part of the standard rotation. Making use of the vast Fort Irwin reservation and extremely liberal safety rules, the NTC gunnery phase is controlled by the unit chain of command. There are no safeties, no range flags, and no administrative actions to conform to range control regulations. Other than the fact that the targets are not really manned and fighting back, it is full-bore firepower and movement. Tanks, heavy machine guns, field artillery, mortars, attack helicopters, Air Force jets, and even rasping Vulcan Gatling cannons blaze away.

The live-fire exercise is the only "canned" part of the National Training Center, consisting of three firing operations run on the northern third of the Fort Irwin reservation. American units trade in MILES on their machine guns, rifles, and tank guns for real rounds, though all units retain the detection systems. TOW, Dragon, and Viper fires are simulated using MILES systems because of the high cost of the missiles and rockets. The ever-present observer controllers act as the effect of enemy fires, dispensing artillery burst simulators, CS riot-control gas grenades, and shots from the all-powerful MILES controller gun. The live-fire phase of NTC features a day defense, a night defense, and a grueling offensive over thirty kilometers of thick obstacle belts, craggy, twisting passes, and wide valley floors.

LFT features an amazing enemy force of black silhouette targets. In the defensive missions the American task force watches successive belts of pop-up tank and BMP silhouettes "move" down a valley toward the U.S. battle positions. The silhouettes change from frontal to flank views as the enemy array appears to move around obstacles and terrain. The targets "fire" with flash simulators, display distinctive hit pyrotechnics when struck, and send up oily smoke clouds when killed. All of these targets have counters that register every hit, MILES detectors to register missile impacts, and internal logic that leaves dead targets stopped in place as the lines advance with appropriate casualty gaps. As the targets close in, they apparently stop and dismount infantry (man-size targets). The targets do not really move—it is an illusion caused by the many lines and columns of target pits and erection machines that cover the valley floor.[4]

The enemy on the offensive mission has small platoon and company defensive positions, which also fire, show hits, and depict lingering kills. LFT's offensive scenario is more famous for its deep, well-built minefields and obstacles near its clots of silhouette defenders. Though the mines are ceramic, real explosives may be used to clear them. The tank ditches and wire aprons are quite real, so that obstacle breaching becomes the key to this mission. As in the defense, a computer controls the enemy targets and counts hits.[5] Controllers furnish a tally of rounds fired by the visiting task force.

Live fire and force on force are combined to create the two-week NTC rotation. The Dragons would be operating on a schedule that started with four days of FFT, then four days of LFT, then the final five days of force on force. Their comrades in 2-70 Armor's task force would do all nine days of FFT in the so-called Southern Corridor, then wind up with the live-fire exercises. The 34th would be the first unit to use the Central Corridor, since the armor battalion would be in the southern third of post for all force-on-force missions, and both units needed elbow room for fighting the OPFOR for the first four days. The Dragons would rotate up to the north for LFT, then come south as the tankers moved up to their live firing. Rotation 1-83 would also be the first trip into the Central Corridor for the OPFOR and the controllers.

The true essence of NTC is not in the MILES or the OPFOR, nor is it in the thick wire and mine carpets in the north. The real learning that came from the Irwin experience came from the operations group. Some of them ran the live fire's computerized array, but most served as observer controllers. OCs were specially selected officers and sergeants who moved with each American platoon, company, staff section, or battalion command group. Besides controlling the MILES and marking artillery fires, the OCs observed the American units as they prepared for, fought, and recovered from their Irwin battles. The OCs came with their own vehicles, provided their own food and fuel, and provided little in the way of encouragement or favoritism to their units. They were there to teach and to watch, and they taught through the use of the After Action Review (AAR).

The senior controller was the chief, operations group. The COG was a craggy, hulking full colonel with a voice like shifting gravel and a mind like a steel bear trap. He controlled the entire rotation, and although the OPFOR had its own leadership, it responded to the COG, since it was a training aid, after all. The OPFOR had their OCs as well. The COG commanded the two teams, the Green Team (Tank Task Force) and the Blue Team (Infantry Task Force). The Dragons were to work with the Blue Team, whose senior controller was a tall, thin lieutenant colonel with a penetrating voice and relentless, searching eyes. The Blue Team had a captain for each company, a lieutenant or sergeant for each platoon (to include the specialized elements such as antitank, mortars, scouts, support, communications, medics, and maintenance). The staff (S-1 through S-4) all had OCs, and a major was the S-3 controller and moved with the Tactical Operations Center. Another major shadowed the battalion executive officer and devoted himself to Combat Service Support (logistics). Each 34th element would be watched and examined at all times.

These OCs were doctrinal experts, undergoing a rigorous training program developed by Combined Arms Training and Doctrine Agency (CATRADA), affiliated with the prestigious Command and General Staff College at Fort Leavenworth. They learned the actual Army doctrine and how to apply it, and those who were not subject matter experts on assignment soon became capable indeed. The OCs worked rotation after rotation with little break, learning the land, the OPFOR, and the usual weaknesses of visiting units. OCs had to be proficient in their duties with MILES, but most important, they had to learn how to watch, record, then teach the application of doctrine.

After each battle, the maneuver company OCs would call their platoon OCs together and tell the unit company commander to gather his platoon leaders in twenty minutes. The OCs tabulated vehicle and soldier battle loss data, ammunition status, rounds expended per weapon (LFT only), and impressions and comments based on the unit's performance. When the company leaders assembled, the company's senior OC would start the After Action Review. CSC platoon OCs also did these reviews.

A company AAR began with the company commander's presenting the intended plan for the battle, not getting into what actually happened. With the stage set the OC would then use questions to touch on points in each of the seven operating systems. The Seven Operating Systems provided the analytical framework to discuss unit shortcomings and, now and then, successes. The seven systems were: Command and Control, Maneuver, Fire Support, Intelligence, Air Defense, Mobility/

Countermobility (engineer work), and Combat Service Support. The senior company OC guided the discussion with frank, biting questions, glossing over very little in exposing errors of judgment and execution. When all relevant areas had been discussed, platoon OCs were asked for brief comments, then the assembled unit leaders were asked for general remarks. It all took about a half hour.

After the company AAR, platoon OCs conducted platoon AARs with all the soldiers and sergeants, getting into the nuts and bolts of what happened and why it happened. While the

The Seven Operating Systems

1. Command and Control
   a. Troop-leading procedures
   b. Facilities (TOC, alternate, command group)
   c. Communications/Electronics
2. Maneuver
   a. See the battlefield
   b. Fight as a combined-arms team
   c. Concentration of combat power
   d. Use the defenders' advantages
   e. NBC defense
3. Fire Support
   a. Tactical air
   b. Artillery
   c. Mortars
4. Intelligence
   a. Direct collection
   b. Collect information
   c. Process information
   d. Disseminate and use
5. Air Defense
   a. Support scheme of maneuver
   b. Employment
6. Mobility/Countermobility
   a. Mobility (breach obstacles)
   b. Countermobility (build obstacles)
7. Combat Service Support (CSS)
   a. Plans and facilities
   b. Vehicle recovery
   c. Maintenance
   d. Supply
   e. Administration
   f. Medical

platoons debriefed, the company senior OC went to a central location in the battalion sector to provide input to the battalion's senior controller for the battalion AAR. The battalion task force's company commanders, CSC platoon leaders, battalion commander and staff, executive officer, and all attachment leaders assembled for this AAR about two hours after the battle ended. These AARs were always well attended by the brigade staff and commander and usually attracted assistant division commanders, the COG, the commanding general of the rotating units, and the brigadier general commanding the NTC. These mighty onlookers had no effect on the proceedings, as the senior controller went through the general plan, the seven systems, and the task force losses and enemy kills with merciless efficiency. OPFOR leaders gave their side of the battle. Embarrassing questions and comments were the rule, and the senior controller explained doctrinal errors as he went along. The battalion commander, so typically a lord in his own realm, often squirmed in the harsh light of this criticism, with his raters in the Great Game listening and looking on. Excuses were unacceptable, and personal offense was no excuse. As the controllers liked to say: "Do not be thin-skinned." So the dirty laundry all came out, and failures were scrutinized in exquisite detail. This bloodletting usually ended with comments by the COG, the Irwin CG, and visiting unit ADCs or CGs. It took two to three hours.[6]

This, in summation, was the structure of the National Training Center that awaited the Dragons in October 1982. A tough, well-equipped, highly trained OPFOR regiment, a realistic MILES hit/loss system, a demanding live-fire exercise, and uncompromising observer controllers all pointed to a very difficult two weeks indeed for the 2d Battalion, 34th Infantry.

Preparing for Fort Irwin training would be hard enough for any unit, but it was particularly trying for the Dragons at swampy, heavily forested, thickly undergrown Fort Stewart, Georgia. As far as Rapid Deployment Force missions, Stewart was well sited for deployment contingencies with its nearby deep-water port of Savannah, Georgia (not to mention fine facilities at neighboring Charleston, South Carolina; Brunswick, Georgia; and Jacksonville, Florida), and the heavy-duty, long runway at Stewart's satellite, Hunter Army Air Field (in Savannah proper). However, one would be hard pressed to find a place less like a desert than the lush, steamy southeast Georgia post.

The 34th first got wind of its National Training Center rotation after the triumphant conclusion of its no-notice air movement and field exercise at Fort Bragg, North Carolina, in February 1982. DRAGON TEAM 3-82 had been a real test of endurance and leadership, and it contributed measurably to the battalion's reputation. Still, Bragg was not the desert, and the 82d Airborne opposition was not the Irwin OPFOR. With brigade and the 2-70 Armor, the Dragons' leadership turned to the thorny problem of training for sand and rocks in a swamp.

Brigade exercise DESERT FORGE was the result. Designed by the old brigade commander, it was executed by the new colonel with little change. For the 2-34 units, the field training was continuous from the second week of August to the third week of September 1982. DESERT FORGE was truly unusual, with brigade pulling in numerous favors all the way up to Department of the Army to stabilize almost all troops in the deploying units. The 34th got new men, but men due to move to other units were extended for the NTC, to include the battalion XO. Because of this freeze on transfers, the Dragons swelled to nearly full strength and built trained gun crews and proficient rifle squads. In an Army of constant turbulence (because of the policy of transferring individuals, not units), the Dragons were relatively constant.

The DESERT FORGE training built on this corps of stable troops, many of whom (especially the leaders) had been in the 34th a year or more, participating in BOLD EAGLE and DRAGON TEAM. Brigade prescribed what was to be done; the Dragons figured out how to learn the required skills. The learning was in stages: first at platoon, then at company. There was little battalion-level work; Stewart's pathetic twenty-foot hills and two-kilometer-by-one-kilometer open areas did not really allow for anything meaningful.

Training was intense, with lavish use of ammunition (live and blank) and full MILES device integration. Rifle platoons trained in their companies for a few days, then underwent a realistic live-fire attack with full mortar support and little artificial safety constraint. The riflemen then underwent platoon ARTEPs (an Army Training Evaluation Program is a graded, critical look at the platoon's performance on basic missions). The tasks checked were platoon defense of an open area, movement to contact (an attack to find an unknown enemy position), and a tough, complicated night attack. Obstacle breaching and chemical defense were integrated into the movement to contact. The graders were not slouches—the CSC commander handled the movement-to-contact lane, the HHC commander the night attack (with the aid of the S-3-Air), and the platoon's own company commander checked the defense. A full inspection of platoon equipment maintenance was included.

Once the platoon-level missions were wrapped up, Company C went over to the tank battalion, and Company C, 2-70 Armor, came over. All companies were task organized with A and B mech heavy (two infantry, one tank platoon) and the attached Company C also mech heavy (two infantry, one tank). The companies trained for a few days on their own, then moved to the post tank ranges to run a Combined Arms Live Fire Exercise (CALFEX). The CALFEX featured a deliberate attack across an open tank range of rolling berms, supported by heavy artillery, mortars, A-10 jets, and Army Cobra attack helicopters. To reach the objective, a low red-clay dirt pile three kilometers away, the company team would need to fire armed TOW and Dragon missiles, maneuver aggressively supported by its own fires from tanks and machine guns, then breach a wire tangle with engineer demolitions. It was a large-scale, demanding mission with few constraints.

Following the CALFEX, the companies were evaluated on the ARTEP missions defend in sector (using the depth on a large area against the rest of the battalion) and company night attack (featuring still another obstacle breach). MILES was used, though a shortage of controllers and unfamiliarity with the equipment hurt this facet of the operations. After company ARTEPs, everyone but Company B took a thirty-six-hour break and went in for showers and a rest, parking vehicles under guard in the field.

Company B was left out by its commander's request, as it alone would defend a wide-open field against the entire 2-70 Armor (with Company C, 2-34 Infantry, attached) in a graphic display of what a huge target array might look like. Company B's new commander dug in deep, had his men scrounge wire and string it without engineer support all across the big drop zone, and assembled a giant kill zone on the armor unit's avenue of approach. Company B's men worked diligently and well. When the demonstration occurred in front of the brigade's officers (it was part of a class by the brigade colonel), 2-70 Armor lost half of its vehicles but made it through Company B. The lesson was obvious to all, but especially to Company B. It would take more than concertina wire and aimed shots to devastate a determined, numerous enemy. It would take mighty barriers.

The final phase of DESERT FORGE consisted of a few days of battalion maneuver, 70th Armor versus 34th Infantry. This did have MILES, but it was not well controlled, swiftly degenerating into the usual driving around and over that typified large-scale umpired exercises. The train-up ended after the two battalions tired of running around the western half of Fort Stewart's pine stands, red clay trails, and dried swamp beds.

The 34th had effectively trained its scouts, heavy mortars, company mortars, TOWs, and Tactical Operations Center on DESERT FORGE. These elements were integrated, and the special combat platoons also were evaluated on several ARTEP missions. The attached tank company was with the 34th for half the exercise and had been examined in detail. Engineers, air defense, and ground-surveillance radars had been present but not really checked out in full. Just as worrisome, the battalion's combat service support troops and equipment had not been heavily stressed or evaluated. Supply lines were short and garrison was close; there was no rear-area enemy threat. Worst of all, the Fort Irwin loss-reconstitution system of reports and evacuation was not really tested, though it was tried halfheartedly on the battalion operations.

The battalion commander of the 34th had made a few assessments based on DESERT FORGE that would color his plans, particularly early in the Irwin rotation. He himself had missed a week of the exercise (platoon ARTEPs, company CALFEX) because of a death in his family. Of his line units, A Company seemed a bit shaky, with problems in all three platoon ARTEPs, a confused company CALFEX, and an indifferent company ARTEP performance. These were a bit disquieting, as the lieutenant colonel was counting heavily on his most-experienced company commander and on the company's three lieutenants. Finally, he dismissed the "seeming" weaknesses as aberrations.

Company B had turned out to be a pleasant surprise. Its three rifle platoons had put in strong ARTEP performances, demonstrating a uniformly high standard of battle drill, particularly in dismounted assaults and obstacle breaching. Even though the 70th had penetrated its position on the brigade demonstration, Company B's dispositions, gunnery, and aggressiveness (as well as a huge amount of barbed wire collected by the company) had destroyed about half of the attackers, pointing to what would be possible with full engineer support and a lot of mines. B Company's new commander seemed competent and his three and a half years in the battalion had made his transition a smooth one. This company would be a reliable unit, it appeared.

Company C, 2d Battalion, 70th Armor, seemed to be the weakest of the three line units, though its commander was still learning. The battalion commander fretted over the tankers, as the new captain inspired confusion on occasion rather than confidence. However, the tank crews were the same old Company C that had gone to BOLD EAGLE and DRAGON TEAM, so perhaps it would all work out. The tanks, however, were a question mark.

The scouts and heavy mortars seemed solid. The big Antitank Platoon had gotten a lot of practice, and it would be a key force, especially if the tanks proved unreliable. As far as attachments, the engineers had not been asked for much, though their platoon leadership had enough trouble handling the minor tasks assigned. The air defense units were not really examined at all, and the ground radars were of little use in the small open areas at Stewart. Fire support on the CALFEX was adequate, though it was a trifle "canned." The real-fire planning system was never checked.

The area of logistics was the greatest "gloss over," with the calm battalion XO soothing the lieutenant colonel's anxieties about administration, supply, and maintenance. Potential control and procedure problems here went unnoticed—there was so much to do just in the fighting units, it was thought. This omission would hurt.

In the end it would come down to the only major part of the 34th not yet discussed—its fine young soldiers. The recession of the early eighties had given the volunteer Army a pretty high caliber of GI, many with college educations. Collegian or farm boy, ghetto gang member or suburban high school athlete, it mattered little. If led with any sort of capability, these infantrymen showed boundless innovation, drive, and stamina. Many Dragon soldiers had served in the Ranger Battalion at Hunter Army Air Field before moving to Stewart (some were transferred for disciplinary infractions, others because they had been exhausted by the Ranger regimen), and these former parachute troops were extremely motivated and skilled. Sergeants and junior officers learned quickly that these young men, these latest versions of *l'enfant*, were typical youths in many ways— easily bored at times, hotheaded, mischievous if left with nothing on their minds. Still, these boys were not children. They knew how to throw grenades, call for shattering artillery shells, narrow their eyes to slits to punch machine gun bullets through man-size silhouettes, slash into rubber bayonet dummies, and move like slow vengeance through the midnight swamp. When the time came, these men would kill with the same ruthless efficiency their older brothers and senior NCOs had shown in Vietnam. They complained about constant field problems, but most of them liked training and were good at their duties. Their abilities would atone for many commander miscalculations. The only thing left now was to go to Irwin. Time for practice had run out.

NTC Rotation 1-83 was the core of an exercise involving deployment and redeployment to Irwin, all under the planning name MOJAVE VICTORY II. The tank battalion and 2-21 Infantry had already been to Fort Irwin (pre-NTC) in November 1980, which constituted MOJAVE VICTORY I. MOJAVE VICTORY II was the aegis for all of 1st Brigade's planning and movement with regard to the October 1982 mission at the National Training Center.

The mechanics of moving a brigade-minus from the Atlantic coast to the Pacific coast are beyond the scope of this study, but suffice it to say that the 24th Division's experience on many RDF exercises was put to good use. Some equipment was moved by railroad, and the troops were flown on chartered commercial jets. In a nasty surprise the 34th found out before DESERT FORGE that it would not use many of its own vehicles but would draw out of an equipment site at Irwin run by Boeing Services International (the same Boeing that builds 747s and B-52s). This yard of combat gear and vehicles was intended to save money by limiting cross-country transportation costs. Unfortunately, the beating the equipment sets took rendered them less than adequate for the intense demands of NTC training.

In the 34th the equipment draw began on 1 October 1982, a week before the battles were due to start. The 1st Cavalry Division was turning in tracks and tanks at the civilian-contracted yard when the Dragons arrived. The equipment was running but not in good shape, with electrical charging problems prevalent and suspension systems in need of new road-wheels and tread shoes. The wheeled vehicles definitely looked like carcasses, though they did run. The Dragons' rail cars carried a few tracks and trucks, but not enough to avoid using the Boeing yard's creaking inventory. This worn-out stuff would be yet another cross for the 34th to bear.

Besides not having very good equipment, the Dragons ended up with less equipment than they needed. Rifle platoons had only three, not four, M113 APCs. Six ITVs were replaced by old M220s, TOW launchers in a basic M113 cargo hatch, lacking the big cantilever "hammerhead" launcher. CSC had no recovery vehicle to pick up its maintenance failures. The tank company was short three M60s—the fourteen it had were M60A1s, without the fine thermal gear or laser range finders of the 70th's own M60A3s. The rail-loaded tracks and trucks from Stewart were mainly command vehicles—they were reliable, but they would not do the fighting. The whole draw was an around-the-clock struggle to get workable equipment out of the lackadaisical civilian contract personnel, who too often were on another wavelength. As a result, the move-out on 6 October was delayed until after dark in an attempt to piece together a few more tanks and TOWs. It all looked cruel and unnecessary, but considering that the European pre-positioned equipment installations may be pretty shot up by the time RE-FORGER units reach them, or that RDF ships and aircraft may not arrive in one piece, the equipment situation was by no means unrealistic.

While the advance party drivers and mechanics drew equipment and the bulk of the troops flew in on daily sorties to Norton Air Force Base (ninety-odd miles southwest), the company and battalion leadership began reconnoitering the convoluted Central Corridor, trying to commit the wadis and dark, basalt-covered hills to memory. The post was not new, though the central region was novel. Most of them had been out to the NTC for a weekend terrain walk on the Southern Corridor (courtesy of the Air Force's Military Airlift Command) in July 1982 under the old brigade commander. The A, B, and CSC commanders had been out for two weeks in April 1982, refereeing the California National Guard and 82d Airborne Division in GALLANT EAGLE 82.[7] The battalion commander and his subordinates looked over their future field of play. They met the observer controllers of Blue Team, got briefed on the NTC rules, and watched and fought the battle of the Boeing yard

TF 2-34 INFANTRY EQUIPMENT

Type	Authorized	Source Rail	NTC Yard	Total On Hand	(+) or (−)*
M113	42	8	26	34	− 8
M901	17	7	4	11	− 6
M220**	0	0	6	6	+ 6
M125	6	0	5	5	− 1
M106	4	0	3	3	− 1
M577	6	2	4	6	0
M578	3	1	1	2	− 1
M88	2	2	0	2	0
Attached Tank Company†					
M60	17	0	14	14	− 3
M113	1	1	0	1	0
M88	1	0	1	1	0

* (+) or (−)—Difference between authorized and total on hand.
** The M220 is an M113 with a single TOW launcher in the cargo hatch. It was issued as a substitute for M901 ITVs.
† No other attachments included. Company C, 2-34 INF, detached and shown as such.

with their disgusted executive officers and motor sergeants. The days crawled by, moving toward 6 October, as the troops built a city of pup tents near the Boeing motor pool. Senior sergeants and battalions set up command posts across the street from tent city in a string of peeling, orange-painted boxcar bodies resting on a sand-scrabble flat. MOJAVE VICTORY II was moving toward its key segment.

In the early afternoon of 6 October 1982, the commanders and staff (and vigilant OCs) of Task Force 2-34 Infantry gathered behind the Dragons' moldering boxcar, planting themselves in front of the sprawling reservation map to hear the plan for the first mission. The CSC captain was gone—his wife had just delivered a baby in Georgia, and he was winging home, his XO taking over. The battalion S-3 called the briefing to order, checked the roll to insure all attachments were present, then began the order.

The mission was movement to contact—in other words, to attack to find and fight the enemy in a zone of action. The zone was, as expected, the Central Corridor, and the plan went into great detail about seizure of objective hills, movement axes, and coordination between teams. The task force would have three mech-heavy teams, with Team A in the north, Team B in the south, and Team Tank following Team A. A provision was made to cross the Barstow "canal" (really the north-south road and instrumentation cable conduit), using the scouts, engineers, and a helicopter insertion by one of the tank team's infantry platoons. The artillery and engineer officers explained their roles. It was nothing strange, except the fact that the zone stretched on forever, well over fifty-five kilometers.

To get into position, the task force would have to drive to an assembly area on the far side of massive Tiefort Mountain, using a thirty-eight-kilometer route that they all thought they had reconned. The task force would move at 2100 that night, totally blacked out, and form a huge perimeter on hill 720 to await the 0630 attack time the next morning. The usual quartering parties (unit guides) would move out with the Scout Platoon before nightfall to mark the route. It all sounded easy enough. Nobody was tired, everybody would grab one last leisurely meal (except the TOW and tank crews, who were still feverishly drawing vehicles), then move out after dark.

The briefing was a bit long, with the order taking over an hour. The commanders and special platoon leaders left to brief their subordinates and marshal their troops and vehicles. Who could have thought that the armor task force was independently planning a movement that would cross the 34th route at two locations close to the Dragons' starting point or that 2-70 would be moving at 2100 as well or that brigade fumbled the coordination requirement? Who could have thought that night in the desert is as dark as the inside of a black sock in a cave? The motor pools were bright with flashlights and busy with final preparations, ammunition stowage, and last minute orders and communication checks as synchronized watches crept around towards 2100. Engines roared to life, many of the NTC tracks requiring jump starts to allay the effects of weak batteries or damaged charging harnesses.

It was 2100, and the first Dragon track (from Company B) crossed the start point at the hardtop road, right near the nearly abandoned tent city. With a gush of throaty exhaust B Team commander's M113 clanked slowly into the coal black night.

Notes

1. Carl Von Clausewitz, *On War*, edited by Anatol Rapoport (New York: Penguin Books, 1983), 164.

2. John Train, "With Our Forces in West Germany," *The American Spectator*, vol. 16. no. 2, February 1983: Staff Sgt. Ann Keays and Staff

Sgt. Rico Johnston, "REFORGER," *Army Trainer*, Winter 81/82, 34–39. The soldiers' comments quoted are particularly interesting.

3. Department of the Army, *TB 9-1200-209-10 MILES. Multiple Integrated Laser Engagement System* (Rock Island Arsenal, Ill.: U.S. Army Armament Materiel Readiness Command, February 1981), 4, 5, 11, 12, 15. All MILES information comes from this manual. See also Staff Sgt. Rico Johnston, "MILES," *Army Trainer*. Winter 81/82, 26–28.

4. Maj. Randolph W. House, U.S. Army, "NTC Live Fire: One Step Closer to Battlefield Realism," *Military Review*, March 1980, 68–70.

5. House, "NTC Live Fire," explains the testing at Fort Hood that led to the design of the Irwin live-fire missions.

6. First Sgt. Michael Brown, "Live From NTC—It's the War," *Soldiers*, February 1984, 27–28. The Brown article describes AARs held in the Star Wars trailer, using full-technology feedback. Though the general flow was similar, TF 2-34 was evaluated under a manual system.

7. Col. E. L. Daniel, *After Action Report, Mojave Victory II* (Fort Stewart, Ga.: 1st Brigade, 24th Infantry Division [Mechanized], 23 November 1982), 9. The 2-34 commander felt leader recon trips to the desert were one of three means to prepare a unit for NTC. The other two were TOC drills on orders and DESERT FORGE.

Chapter Five

Movement to Contact (I)

*"Most offensive operations begin with a movement to contact. A movement to
contact is usually characterized by a lack of information about the enemy."*
      FM 71-1 The Tank and Mechanized Infantry Company Team,
                 Coordinating Draft[1]

*"If one knows where and when a battle will be fought his troops can march a
thousand li and meet on the field. But if he knows neither the battleground nor the day
of battle, the left will be unable to aid the right, or the right, the left; the van to
support the rear, or the rear, the van. How much more is this so when separated by
several tens of li, or, indeed, by even a few!"*

                Sun Tzu, The Art of War[2]

Darkness smothered the columns that moved slowly out of the
garrison area after 2100 on 6 October. Fine, bone white dust
rose behind each tank and APC as the Dragons uncoiled onto
their wide trail that led them first north, then east to hill 720.
The moon had not yet risen, and the tiny stars did little to guide
the lumbering files.

The route that Task Force 2-34 was taking was thirty-five-
kilometers long, pushing north along the hardtop Barstow Road
(a "canal" for problem play), then turning east as it passed the
gargantuan bulk of Tiefort Mountain. The battalion task force
would continue east, finally halting around the base of hill 720,
a flat outwork on the northeastern tail of the Tiefort massif. To
simplify the whole operation, the task force was moving slowly
(less than twenty-five kilometers per hour) in a long column of
company columns, playing a battalion-size version of follow
the leader. Every company had sent out a guide team of three
men with the Scout Platoon to meet the incoming elements at
the end of the eastern straightaway and to walk them into the
assembly area. The concept could not be more clear-cut.

The fog of war rolled in thickly and swiftly enough. The
tank battalion task force had chosen the same start time, but
somehow managed to cross its vehicle stream with that of the
Dragons right near the start point, although 2-70 Armor was
heading south to its own zone. Part of the Antitank Platoon was

TASK ORGANIZATION: TF 2-34 INFANTRY
7 OCTOBER 1982

Team A

Company A (−)
3d Platoon, Company C (tanks)

Team B

Company B (−)
1st Platoon, Company C (tanks)
1 AT section (+ 1 squad)

Team C

Company C (−)
3d Platoon, Company B (OPCON to TF for air assault)
3d Platoon, Company A
1 AT section

TF Control

Scouts
Heavy Mortars
3d Platoon, Company B (−) (OPCON for air assault)

Not Under Control (Disorganized)

AT Platoon (−) (attachment not made to Team A)
DS Engineer Platoon (no attachments made to line units)

OPPOSING FORCES (OPFOR) MOTORIZED RIFLE COMPANY

1 Motorized Rifle Company (MRC) (10 BMP infantry vehicles)
1 Tank Platoon (4 T-72 tanks)

still just outside the Boeing yard, hurriedly inventorying its last
few M220 TOW vehicles. The AT Platoon leader was surprised to see a pile of dirty black boxes behind the long-
departed parking spots of the Scout Platoon. He went over and
found the scouts' night-vision devices, to the tune of $5,000
per copy. The scouts, meanwhile, were reduced to using the
Mark I eyeball at the distant release point.
  One of the Improved TOW Vehicles that had already left the

motor pool area suddenly lighted up the long, cloudy track march with the steady yellow flashing of its MILES kill-indicator light. A report went in to the 34th Tactical Operations Center, with the hit attributed to enemy action. So the OPFOR were starting already, were they? In fact, all that had happened was a malfunction in the TOW track's MILES harness, but nobody could have known that. The Dragons crept on even more cautiously, night-vision-goggled crews straining to see through the choking dust and inky night.

As if the crossbuck near the Boeing yard were not bad enough, the Dragons soon discovered an artillery battalion hot on the rear of the 34th's last APCs. With the timetable slipping into fantasy as the dust boiled up and night closed in, the Dragons' lead elements made an error in navigation that threw everything into the trashbin. Team Bravo, its commander confused by the blended silhouettes of the Tiefort outcroppings, turned to the south without meeting its guides. The Heavy Mortar Platoon, CSC headquarters, and most of the Antitank Platoon (those not completing their draw) followed. Nobody had bothered to give the guides radios, and the scouts were not answering any calls. Everyone guessed the OPFOR had gotten the guides. Instead, it was the result of stupidity. Thus the guides were presumed lost when they had not yet been reached, and a major portion of TF 2-34 set up an assembly area at the base of hill 760, seven kilometers west of hill 720. To further confuse the issue, the TF TOC received reports that everyone

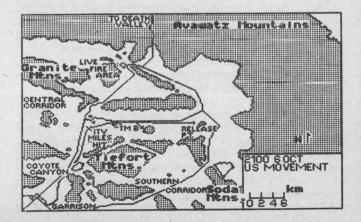

was in position as planned. Team A and Team Charlie Tank tied in, but neither reported CSC and Bravo to be absent.

The TF command group and TOC, meanwhile, pulled into a position a kilometer north of hill 720, outside of the incomplete perimeter. The battalion commander thought everyone was lost, a logical deduction at 0130 on the 7th when all units reported closure and he could see nobody. (The possibility that he himself was misoriented did not occur to him, any more than it did to Team B, the errant CSC platoons, or the rest of the command group.) The road was choked with artillery behind the battalion, and the moon was still fat and low on the horizon of the black desert. The option chosen to resolve the mess was to do nothing and hope for the best.

In the night the wind blew gently but steadily across the scattered, nervous task force troops. The units on hill 760 took their bearings, discussed the issue with the CSC XO (acting commander), AT lieutenant, and Heavy Mortar Platoon leader and finally agreed with the commander of Bravo Team that they were in the right place since that young captain was usually dead right.

This time he was dead wrong. As the scouts and engineer recon force inched to the Barstow canal in the small hours of 7 October, Team B deployed into attack formation at the foot of hill 760, ready to push west at 0700 just after sunrise. The only problem was that they were all facing due east.

The idea behind a movement to contact is to locate the enemy, test his dispositions and strength, then act before the enemy can react to the moving force. The initial contact must be made with the smallest possible element, thereby allowing the bulk of the task force to maneuver to destroy the enemy. A movement to contact orients on the enemy, not on terrain, although an initial "march" objective is designated to provide a direction for the force hunting the opposing units.[3]

What makes a movement to contact so tricky is the utter dearth of hard intelligence about the opposition. Once the enemy is located, the moving force could find one of several situations. The best of all would be a small, stationary enemy unit that task force–led troops could easily crush and brush aside. Next best would be a slightly larger, stationary enemy force that the lead element would fix by aggressive fires and movement while the rest of the task force came up to eliminate the hindrance. Third, the lead elements of the task force might

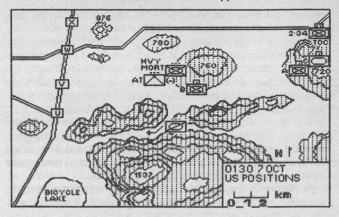

fix the enemy and let the bulk of the task force bypass the stationary hostiles, though it can be hazardous to leave live, intact enemy roaming around one's rear area. Finally, the enemy could prove to be very powerful, necessitating a hasty defense to prepare a set-piece, deliberate attack, or even a full-scale defense in the face of a major enemy offensive. The greatest nightmare was surely the fear of striking an OPFOR regiment on its own "approach march." In that case victory would go to the unit that first recognized the situation and ambushed the other.

The 34th's plans for its 7 October mission were not really first-rate. Faced with a wide zone and a canal to cross, the task force had opted for two up, one back, with Team A leading in the north and Team B in the south. Team Charlie Tank was to follow Team A and provide an infantry platoon to helicopter across the Barstow canal and secure the far side. The real danger here was that the task force would hit the enemy with both lead teams at once, leaving little combat power free to maneuver if the OPFOR was deployed in strength on a wide front. Additionally, the battalion seemed fixated on its geographic objectives, and its operation order indicated enemy units might be bypassed to strike into their rear areas. This was not in keeping with the movement to contact's orientation on locating and attacking the OPFOR units. The role of the scouts was clear as far as finding and marking "ford sites," though their duties after that point were unclear. Worse, the Antitank Platoon leader had not fully posted his map and had missed part of the order with a resultant information gap among the task force's primary antitank units. Additionally, Team A's TOWs had not linked up. Finally, though the engineer platoon leader was with the scouts to check the canal, his squads had not attached themselves to any of the maneuver teams, leaving the task force short of obstacle-demolition capability at its leading edge. All of these considerations were aside from the navigation troubles that were dissolving even this flawed plan.

The basic rule of military movement (unchanged since the Romans) was to move in column, fight on line. American Army doctrine in 1982 prescribed movement techniques based on the column, even in the face of enemy action. Dismounted infantry, mounted infantry in APCs and tanks in platoons, and even platoons in companies were all taught to move in long, staggered files, swinging on line only to assault. The result was that the Dragons were trained to use formations that made long moves easy to control and that put only a small chunk of fighting power out front. However, pulling units into an assault line or reacting to flank threats was much harder. In his day Napoleon had solved the line/column controversy by adopting the *order mixte*, a complicated column with subordinate units on line to speed battle drill. What the Dragons needed was an intermediate formation that platoons could use, whether or not the company was in column or on line. But doctrine had yet to return to then venerable World War II–era wedge in its search for a mixed order tactical formation,[4] so the Dragons at NTC were stuck with evolving battle drills from the column. As a

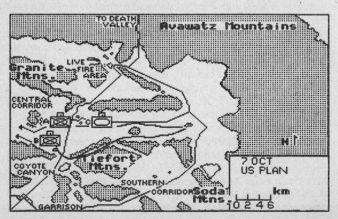

result, units had a tendency to dribble strength straight forward into a firefight, like sausage into a grinder.

Even though columns were the rule at company team and platoon levels, the task force was moving in a line, since the two lead teams were in parallel columns. Trying to move a

Movement Techniques

Travelling	Travelling Overwatch	Bounding Overwatch

long distance with units abreast is rather difficult, since one or the other invariably crosses easier ground or fewer enemy. Besides not knowing much about the OPFOR alignment and strength, the terrain west of the Barstow canal did not lend itself to cursory map reconnaissance. The general flow of wadi cuts was perpendicular to the Dragons' motion, and it was by no means anything like the "open desert" suggested by most of the doctrinal literature. The fight in the wadis would be a battle of compartments and foot infantry, not speeding tanks. But nobody knew that yet; the order from brigade prohibited ground reconnaissance into The Washboard, as the wadis west of the canal became known. This engagement would be the first time any NTC rotation used the Central Corridor.

Sunrise came within the hour before the 0700 start time. It revealed to the TOC and Team B just how far off position they were. Team B quickly reoriented as the desert lighted up, and the other two teams shook out of the assembly area. However, Team B did not report its incorrect location, well across the line of departure. The scouts had moved through the defile between Tiefort and ridge 955, reaching and marking the crossings without incident. The platoon designated for the helicopter assault (3d Platoon, Company B, attached to Charlie Tank for 7 October and directly to TF 2-34 for the air operation) was in its pickup zone, waiting on the swift UH-60 Blackhawks from 24th Combat Aviation Battalion.

Task force communications planning demanded radio silence prior to contact with the enemy. By doctrine, wire and field phones should have provided sure internal commo within the assembly area. The 34th had laid no wire, not even within companies. Had a wire net been attempted, Team B, CSC, and the TOC itself might have gotten pulled into their proper spots on the perimeter. But no attempt was made, and the TOC and command group (the colonel and his artillery and Air Force fire support officers) hoped for the best at 0700.

Predictably, what they got was something less. At 0700 Team A reported some problems that would delay its attack time (later attributed to a late wakeup for the company). Team Charlie Tank, despite its follow-up role in the plan, jumped ahead and actually crossed the line of departure a few minutes early, fortuitous in light of Team A's slowness. The air assault went off quite well, landing without enemy interference. As for Team B, it was already well across the LD, and its commander decided to pretend as if all were well, which it essentially was.

By 0705 the TF had caught up with Team B anyway, and Team A had fallen in behind Team C. The canal crossings had been evaluated and marked, and the command group was following Charlie Tank.

It took some time to move across the wide valley, though the sight of the task force deployed with two up and one back was quite impressive. For the first time many of the soldiers saw just how many tanks and APCs really went into a battalion. It was a vision never seen in the dense pines of Fort Stewart. The task force began to spread out among the creosote bushes, its teams in open columns as they sped up to reach the river. There was a problem already with something known as mutual support, though it was not recognized. Mutual support demands that the fighting teams stay in range of each other, with about 1,500 meters being optimum. If one team hits trouble, the others can see the enemy threat and support by fire. But the Dragons' company teams were already drifting more than three kilometers apart.

Team B had the mission of clearing the small, tight valley formed by ridge 955 and the Tiefort Mountain complex. This pulled Team B well out of sight and support of the other two teams during the last ten kilometers east of the river. The scouts had been through before dawn and reported it clear. Even so, Team B was to drive through again and look for the enemy.

As Team B entered the narrow opening of the canyon, an incident occurred in Team C that slowed momentum east of the

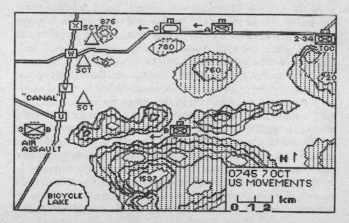

crossing sites. The enemy had finally put in an appearance, opening up an artillery barrage on the northern teams (the OPFOR had yet to sight Team B to the south). The observer controllers fired airburst charges (like giant cherry bombs) and began "killing" exposed tank loaders and infantry until Charlie Tank got the message and slammed the hatches of the APCs and tanks. Only three casualties were assessed, though the team reduced speed as it tried to stay on course using the small, thick periscopes around the sealed hatches.

One real casualty resulted: it was a serious one, at that. The Team C commander struck himself on the head with an APC cargo door, tearing a large, bleeding rent in his scalp and knocking himself out. The possibility of cranial fracture or concussion demanded quick medical evacuation. So it was that at 0815 Team C halted to change command to the executive officer and to await an actual medical evacuation helicopter from Fort Irwin garrison. Team A passed around the confused tank element, coming under artillery as it did so. Team B reached the end of its defile in the south and stopped to overwatch Team A's river crossing. Team B was also barraged by artillery, and it was almost four kilometers to the south of Team A and could not deliver direct fire support. Team B should have pressed on and crossed at the southern sites. The TOC got wrapped up in medevac procedures and allowed Team B to sit and eat artillery shells. It would be almost forty-five minutes before Team B crossed the canal.

As the Team C command was shifted, Team A began moving across the canal, urged by the impatient battalion commander. The OPFOR artillery caused most of the task force to operate "buttoned up," which meant driving slowly with only the view offered by the vision blocks. On the M113s the powerful .50-caliber machine guns swung unattended above the slammed hatches. Squad leaders, platoon leaders, and company commanders, who ride in the big cargo hatch behind the APC's small machine-gun cupola, were blind in their crowded tracks, struggling to move near the machine gunner's vision blocks and tied to the radios. Since the real Soviets like to mix in nerve gas and blood agent with their high explosive artillery shells, the task force had donned stifling protective masks at the first sign of OPFOR indirect fire. The Dragons were already wearing the charcoal-impregnated chemical protection suits in deference to OPFOR chemical capacities. Given all of this, the

OPFOR's artillerists could be well satisfied with the slowing and disruption their calls for fire were causing.

The proper U.S. response would be to fire counterbattery with its own artillery and use its heavy mortars to generate a big smokescreen to cover the open canal line and the struggling Team Charlie Tank. But the Dragons' fire support officer and his company fire support team officers had not done their homework. Working with an "out-of-the-can" generic fire plan invented during a map study back at Fort Stewart, the fire support men had not created a plan that would protect the canal crossing and search out likely enemy locations for preplanned targets. The preplanned missions were arbitrarily dotted on bits of high ground around the Central Corridor. The heavy mortars, a potentially fine source of smoke rounds, did not even have a copy of this inadequate fire plan. Team A's mortars were also in the dark, and no fires at all had been planned at the company team level in Team A. Most damning, the final fire support plan was never given to the FIST officers in the companies, the scouts, or the Antitank Platoon. The young artillery lieutenants were told to use the "made-at-home" version. After all, artillery was "never played in most exercises." But NTC is not "most exercises."

So Team A crossed in full view of the watchful, hidden OPFOR and moved slowly toward hill 910 on its own. Hill 910 was a crag just east of the major feature in the Central Corridor, the hill 1161/1195 conglomerate. It was not a designated intermediate objective, and Team A intended to pass south of it

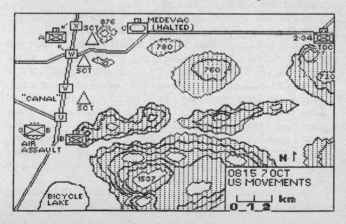

and press on to the west on the valley floor. Team B was crossing to the south by 0930 as Team A pushed on, and the XO of Team C was finally moving out. The 34th battalion commander, gratified that things were getting unstuck, exhorted Teams A and B to move out smartly, neglecting the wide gap between them.

The TOC redirected Team C to follow Team B in the south when it was realized that the dismounted air assault platoon's vehicles were with Charlie Tank's column. The scouts languished at the canal crossing, lacking a real follow-on mission. Antitank Platoon was following Team B but had lost communications with the TOC; lacking an operations overlay, the AT Platoon leader had no real concept of what to do. He just followed along, as did the heavy mortars (still without a call for fire).

As Team B came up even with Team A (the ground to the south being flatter), the TOC and the colonel were unaware of more serious troubles. Team A had left three of four tanks broken down on its route of march, as well as a squad APC. With no ITVs (recall, they had failed to link up the night before), Team A disposed one tank and five squad tracks; this was just an oversize platoon. Team A's mortars were out of the picture, having no orders and no fire plans. Team B to the south had dropped two tanks for mechanical reasons and lost a mortar carrier at the canal to enemy artillery. The TOC knew about Team B's losses. Team A's losses had not been reported, and Alpha was presumed at full strength. All this and not one round of direct fire had been shot.

At 0945 the OPFOR fired at Team A from hill 910 and the Little Black Rockpile a kilometer to the southeast. Team A identified an enemy "tank" (really a BMP) at the rockpile and stopped to return fire, knocking it out. Two BMPs took up the fight from hill 910, and Team A's movement ground to a halt as vehicles scrambled for cover. The battalion commander, judging the force on 910 to be a security position, pressed Team B onward to the west. That was a valid deduction. It was confirmed by a hard readout from an air recce mission that placed a motorized rifle company (MRC) near benchmark 934, just inside the wadi rills called The Washboard. The colonel expected Team A to brush aside the security units and join Team B in attacking the MRC. It was 1000 hours.

Far to the rear, Team C was still at the canal, just beginning to cross. The XO had no idea of the tactical plan, other than the

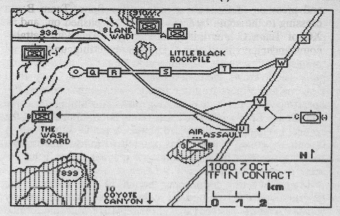

cryptic scribbles on his absent commander's map, and was not conversant with the changing situation. He had been worrying about his maintenance responsibilities (the old Boeing yard tanks were junkers) and had not bothered with the shooting war. About all he knew was that he would go to the south and had to pick up the helicopter assault platoon en route. The colonel and the TOC could not raise him on the battalion command net and relied on visual reports from Team B's trail units to keep track of Team C. The battalion commander needed the Team C force quickly.

At 1015 Team A was fully engaged at hill 910, its commander off the battalion net. Team B entered the ups and downs of The Washboard and spotted the enemy near benchmark 934. Using the cover of the broken ground, Bravo went right by, trading a few desultory shots as it bypassed most of an MRC. Neither side took any losses. Elated by Team B's "breakthrough," the colonel ordered it to continue on at maximum speed. He hoped Team A and Team C were moving to follow along.

The 34th had no such luck. By 1030 Team A was reduced to a few headquarters and mortar tracks, its combat power destroyed in a slugfest east of hill 910. Team A had gotten a "T-72" (that was, in fact, a BMP) and two more BMPs, but it had cost the command track, the only tank left, and five squad tracks. The team commander was "dead," and Team A was finished. It had tried a mounted charge and had gotten picked apart.

Team Bravo, far out ahead of the wreckage of Team A and the muddled Charlie Tank, had finally struck an enemy tank platoon near benchmark 999, three kilometers west of the enemy main body. Like Team A, Bravo went in mounted, its lead infantry APC actually ramming a fleeing T-72 in a twisting gully (both crews were destroyed).[5] Bravo's infantry fired Dragons and Vipers from the hatches with some success, cooperating with the two remaining tanks in eliminating three reinforcing BMPs without loss. Team B continued east, the colonel having finally contacted Teams A and C. With Team A essentially gone, Team C was ordered to follow up Bravo's seeming success. In other words the colonel threw in his reserve to press the enemy.

Team C's acting commander thought he was doing so, but he had in fact committed the colonel's reserve for him by straying over the eastern ridge of the big 1077 hills that formed the south wall of the Central Corridor. Unaware of the ground plan, the errant XO entered Coyote Canyon just as Team A was caving in to the north.

With Team C out of zone, Team A out of action, AT Platoon out of communication (with a sizable part trailing Team C into Coyote Canyon), and fire support wretchedly ineffective, the exasperated colonel pressed Team B to continue. The Dragons had five squad tracks, three TOWs (two ITVs and one old M220), and two tanks against the OPFOR's three T-72s and four BMPs scrambling to cut off Team B. The ten- to fifteen-meter wadi embankments split up and masked Bravo's overwatch, lengthening the company's column into little packets on the folds and dips. Using a better knowledge of the ground and the value of shooting along the grain, two T-72s finally held up Team B near benchmark 1075, blowing away both M60 tanks in a few seconds. To the rear a BMP nailed an ITV, signaling that Team B was now cut off and in deep trouble should the enemy dredge up some more forces. The OPFOR had had enough, however, and withdrew. At 1110 the TOC (still way back near hill 720 and barely audible) passed a "halt and defend" order to the task force. The colonel had to relay the command to Team B. In Coyote Canyon Charlie Tank was finally getting its bearings as the halt order came. Team A's acting commander acknowledged.

The first battle was over, but not quite. The radios crackled to life with word that the After Action Review was scheduled for 1400 hours.

* * *

The first After Action Review, held in the shadow of hill
1195/1161, was not a pleasant experience. By umpired exercise standards the Dragons had not done too badly: after all,
hadn't Team B driven way past the enemy? But this was not
BOLD EAGLE or REFORGER, and there was a definite ac-
counting for such sloppy tactics.

The AAR began with the brigade operations officer stating
the generalities of the brigade order given to the 34th. Then the
battalion commander went through his force disposition and
plan, followed in turn by Team A, Team B, and the Team C
XO. Thus far the windy little hillside seemed cordial enough.
Maybe the big blunders had gone unnoticed in the general
confusion.

However, the NTC is unforgiving by design. The AAR continued and grew markedly harsher as the brigade commander
listened intently from the rear of the knot of Dragon leaders and
observer controllers. The OPFOR commander, dressed in his
distinctive olive uniform, stood up and gave his view of the
battle. He had only a BMP company plus four tanks, a visible
shock to most of the 34th's leaders, who thought there were at
least two MRCs (one at hill 910, one passed by Team B). The
OPFOR commander was able to stay well within his plan,
which had platoons forward at 910/rockpile and at the edge of
The Washboard in the south, with tanks and the third BMP
platoon back and centered. He had employed no mines or
ditches, nor had he used chemicals with his observed artillery

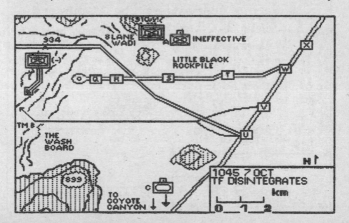

fires. The OPFOR leader said he had employed, however, his usual washboard defense to slow and finally stop Team B. The OPFOR commander explained the washboard positioning system of alternating firing lanes in the low, rolling ground and added that Team A was easier to eliminate since it had elected to move in the open without suppressive fires.

The Blue Team's chief controller was not a word mincer. He went right to work, hitting some of the major errors and omis-

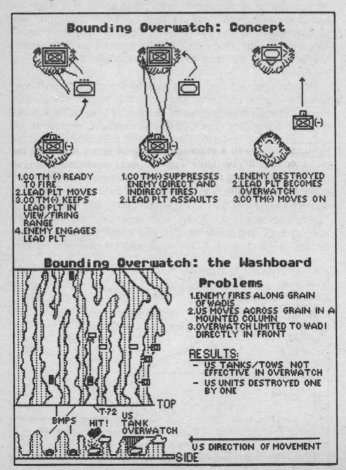

Bounding Overwatch: Concept

1. CO TM (-) READY TO FIRE
2. LEAD PLT MOVES
3. CO TM (-) KEEPS LEAD PLT IN VIEW/FIRING RANGE
4. ENEMY ENGAGES LEAD PLT

1. CO TM (-) SUPPRESSES ENEMY (DIRECT AND INDIRECT FIRES)
2. LEAD PLT ASSAULTS

1. ENEMY DESTROYED
2. LEAD PLT BECOMES OVERWATCH
3. CO TM (-) MOVES ON

Bounding Overwatch: the Washboard

Problems
1. ENEMY FIRES ALONG GRAIN OF WADIS
2. US MOVES ACROSS GRAIN IN A MOUNTED COLUMN
3. OVERWATCH LIMITED TO WADI DIRECTLY IN FRONT

RESULTS:
- US TANKS/TOWS NOT EFFECTIVE IN OVERWATCH
- US UNITS DESTROYED ONE BY ONE

TOP

BMPS   T-72   US
        HIT!   TANK
               OVERWATCH

US DIRECTION OF MOVEMENT

SIDE

sions. Under command and control subjects, the chief controller pointed out that the task force order was unclear about how to orient on the enemy, with the result that dangerous OPFOR units were bypassed to get to unimportant terrain objectives. The order left the pickup of the air assault platoon in doubt, since Charlie was supposed to move in the north and the helicopters had landed that infantry in the south. Of course, most criticism was reserved for the tendency to allow teams to move without regard to mutual support (or, as in Team B's case, to order such action). This lack of control over the companies was discussed at length in light of the bungled night road march, the confusion at the line of departure, the out-of-range overwatch provided by Team B at the canal, Team B's independent movement past most of an MRC, and Team C's wanderings in Coyote Canyon.

The TOC was taken to task for losing track of Teams A and C, not giving the scouts a follow-on mission, and not making any attempt to move forward to follow the battle. The TOC and Team A were both noted for inaccurate reporting and outright nonreporting, with a resultant confusion about just what had occurred at hill 910. Only Team B went unscathed there, although that element as well had failed to pass some important information. Teams A and C spent too little time on the battalion command net, pleading communications difficulties that took radios off line. Since they were talking only to their own platoons, not the TOC, their status was uncertain for most of the operation.

The Antitank Platoon and engineer platoon lieutenants were brought forward and ripped to shreds for failing to make attachments and contribute to the mission. The two young officers, dusty and dejected, could offer no excuses for their inabilities. The TOWs were sorely missed all day, and they could have helped at 910, though not in the successive cuts of The Washboard. The TOW platoon leader was extremely embarrassed as his failures to attend the whole OPORD, post his map, navigate, maintain communications, and move tactically were examined in depressing detail.

The fire support fiasco was also scrutinized, and the planning mistakes and missed signals were fully listed. The battalion commander winced as the chief controller noted that Team A, fighting in close at hill 910, had not called one mission from its mortars. The battalion Heavy Mortar Platoon leader was scorched for his inactivity. Most embarrassing, the FSO had

approved (and even repeated) a 155-mm fire mission on Team
A that resulted in simulated casualties. Consequently, two of
the few missions fired hit friendly troops. The OPFOR leader
noted that the U.S. artillery had not been a factor in his operations.

The intelligence area was covered, with the S-2 under fire
for failing to tell the commanders just how the OPFOR was
likely to be laid out. The Soviets (and the OPFOR) set up a
rather regular defense pattern, similar at all levels. Two up,
one back, fire sack in the middle: that is the typical setup,
regardless of terrain. The depth platoon may provide security
positions and guard artillery observers in front of the two for-

LOSSES: 7 OCTOBER 1982

	Tanks		APCs		TOW/Sagger	
	Start	Lost	Start	Lost	Start	Lost
Team A	4	1	10	6	0	0
Team B	4	2	11	2	3	1
Team C	4	1	8	2	2	0
CSC	0	0	5	0	0	0
Bn. TF	12	4	34	10	5	1
OPFOR	4	1	10	6	0	0

Source: *Take-Home Package, Task Force 2-34 Infantry*, pp. III-A-1-1, IV-A-1-1.

TIMELINE: MOVEMENT TO CONTACT
7 OCTOBER 1982

6 OCT 82-1300:	Battalion OPORD
6 OCT 82-1700:	Company OPORD/Movement order (B Company typical)
6 OCT 82-1715:	Nightfall
6 OCT 82-2100:	Units depart for assembly areas
7 OCT 82-0130:	Lead 2-34 Infantry elements close in presumed assembly areas
7 OCT 82-0700:	Line of departure time/time of attack
7 OCT 82-0815:	Barstow River crossed (by Team A); Team C CO injured
7 OCT 82-0945:	Team A engaged at hill 910; Team B across in force
7 OCT 82-1015:	Team B bypasses lead enemy elements
7 OCT 82-1030:	Team C moves into Coyote Canyon
7 OCT 82-1110:	TF 2-34 Infantry asssumes hasty defense
7 OCT 82-1130:	Company After Action Reviews
7 OCT 82-1400:	TF After Action Review

ward platoons. This information was not rehashed prior to the mission. More to the point, the colonel did not react to the hard data on the MRC despite his movement-to-contact mission. Instead of fixing and crushing that OPFOR unit, he hit it piecemeal, one element at a time.

The 34th losses had been heavy, with even Team C losing a few vehicles to pounding artillery near the canal. The OPFOR was down to half strength but still combat effective. The 34th was at two-thirds strength (less when maintenance failures were considered) and utterly disorganized. Loss summaries were a sobering postscript to the day's mission.

The battalion commander was professionally chagrined. The Dragons had displayed an unusual degree of ineptitude. Only the scouts and, maybe, Team B (if one excuses that unit's inability to find its way at night) had done anything worthwhile. Team A had failed miserably; Team C had never been anything but a field artillery target. The Antitank Platoon was ineffective. The whole fire support structure, the great explosive hammer that could even long odds and amass fighting power, had been utterly inadequate. Team commanders couldn't even stay on the radio. All these disasters, yet the task force had faced but a single MRC without obstacles, chemicals, smoke, or night to further screw things up.

Tired, beaten, soundly embarrassed in front of rating superiors, and barely started on the great exercise, the Dragons gathered after the AAR to prepare for the next mission. There really was no use in looking back now. There was not enough time.

Notes

1. Department of the Army, *FM 71-1 The Tank and Mechanized Infantry Company Team, Coordinating Draft* (Fort Benning, Ga. and Fort Knox, Ken.: U.S. Army Infantry School and U.S. Army Armor School, April 1982), 4-3.

2. Sun Tzu, *The Art of War*, translated by Samuel B. Griffith (New York: Oxford University Press, 1982), 99.

3. *FM 71-1 The Tank and Mechanized Infantry Company Team, Co-ordinating Draft*, 4-24 to 4-25.

4. Formations completely dropped out of the 1977 how-to-fight manuals, though they are in current battalion and company literature. The *FM 71-1 Draft* of April 1982 has a discussion of formations on pages 4-13

through 4-15, although the 34th units did not employ the line, Vee, or wedge at Irwin within companies.

5. The author's armored personnel carrier was just behind the track that rammed the T-72.

Note: Other sources for material in this chapter include: interviews; Department of the Army, *Take-Home Package, Task Force 2-34 Infantry* (Fort Irwin, Calif.: National Training Center, Training Analysis and Feedback Division, 22 October 1982).

Chapter Six

Deliberate Attack

"Hektor, attacking, tried to break the lines at that point where the Akhaian soldiery was thickest, and their gear the best. But not with all his ardor could he break them."

Homer, Book 15, **The Iliad**[1]

The brigade operations officer pulled the battalion commander and battalion S-3 aside after the After Action Review. The lieutenant colonel was in no mood to move on to new problems, but NTC is a lot like war; there are no breaks. The brigade operations officer spread his map across the battalion commander's dusty jeep hood. On that flapping paper were the symbols that marked out the job for 8 October 1982. The mission indicated: deliberate attack.

An attack is an offensive operation, focusing on either the destruction of enemy units or the seizure of key terrain, or both. Attacks are divided with regard to time as well as to purpose. Hasty attacks are quick, on-the-move actions to take advantage of immediate opportunities. Hasty attacks are launched from the march, usually with incomplete but promising information about the enemy.

A deliberate attack, the Dragons' mission for 8 October, is typified by more time to prepare and to find out about the opposition. Deliberate attacks are preceded by a buildup of supplies and an extensive intelligence-gathering patrol effort. The artillery plan and ground maneuver plan usually cover only a little ground (compared to a movement to contact), but that is to be expected given that deliberate attacks are launched against well-defined objectives, not into an ill-formed, deep zone.

The Dragons were issued a full brigade order at 1630 on 7 October. The brigade specified a limited thrust to take out a motorized rifle company located at the west end of The Washboard, just south of dry Nelson Lake. The enemy was within six kilometers of Team Bravo's forward positions, so the attack would be a short (and, it was hoped, violent) strike to eliminate

95

the located OPFOR resistance. The time of attack was set for 0700 8 October 1982. Brigade did not specify techniques or tactics, only time and objective. The 34th's attack at 0700 would be simultaneous with an attack by 2-70 Armor far to the south. Such coordinated brigade attacks would typify real operations, particularly since the armor, like the Dragons, had suffered a reverse in the initial movement to contact. The OPFOR had been found and sized up. Now it was time to destroy them.

There were two things going in favor of the 34th that late afternoon as the company commanders gathered around the colonel and his S-3 to get a warning order for the upcoming attack. The first was that the mission was an easy one: the concept was simple and the objective was close. The second positive element was that the enemy force appeared to be small and fixed in location. After all, the Dragons had wiped out half an MRC on their first mission, even with all the bumbling and fumbling. So the 34th should be able to handle the OPFOR on 8 October.

Negative elements predominated, however. For openers, only Bravo had experienced The Washboard phenomenon, but the whole task force would have to traverse and fight in that world of ditches and rills to do the attack. Second, the task force was spread from hill 720 all the way to benchmark 1075 in the center of The Washboard. Team C was way back near the canal (having emerged from its Coyote Canyon detour). Team A lay grounded out near hill 910. The TOC and trains were back near hill 720. The scouts and heavy mortars were concentrated near the Barstow canal. The antitank and engineer platoons were lost somewhere in zone, with only fragments reported in. Thus, it would take awhile to pull the Dragons back together.

Time was the third problem, and it was a serious one. It would be dark by 1700 or thereabouts, and wandering around in the dark in the Central Corridor was not a happy prospect. By 0700 the next day (14½ hours after the warning order), the 34th would have to design a plan; issue an order; pull its units on line with Team Bravo; reorganize; order replacements; evacuate "dead" and "wounded"; resupply food, fuel, and ammunition; patrol the enemy lines; and do something about repairing and recovering broken combat vehicles.

Maintenance, in fact, was the final trouble. The numbers there did not look good, and unless mechanical miracles occurred in the darkness, the Dragons would go into action in the morning far below strength. Team A was the worst of all, reduced to five squad tracks and the captain's APCs. Every Alpha tank (four) was inoperative, and Team A still had no TOWs. Thus, Team A became Company A (−) with just two platoons of mechanized infantry, one platoon with but two APCs.

Team Charlie was short two tanks, but still had four running, along with two full-strength infantry platoons and six TOWs. Team B was also short two tanks, which left Bravo with only two M60 main battle tanks. Nobody knew where the majority of the Antitank Platoon had gone (not even its lieutenant), but the scouts and heavy mortars were intact. Alpha's plight would heavily influence task force planning.

Sunlight was fading to the west, beyond NASA's huge Goldstone tracking station hidden in the next valley. The colonel gave 2100 as the time for his order and sent his leaders into the twilight to gather their lost sheep and feed the few they still had a handle on.

The company teams and CSC platoons faced two complex and demanding sets of necessary activities as the sun dipped below the horizon. On the one hand, the units had to clean up the mess made by the 7 October operation, a coordination drill that would tax the 34th's unsteady logistics chain to its limits (and beyond). On the other, there was a battle to fight, and more than a few tired young infantrymen and scouts would need to push out and discover just what the OPFOR company was doing south of Nelson dry lake. These two strenuous efforts would insure that, for the second night running, the majority of the 34th would get very little rest.

Logistics, the "other war" at NTC (and in real combat), had reared its head rather early in the game at Fort Irwin. Most exercises at Fort Stewart (and even REFORGERs in Germany and TEAM SPIRITs in Korea) concentrate solely on the maneuver battle. These traditional "count noses and roll dice" training games make the assumption that the logisticians will get training out of simply keeping the units racing along. But there is more to combat service support than mere operation of fuel dumps.

Combat Service Support (CSS), the seventh operating system on the NTC list, is examined in the same detail as everything else at Fort Irwin. Units must not only resupply

TASK ORGANIZATION: TF 2-34 INFANTRY
8 OCTOBER 1982

Company A (−)

Company A (−)

Team B

Company B (−)
1st Platoon, Company C (2 tanks)
1 AT section (+ 1 squad)

Team C

Company C (−) (4 tanks)
3d Platoon, Company B
3d Platoon, Company A
3 AT sections

TF Control

Scouts
Heavy Mortars

Not Under Control (Disorganized)

AT Platoon (−) (attachment not made to Team A)
DS Engineer Platoon (no attachments made to line units)

OPPOSING FORCES (OPFOR) MOTORIZED RIFLE COMPANY

1 Motorized Rifle Company (MRC) (10 BMP infantry vehicles)
1 Tank Platoon (4 T-72 tanks)

themselves (as in any field training), but must also care for
simulated casualties, repair "battle-damaged" vehicles, bring
up ammunition for the MILES devices, keep track of unit losses, order replacements, and secure the trucks and supplies
in the rear area against OPFOR guerrillas. The observer controllers for logistics kept track of all of this with unforgiving
scrutiny.

CSS activities in the 34th, like those in any battalion task
force, are centered within three levels of trains. At the company echelon, one finds three armored vehicles in the company

trains. Two of them (the maintenance APC with tools, mechanics, and spare parts and the attached medic track from HHC with stretchers, corpsmen, and aid equipment) are M113A1s or A2s. The other is the ungainly M578 recovery vehicle, a twenty-seven-ton, wide-tracked, lightly armored beast characterized by its big, square turret mounted far back on its flat hull. This turret has a boom with winch, not a cannon, and also mounts a heavy-duty cable and drum under its lightweight crane. The M578, sometimes called a VTR (for vehicle, tracked, recovery, its property book nomenclature), has a driver and two men in its big turret cab. One mechanic in the cab fires the .50-caliber, which can defend the VTR from air or ground threats.

These three tracks work for the company executive officer, who is the infantry unit's logistical master. This armored trains force stays well forward in movement or defense, and it usually includes the communications/alternate command post track, detached from the company command section for the XO's use. The motor sergeant supervises the actions of the multicapable VTR and his heavily laden maintenance track, and usually gives a mechanic to each fighting platoon to provide a little depth to coverage. The medical section chief runs the aid track, and like the motor sergeant with his mechanics, gives an aid man to each platoon for immediate reaction to wounds.

The company trains have another element that comes forward during lulls in combat under the first sergeant and/or supply sergeant. This element is made up of the supply truck,

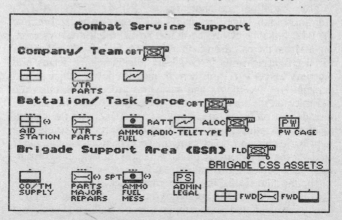

the maintenance truck (more parts and tools), and a few jeeps. The "wheels" usually stay at the battalion field trains, well out of enemy direct fire and mortar range, coming forward to resupply food, ammunition, and vehicle parts. The first sergeant also brings up mail, replacement soldiers, and information from the rear areas. He takes the bodies of the dead, the lightly wounded (the seriously hurt leave immediately on the medic M113), routine supply requests, and empty water and oil cans back to the battalion trains. By 34th standard operating procedures (SOP), the wheels were to come up only under cover of darkness.

The elements at the second level of logistics were the battalion combat trains. Like the company's armored medics and mechanics, the battalion combat trains were intended to be small, mostly armored, and close to the action. At the combat trains one could find the S1/S4 M577 armored command post carrier, the communications platoon radio-teletype M577 (to send and receive messages from brigade), the battalion aid station M577 for quick treatment and stabilization of the wounded, the maintenance forward with the big M88 recovery vehicles (based on tank chassis), and the support platoon's forward site with fuel and ammunition trucks. The combat trains were under the S-4 and ran the battalion's prisoner-of-war cage in a nearby area as a subsidiary duty. The fuel at the combat trains was for emergencies, and the ammunition consisted of high-usage items such as tank rounds, TOW missiles, mines, and mortar projectiles.

The battalion combat trains S1/S4 track (ALOC, Administration-Logistics Operations Center) was the brain of the 34th logistics effort, coordinating the truck convoys coming up from the battalion field trains with fuel, food, and ammo for the fighting units. "Quick-fix" maintenance teams and recovery assets left from here to pick up down vehicles, and personnel replacements and casualties processed through the S-1 track on the way forward or back. The combat trains were intended to move as frequently as the TOC, and the clerks, medics, mechanics, and support truck drivers had to dig in a tight perimeter and erect camouflage nets at each stop. On 7 October the vital combat trains were still far behind the frontline, back across the Barstow road.

The third level of CSS, and farthest back, was the battalion field trains. Part of the sprawling brigade trains, the battalion field trains were under the support platoon leader and consisted of the 34th's supply dumps of fuel and ammunition, its heavy maintenance teams pulling engines and troubleshooting transmissions, and its field kitchens putting out (at NTC, at least) one hot meal for dinner every day. The battalion field trains were made up of wheeled maintenance and support platoon vehicles, plus the company first sergeants with their supply section wheels. The field trains also included an administrative center for the battalion personnel/legal/finance clerks and a supply center for processing routine requests for supplies other than food, fuel, or ammo (which came pretty much automatically). These units were generally beyond enemy cannon artillery range.

The battalion field trains were part of the brigade trains, a nearly immobile conglomerate that resembled a Vietnam-era base camp. Brigade disposed a forward supply company (administering mountains of ammunition, bladders and drums of fuel and oil, pallets of C-rations, and giant tractor-trailer rigs loaded with barbed wire, steel rails and plates, and wooden construction materials), a forward support maintenance company (with bins of parts, major engine and drive train spare assemblies, and trained maintenance technicians with specialized lift, testing, and repair equipment), and the medical company (with medical supplies, a little holding hospital, and a nonanesthetic surgical ward). Brigade even had a shower and laundry facility, courtesy of XVIII Airborne Corps troops. At Irwin the brigade trains (and battalion field trains) were located permanently in the valley between ridge 955 and Tiefort Mountain, the same passage cleared by Team B on the 7 October movement to contact. The brigade trains were arrayed tactically but were not under evaluation or subject to OPFOR attacks.

The idea of these three layers of trains was to push forward vital supplies to keep the battle going. Besides resupply going forward, there was also a steady backward flow of injured men and damaged equipment moving to the aid stations and maintenance sections. In 1982 the newest draft field manuals were beginning to speak of "logistics packages" or "log packs," a concept in which each company team's first sergeant would come up with the hot food from the field trains, stopping at the battalion combat trains to pick up a fuel truck and ammo truck (the pickup could also occur at a remote Logistics Release Point). These combined convoys could then roll to the company positions with everything at once, allowing security in numbers for the trucks and a quick, thorough resupply for the forward forces. The 34th, however, did not use log packs.

In the Dragons the company XOs had to request fuel and ammo, then pick up those items from the combat trains. Ammunition had to be carried in company vehicles. The time of the pickup could vary, but as noted earlier, it had to be after dark. The battalion's three fuel trucks had to fuel the three line companies and all of the HHC and the CSC platoons as well, and they were parceled out on a "first come, first served" basis. The XO with the fuel tanker had to guide the truck forward to his company, then hand-carry it back to the combat trains. Whoever was next in line could get it at that time. The tank and pump units (TPUs) had 800 gallons of diesel, a trailer of gasoline, and some small cans of the varied oil and grease used by M113s and M60s. The trucks had no radio communication to contact the ALOC, hence the requirement to stay with the company XOs. Navigation among tank and pump crewmen was rudimentary at best.

While the XO grubbed around the combat trains for fuel trucks and ammunition, the first sergeant brought up food from the distant field trains. Between the food and fuel/ammo, it was not unusual at Fort Stewart to wait all night, with the expected effects on night operations, let alone rest plans. At Fort Irwin things would exceed even the worst Fort Stewart situation.

Was a nightly refuel really necessary? After all, an APC had a 95-gallon diesel fuel capacity (3.16 miles per gallon), and an M60 tank had 375 gallons (.83 miles per gallon), and both could go 300 miles without refueling. However, consider that the 34th had to refuel sixty-six M113-type vehicles and fourteen tanks every day, plus many trucks. With only 2,400 gallons of diesel in its TPUs, the 34th could afford to give each vehicle only thirty gallons a night before the tank trucks ran dry, and even less if the 2½-ton and 5-ton trucks needed fuel. The name of the game was to "top off," otherwise, things would drain down to a point where the Dragons' puny TPUs could never refill them.

The situation after sundown on the 7th was complicated by two factors unique to Fort Irwin, though certainly not to real war. First, the teams and platoons had taken equipment losses that needed to be called in to the ALOC, "casualties" that had to be evacuated to the aid station, and "dead" that had to go to graves registration. Second, the first sergeants were experiencing the route into The Washboard for the first time, trying to find units that were in the process of moving up on line with Company B in the deepening gloom. The scouts were well forward looking for the enemy, but they still needed supplies and repairs. Only God knew where the TOWs (and pieces of the company teams as well) had wandered.

If the 34th had been using log packs, the supplies would have been moving simultaneously, and the XOs could have found the first sergeants at one spot (the canal crossing site, for example) and led them up to the fighting units with food, fuel, and ammo. Instead, first sergeants with food drove past XOs looking for the combat trains, all in the ups and downs of the night-enshrouded Washboard, and all, of course, without lights. The ALOC received most of the loss reports, but trucks laden with the raw materials of combat were busy floating around searching for consumers, and the logisticians of the 34th could do nothing to diminish the confusion.

CSC, without its commander and saddled with an unambitious first sergeant and a widely dispersed set of critical platoons, was in the worst situation. The XO had to attend the battalion OPORD, find his platoons, and somehow insure they all got fed, fueled, and rearmed, all simultaneously. It was just not going to happen.

Charlie Tank, also minus its commander (out with the freak head wound), was in a similar bind. The harried XO was very happy when his captain returned to the battalion TOC just before the OPORD, sporting a square white bandage on his stitched-up forehead. Company A (−) was trying to repair its broken-down tanks and tracks, scattered all the way back to hill 720. Only Team B, its first sergeant and XO having coordinated with its captain prior to the afternoon AAR, had its logistics in order. Everybody there ate and fueled. But even in Bravo the captain, XO, and first sergeant had elected not to evacuate any "casualties" or "bodies" until the sun came up. Navigation had gotten that difficult.

The CSS breakdown in distribution was owing to a poor system and very little help from battalion. Leaving the entire resupply and maintenance effort to the company teams was not in accord with the "push forward" doctrine. The idea of using a "garrison"-style request and pickup system, rather than letting battalion S-4 assemble and dispatch log packs tailored to each company's needs, was an inadequate, unimaginative response to the stresses of the NTC. CSS demanded as much initiative and commitment from the battalion S-4 and his assistants as maneuver demanded from company commanders. It was not there on 7 October 1982.

It is evident that the Dragons were betrayed early by their untested logistics network. A Company was in deep maintenance trouble, Team C was not fully refueled, the scouts did not eat, and the bulk of the Antitank Platoon remained unaccounted for. Nobody got ammunition (though it was direly needed by everyone), and almost a third of the task force did not eat.

One of the most common statements made in military histories is the one about the unit conducting "aggressive patroling." There seems to be a general agreement that one should patrol (aggressively, of course), and there is a good reason for that belief. Patrolling boils down to a battle for information, and patrols are simply small elements sent out either to look for data about the enemy and terrain (reconnaissance) or to keep the enemy recon effort at arms length (combat patrols).

Patrolling is a means of keeping contact with the enemy so that he cannot slip off unnoticed. Patrols are designed to control the empty stretch between the enemy and the Americans, with the theory that he who controls this "no-man's-land" will de facto control the information flow. The problem with patrolling is that it takes time to patrol correctly, and it takes manpower that is often needed to hold defensive positions and to replenish and refit. Also, the soldiers must rest sometime. In a typical, full-strength rifle company, with tanks attached and one mech platoon detached, there are few men available for extensive patrolling unless that is the unit's prime effort (and it is seldom the sole effort). If the two rifle platoons left were at full strength (thirty-seven men each), only seventy-four men would be available to patrol. Sending out more than two squads (twenty-two men) thins the lines beyond the danger point. Under all circumstances, however, observation/listening posts would be deployed to secure the American positions. These two-man OP/LPs, one per platoon (even the tanks put one out as a matter of course), are security "patrols" in a sense, denying the enemy close observation and preventing surprise enemy assaults.

Once the OP/LPs were out, a two-patrol schedule for a mech-heavy team would result in two of six squads on patrol, two of six rifle squads on security, and the last two sleeping, cleaning, fixing, eating, or attending to the APCs. The mortars would keep one tube ready to fire (in support of the patrols) and one gun squad out in local security. The ITVs would keep one track in each two-TOW section awake and in security. The tank platoon would man its OP/LP and keep one man per tank awake and up in the commander's cupola. In general, to patrol "aggressively" is to surrender time and men who need to help with refitting and rearming and who need to rest to be fresh for the main engagement. Still, it is necessary to dominate the reconnaissance struggle between the two sides.

The 34th, in accord with doctrine, derived its patrolling requirements from the S-2 and his intelligence section. The S-2 talks to the S-3 (operations) and figures out what knowledge is needed to successfully fight the upcoming engagement. The S-3 then allocates the missions to the intelligence-gathering elements at hand. The scouts (who exist to reconnoiter) will usually get the deeper-look duties, and they tend to patrol mounted on a wide front. Specific, close-in areas and routes are given to the line companies. All patrols must be briefed on what to look for and what to do if the enemy shows up unexpectedly (recon patrols usually run, combat patrols usually fight).

On 7 October the TOC (S-2 and S-3) determined early that it needed to confirm a flanking route into the presumed enemy position, and that the battalion headquarters wanted to confirm that the OPFOR company was still in its lair just south of Nelson dry lake. The TOC recommended to the colonel that the scouts get the mission of watching the enemy and that Team B and Company A (−) move out to examine the route into the MRC's defenses. The directions for these patrols would be issued at 2100 at the battalion order.

The 2100 operations order at the Tactical Operations Center was delayed a few minutes waiting for the A Company commander. The TOC had moved well forward into the big Eight-Lane Wadi just south of the dark 1161/1195 hill mass. When the order kicked off in the dimly lighted canvas extension that linked the S-2 M577 to that of the S-3, it was evident that the TOC had recovered from the first mission and was already in good form. This time the plan was simple yet cunning and complete. The OPFOR had eased matters by drawing up in the far west end of The Washboard. The tanks and TOWs of Charlie Tank would move to the roll of high ground just north of benchmark 1075 to fix the OPFOR in their position with suppressive fires. Meanwhile, Team B and the weakened Company A would skirt the base of the 1214/1406 range of steep hills that formed the south wall of the Central Corridor, turning north and coming on line just past benchmark 1075. Bravo to the west and Alpha to the east would steamroll the enemy, moving with the grain of the wadis north toward Nelson Lake. If the MRC tried to flee to the west, he would crest the last few rolls of The Washboard (right in the sights of Team C), having to move across the wadis rather than with them. The flank attack massed combat power, and the map graphics and oral instructions were clear and concise. It all depended on two reasonable assumptions: first, that the enemy would stay where he was, and second, that the southern flanking approach was passable. The patrolling effort was the key to verifying these assumptions. The orders briefing ended by 2200, and despite some of the usual meandering caused by picking one's way through the desert night, Team B and the scouts were out on patrol by 2300.

The competent planning in the TOC was not equaled by the execution in the field. Company A (−) sent off only one patrol, about midnight, which never made it past benchmark 1075. Team B sent one patrol at 2300 and another at 0130, both of which found the route to be clear to the objective, though fairly tight. The problem was that the avenue was not clear, as Team B would discover on the attack. The scouts moved out and established OPs in the hills overlooking the OPFOR but withdrew from them at first light to move to a screen line on the task force southern flank (to provide early warning into Coyote Canyon). The scouts had seen the enemy, but their surveillance was broken just prior to the attack when it was needed most. The flank screen, while doctrinally sound, pulled them out of their OPs at a critical juncture.

The greatest execution failure was the S-2's mistake in not getting a thorough debrief of the scouts or the company patrols, relying instead on a line or two over the crowded command radio net. Because of that, much valuable intelligence was not disseminated. Company A, for example, had no idea that the approach to the objective was a narrow wash at the base of the hills, barely capable of holding two tracks abreast throughout most of its length. In other words, while there was a collection of information, there was no analysis and only minimal sharing of the knowledge gained. As on 7 October, the greatest intelligence was provided by dawn's revealing light.

*   *   *

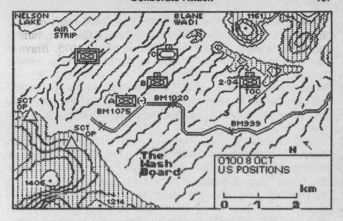

The sunrise of 8 October 1982 heralded another warm, clear day in the California desert. In The Washboard, vehicle engines revved and sputtered as the task force completed preparations for the 0700 attack. This day there would be no late units at the line of departure. The command net was subdued and businesslike, and it looked like it would be a good day. True, there had been trouble fueling and feeding, some units were lost (though the rump of Antitank Platoon was now with Team C), and ammunition stocks were down to half for the numerous MILES devices. Nevertheless, the general feeling was of sound organization and purpose.

One unusual incident occurred in Team B as it lined up about 0645. The Bravo XO was shocked to see the lieutenant from 3d Platoon, Company A, walking unsteadily down the wadi to the rear of Team B's maintenance tracks. This officer was cross-attached to Team C. What made the lieutenant's behavior doubly odd was his lack of helmet, load-carrying combat belt and suspenders, and even weapon. All he had was a chemical protective mask. The XO ran down to see what was up and was met by a wild-eyed stare and some unintelligible babbling. Recognizing the symptoms of heat injury or exposure, the quick-thinking B Company XO summoned the chief medical aidman and sent the delirious young man to the battalion aid station. The XO wondered how the Alpha Company lieutenant had gotten himself into such a state only two days into the exercise, then looked at his own scabrous lips and violently sunburned hands. The desert had its own tolls to collect.

At 0700, the fire support officer fired a simulated artillery preparation to stick the motorized rifle company in its holes, and the task force moved out. Team B and Company A crept slowly into their cramped avenue of approach, weaving along in wary, strung-out columns. Team C moved boldly forward to its overwatch position. The TOC got word that the heavy mortars and scouts were in their proper spots, and the command group moved out with Team C to observe the attack on the objective.

The overwatch team (Team C) was set up by 0730, but Team B and Company A were not moving nearly so fast. The column formation can be easily delayed by the smallest resistance, and Team B's lead infantry tracks were quite cautious as they inched along the tight washway. By 0800 they were just about in position to come on line and turn north. The OPFOR had established a thick minefield athwart the avenue to complicate that maneuver.

Team B was skilled in minefield breaching (the engineers were back near the TOC, still somewhat disorganized), and its lead platoon found a bypass by 0815, covered by smoke grenades and simulated mortar white phosphorous smoke rounds from Team B's 81-mm section. But things had been delayed a little too long, and the OPFOR was onto the plan. Team C could see dust that indicated the OPFOR was moving south, not west. The MRC was counterattacking toward the minefield and the smoke clouds of Team B.

The first indication of trouble was the blinking of the MILES

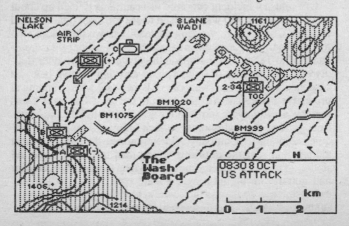

light on the Team B commander's APC, followed in quick sequence by a squad track in first platoon, a tank waiting to skirt the mines, and an ITV back in overwatch. The OPFOR firing was unseen, but dust in The Washboard to the north showed something moving. The Bravo captain was not injured when his track "blew up," but it took time to move to the alternate command track and reestablish communications. In the interim another TOW was lost and the infantry, reacting to contact, turned into the wadis and began chasing the OPFOR ambushers. The lone tank followed, and by the time Team B's commander was back on the air, the company was committed to a slugging match in The Washboard. The infantry dismounted this time, and a long, tiring game of cat and mouse ensued. Team C was unable to help, since the enemy did not move up out of the gullies.

The colonel, frustrated by Team B's slow movement and now forced to alter his plans by the OPFOR maneuver, committed Company A's shrunken platoons through the mortars and maintenance trains of Team B, pushing out to the west to come on line and close off the enemy withdrawal. In essence, Team B would pin the enemy, and Company A, taking Bravo's intended half of the objective, would seal them into a pocket.

The OPFOR were not obliging. In a slow, fighting withdrawal, the BMPs and T-72s backed slowly away from Team B and Company A, avoiding the ineffective overwatch of Team C. The TOC was well aware of this situation, and it listened as the teams ground themselves down in the wadis. If only the Scout Platoon still had OPs on the high ground to the south, the companies in contact could have a better idea of where the OPFOR were going. Instead, the fight was a ground-level columnar firefight, with the OPFOR facing one U.S. track or tank at a time in successive ambushes. (This battle offers another good example of how *not* to deal with the cuts and rises of The Washboard.)

Though Team B had suffered greatly (two squad tracks, the command track, two TOWs, and both tanks were gone by 1000), Company A was intact, and Team C had lost one tank, one APC, and two TOWs to OPFOR artillery and tank fire. The task force was still well in hand and combat effective; and though doing it the hard way, Company A was within about fifteen minutes of sealing off the OPFOR's retreat path. There was consternation at all levels at 1000 hours when the order was issued to all units: assume hasty defense, withdraw to high ground.

The line units thought that the battle had been ended by the controllers, but a quick check with the OCs showed that it was not they who had stopped the action, and there was no AAR scheduled. It was just a change of mission. But why?

The answer could be found in the brigade TOC. At NTC brigade was there to pass the control group's orders to the participating task forces, but, naturally, the brigade TOC tried to get a little tactical practice in the bargain by issuing full plans and coordinating operations. Brigade attached and detached critical combat support assets and ran the gigantic brigade trains as well. On 8 October 1st Brigade, 24th Infantry Division (Mechanized), was conducting a coordinated attack with TF 2-34 in the Central Corridor and TF 2-70 in the Southern Corridor (and a notional task force in the middle in Coyote Canyon just to round out the situation up at brigade). Everything started at 0700, and brigade took the usual reports and passed guidance in accord with the NTC scenario.

At about 0950 brigade S-3 and S-2 sections saw a picture that looked like this: in the Central Corridor, TF 2-34 was making good progress, albeit with heavy losses, toward bagging the MRC; in the Southern Corridor, TF 2-70 had also taken heavy losses and had strong indications that the OPFOR were withdrawing to mass for a regimental-size assault. The brigade commander was apprised of these conditions and issued sensible directions. TF 2-34 was to continue its attack and TF 2-70 was to assume a hasty defense. In the process of sending out these words, the messages got garbled.[2] The tankers to the south were told to keep attacking; the Dragons were ordered to assume a hasty defense!

The results were poor at both ends. TF 2-70 suffered a disaster as it trailed the OPFOR almost to their assembly areas, then got buried by a regimental-scale attack. The 34th was not crushed, but it stumbled into a halfhearted defense, with Company A on the front slope of steep hill 1487, Team B pulling onto the forward slope of hill 1406, and Team C holding in its overwatch position. The fire support officer, pleased with his decent plan for the deliberate attack, did not adjust his plan for the hasty defense. Everyone was still pretty sure that the day's mission was over and that an AAR (and a break) would follow shortly. The Dragons were playing gamesmanship, and they got burned.

The line companies made no serious attempt to disperse, site weapons, or dig in. Team B did not even redistribute ammunition, and Company A called up its wheels for resupply in the lull. The OPFOR, suddenly freed from the closing jaws of a bumbling, but strong, trap, pulled up the wadis toward Nelson dry lake. The Dragons were not ready when the OPFOR came back at them.

The motorized rifle company, with its attached tanks, had lost but two BMPs in the wadi fighting, so its four T-72s and eight remaining BMPs struck A Company very hard from the west at 1045, destroying all but one track and "killing" most of the recumbent soldiers. Team B, alerted to the threat as it saw A Company to its left scrambling on the open hillside, could not swing around in time and lost three more squad tracks and its last TOW. Alpha had gotten one T-72; Bravo's VTR crew accounted for another with some skillful Viper shots. The rest of the MRC rolled on, swinging north to knock off a Charlie Tank APC, another tank, and two more ITVs for the cost of a third T-72. This shameful interlude for the Dragons ended as the OPFOR withdrew back past Nelson Lake. Then the end-of-mission announcement finally came.

The 8 October engagement had a disturbing finale (a reminder that NTC was like warfare, not like BOLD EAGLE), but on the whole it had been a fair performance. The After Action Review at 1430 hit heavily on the logistics failings and the troubled fire support planning sequence (still using parts of a canned, Fort Stewart overlay) and also mentioned the miscue

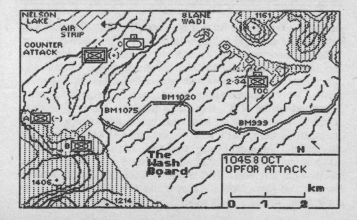

DRAGONS AT WAR

LOSSES: 8 OCTOBER 1982

	Tanks		APCs		TOW/Sagger	
	Start	Lost	Start	Lost	Start	Lost
Team A	0	0	6	5	0	0
Team B	2	2	11	5	3	3
Team C	4	2	7	2	6	4
CSC	0	0	5	0	0	0
Bn. TF	6	4	29	12	9	7
OPFOR	4	3	10	2	0	0

Source: *Take-Home Package, Task Force 2-34 Infantry*, pp. III-A-1-1, IV-B-1-1.

TIMELINE: DELIBERATE ATTACK
8 OCTOBER 1982

7 OCT 82-1630:	Warning order
7 OCT 82-2100:	Battalion OPORD
7 OCT 82-2300:	Company OPORD/Unit patrols depart (B Company typical)
8 OCT 82-0400:	Patrols return
8 OCT 82-0615:	Dawn
8 OCT 82-0700:	Line of departure/Time of attack
8 OCT 82-0800:	Team B encounters minefield and bypasses
8 OCT 82-0845:	TF engaged with enemy in wadis (Company A and Team B)
8 OCT 82-1000:	1st Brigade orders hasty defense
8 OCT 82-1045:	OPFOR counterattack
8 OCT 82-1200:	Company After Action Reviews
8 OCT 82-1430:	TF After Action Review

in moving the scouts from their vantage points. The OPFOR commander admitted to some initial desperation caused by the Dragons' flank attack. The brigade order was not explained; the 34th's lackluster reaction to it was closely evaluated and found execrable. Everyone was treated to the disquieting spectacle of the chief, operations group, then the brigadier general commanding the NTC, take turns lecturing the tired Dragon battalion commander on how to attack with violence and aggression. In the Great Game the colonel's stock took a slight dip, but not the great plunge of 7 October.

There would be another chance on 9 October, but the stakes were going up. The mission: defend in sector. And as the Dragons got a look at the map overlay from brigade, their dirty faces creased with anxiety. Defense could mean only one thing—tomorrow the 34th would meet the OPFOR regiment.

Notes

1. Homer, *The Iliad*, translated by Robert Fitzgerald (Garden City, N.Y.: Anchor Press/Doubleday, 1975), 369.

2. Norman interview; Finley interview. Captain Jack Finley enlightened the author on this particular incident, supplying most of the details used in this account. Apparently, the OCs found this all rather amusing. Captain Raymond K. Norman confirmed the destruction of TF 2-70, which he monitored on the brigade command radio frequency.

Note: Other sources for this chapter include interviews; *Take-Home Package, Task Force 2-34 Infantry;* relevant doctrinal manuals.

Chapter Seven

Defend in Sector (I)

"The shrill ringing of the telephone startled him. He reached for the receiver. Nervously he recognized the regimental commander's incisive voice: 'I hear you left a platoon behind?'

" 'Of course. I received a clear order to do so.'

" 'The other battalion commanders also received this order. Are you aware of that?'

" 'So Captain Kiesel informed me,' he said.

" 'Indeed.' There was another pause. Stransky pressed the receiver to his ear and heard the rushing of his own blood, excessively loud. Then the commander's voice spoke again: 'Are you also aware that the other commanders took it upon themselves to disregard the order?'

" 'No,' Stransky murmured. 'I cannot understand such conduct, sir. I, at any rate, have strictly obeyed the orders I received.'

" 'So you have, so you have, Captain Stransky. I suppose you have not yet had enough front-line experience to use your own initiative whenever the situation demands some adjustments. Unfortunately, there was no time to send revised instructions. Vogel and Korner used their judgement in taking their platoons back with them. I have commended the good sense of these officers in my report to Division.' "

Willie Heinrich, *The Cross of Iron*[1]

In their initial analysis of the defense mission, the battalion commander and his operations officer (S-3) were satisfied that the Dragons could slow and destroy the OPFOR regiment in the uneven, jumbled terrain of the Central Corridor. The heartening performance of the 34th in the 8 October attack, coupled with the recognition of the ease with which the opposition had defended for two days, encouraged the colonel and major to hope for the best.

Time was a problem already at 1630, with night due by 1715. The task force dispensed with a formal warning order so it could get company commanders and special platoon leaders out to survey the Central Corridor with an eye toward stopping a motorized rifle regiment attack out of the west. While the captains and lieutenants fanned out to check the terrain in and around The Washboard, the colonel and S-3 major went to the nearby TOC, along with the battalion executive officer. There were decisions to be made, revolving again around the ongoing difficulties in task force logistics.

The cuts and washes of the valley's rolling floor and the steep-sided hills north and south of The Washboard could best be defended by mixed companies of tanks, infantry, and TOWs. The idea was that the nature of the ground would slow OPFOR momentum, allowing TOWs to engage at 3,000 meters from hillsides, tanks to fight the midrange and close-in battle in The Washboard, and infantry to secure the tanks and missile carriers. However, there were only five tanks (a single full-strength platoon) mechanically operational by 1800 on 8 October 1982; nine tanks were under repair or lost somewhere in the Central Corridor. Two of the functioning M60s were over with Team Bravo, the other three with Charlie Tank.

The TOW situation had taken a turn for the better. All but three of the 34th's seventeen TOWs were under control and in working order. For the first time since the Dragons left their dusty motor pool near the Boeing yard, the Antitank Platoon was fully combat effective. With the tank strength down to only five, the employment of the fourteen TOWs would be critical in defeating the enemy.

The reliance on TOW missiles (typical even in up-to-strength mechanized infantry battalion task forces) demanded the construction of stout obstacles and minefield belts to stop the enemy formations. The antitank missiles were accurate, to be sure, but their time of flight was slow (fourteen-odd seconds to reach 3,000 meters), and they were much more likely to hit stationary vehicles than moving targets. The barriers would be essential to insure "standoff" for the lightly armored, slow-shooting ITVs. OPFOR tanks could fire and hit targets reliably at about 2,000 to 1,500 meters, pumping out shells as fast as they could load. At 2,000 meters a decent tank crew can put three main gun rounds into an ITV before the first TOW strikes the tank. Though under fire (possibly intense), the TOW gunner must track his target as steadily as he can until the missile hits. In an open field engagement, an ITV could kill a tank only if the missile crew shot first at 3,000 meters. Otherwise, the tank's combination of rapid-fire capability and closing speed would overcome the TOW launcher. The key to solving this equation is to emplace thick, powerful obstacles to halt the enemy at that maximum standoff range, keeping the flood of OPFOR tanks at a distance of 2,000 meters. With such large barriers, TOWs could fire, reload, and move between positions

TASK ORGANIZATION: TF 2-34 INFANTRY
9 OCTOBER 1982

Team A

Company A (−)
AT Platoon (−)

Company B

Company B
1 AT section (+ 1 squad)

Team C

Company C (only 5 tanks operational)
3d Platoon, Company A

TF Control

Scouts
Heavy Mortars
DS Engineer Platoon
GS Engineer Platoon

OPPOSING FORCES (OPFOR) MOTORIZED RIFLE REGIMENT

3 Motorized Rifle Battalions (MRB) (31 BMPs each, plus 2 in HQ–95 total)
1 Tank Battalion (40 T-72 tanks)
1 SP Artillery Battalion (18 × 122-mm SP howitzers)
1 Recon Company (3 BMPs, 9 BRDM2s, 5 motorcycles)
1 Antitank Battery (9 BRDM2s)
1 Antiaircraft Battery (4 × ZSU-23-4, 4 × SA-9s)

---

without being overrun in the process. If the barricades were sited well, they would allow the TOW gunners surprise shots from flanking and oblique angles, further aiding the thin-plated ITVs' survivability. Good minefields, tank ditches, and craters would allow a few TOWs to kill a lot of enemy tanks before the enemy tanks could get close enough to threaten the TOWs.

The engineer platoon, therefore, would also be important in the TOC's planning considerations. The mighty M728 Combat Engineer Vehicle (CEV) and the trailer-borne, sluggish D7F bulldozer gave the engineer platoon leader two fine ditch-digging machines (two such "blades" work together to dredge out an antiarmor ditch). With his three squads of engineers (all, at last, under his central direction), the engineer lieutenant had the men and equipment to install some sizable barriers. Since time was short, brigade dispatched a second engineer platoon (with CEV and D7F dozer) to work with the 34th's engineer platoon. There would not be time to dig the tanks and TOWs into hull-down positions since the defenses had to be ready by 1000 the next morning. No, the engineers would have to work all night in the hard-scrabble desert floor simply to create some credible antitank trenches.

The colonel and S-3 turned to the battalion XO for the other part of the engineer lieutenant's requirements. There were no logs in the desert, nor convenient villages to dismember for barrier material. However, the sprawling brigade trains were full of construction timbers, sandbags, and steel plates. Minefields, the deadliest type of barrier and the fastest to install, were composed of many hundreds of heavy antitank and antipersonnel mines. All of those mines were far back in the brigade support area at sundown on 8 October, and it was doctrinally the duty of the Dragons' logistics network to bring the vital mines forward. The battalion executive officer, already juggling the food, fuel, ammunition, loss replacement, and maintenance troubles of the task force, added the immediate movement of a great many land mines to his worries. The S-3 and colonel figured that the mines would be up by midnight.

The mine problem aside, the colonel and S-3, along with the TOC officers, huddled to create a viable task organization. The tanks would have to be consolidated, with Charlie Tank's location (already in The Washboard) the obvious place to do so. Company A, which had restored its maintenance failures and was up to two full-strength rifle platoons, could assume command of the Antitank Platoon and stay about where it was on the slopes of the south wall of the Central Corridor. This would insure flanking TOW shots. Team B would have to do the necessary moving around, giving up its two tanks and collecting back its 3d Rifle Platoon from Team C. With its three TOWs, Company Bravo would shift to the north to cover a dangerous wadi that cut through the bottom of the 1161/1195 feature. The intent of the colonel was that Alpha and the TOWs would stay in position, Team C would fight wadi to wadi, and Company B would keep the quick end run shut off by guarding the Eight-Lane Wadi that pointed like a twisted lance deep into the 34th rear areas.

All of this would compose a *defense in sector*, a tactical mission that focused on destruction of the enemy units rather than on simple terrain possession. The Dragons' conceptual framework was hamstrung by the ongoing Army doctrinal debate on how best to defend, a controversy still unresolved in 1982. The 1976 how-to-fight manuals prescribed the idea of an *active defense*, in which units essentially delayed (trading space as they slowed and beat up the enemy), and lightly committed units were shifted laterally to blunt the enemy's main thrust.[2] The active defense was impossibly complicated, and it rather cavalierly discounted traditional reserves (expecting to yank them out of the neighboring units that were not facing the enemy's main efforts). It had a tendency to degenerate rather quickly into a headlong retreat, with the enemy pursuing American units that were frantically trying to establish subsequent positions. The 1976 doctrine, however, broke the old mold of linear, dig-and-die, two-up, one-back conventional defense. The new operations manual was off the presses, but the 34th at Irwin was still very much attempting to apply the active-defense concept.

The only way units can pull out under enemy attack is to put a strong obstacle out at about 2,000 meters (if closer, it becomes an infantry slugfest, normally termed a *decisive engagement*) and plaster the closing enemy with artillery and direct fire as the OPFOR "hang up" on the wire, mines, and ditches. Without the barriers the active defense is very difficult to pull off, requiring units to expend themselves fixing the advancing enemy while the rest of the Americans pull back to form successive firetraps. The Dragons would have to try it without the engineer work on 9 October 1982. Fortunately, the rolling wadis were athwart the OPFOR axis of attack.

The battalion operations order issued the plan the colonel and his S-3 had created. The S-2 and his intelligence section presented a grim picture of well over 150 enemy combat vehicles sweeping into the battalion sector in the typical Soviet-style mass formation. The enemy would be preceded by reconnaissance BMPs and BRDMs, trying to draw the Dragons' fire, then his battalion columns would array themselves, funneling into the holes in the defense found by the recon troops. The S-2 predicted extensive OPFOR reconnoitering efforts after midnight and gave the expected time of enemy attack as 1000 to 1200 on 9 October. The scouts, already far forward of the line units, were enjoined to keep visual contact with the OPFOR assembly areas, allowing up to forty-five minutes' early warning. The fighting companies were not tasked for patrols beyond local security.

The engineer explained his planned obstacles, but the dark look on the battalion executive officer's face spoke much about the missing barrier materials. In fact, given the length of the supply lines back to the brigade trains and the usual night navigation problems, the "priority" mine shipments did not struggle forward until almost 1100 the next morning. So the task force barrier plan never came to fruition.

The fire support captain, looking harried and disheveled, pleaded with the companies to send in updated fire plans, then disseminated the same old "out-of-the-can" Fort Stewart fire support overlay that had misfired the previous two days, replete with errors and omissions. The heavy mortars were given neither a firing site nor final protective fire missions.

The colonel stood up last, his tired gestures still resolute in the gloomy TOC vehicles. The battalion commander went over the company missions: Team A, the flanking missile fires; Charlie Tank, the gunfight in the wadis; Company B, the defense of the big northern wadi and flanking missile fires, covering the withdrawal of Company C. The key would be aggressiveness and active communication, said the commander. He was certain that the engagement could be won and, having said so, left things to the men who would have to pull it off.

Company B was told to turn over its tanks and to pick up its 3d Platoon at Team C by dawn, hardly welcome news to the bone-tired young captain as he bounced back to his forward positions after the battalion order. It was already past 2300, and the prospect of threading the tracks back through the labyrinthine Washboard in the coal black night was quite unwelcome. Finding Charlie Tank seemed unlikely out in the formless middle of the gullies, so the Bravo captain elected to do something other than what he had been told. He issued his order but stated that the company would move out at 0600 (it was supposed to be nearly in its new position by then, not just pulling out) to avoid further confusion and, just as important, to allow his men some rest. It turned out to be a better decision than he had expected.

The OPFOR, as predicted, slipped in patrols just after midnight, easily infiltrating into the battalion sector. The OPFOR reconnaissance picked out all the major task force units (except the scout screen, which was busily engaged in establishing itself on the heights over the OPFOR assembly areas), identifying Team A, Bravo in the middle, and Charlie Tank in The Washboard. The recon also showed the Eight-Lane Wadi to be utterly unprotected, and the reconnaissance forces withdrew with the false impression that the Dragons had an exposed flank in the north.

The OPFOR patrol near Alpha was not very careful as it remounted its BMP. The noise aroused one of Alpha's listening posts, and a sharp exchange of gunfire occurred about 0445 on 9 October. The enemy called in artillery on the Team A hill locations, then left in the resultant disruption. There were no casualties on either side.

There was an unintended result of the gunfire exchange. Bravo's captain, sleeping fitfully in his dusty chemical suit under the humming radios of his armored personnel carrier, awoke with a start as he heard the clash at the Alpha LP. The thuds of bursting artillery simulators convinced the company commander to arouse his unit and to get it on the road without delay, because he feared an OPFOR attack at dawn. The troops responded with more than the usual haste, and by the time of first light, Bravo's men were deployed in and around the 1161/ 1195 complex. the OPFOR recon efforts missed this critical shift, as it occurred after they had left.

It took almost three hours to fully implement the linkup with Charlie Tank. The tank captain, with the huge, off-white bandage on his injured head, eagerly accepted the two tanks from Company B but grew vague as to where Bravo's 3d Platoon's three APCs were. The Bravo commander found one (with the platoon sergeant aboard), who related that his other two vehicles were lost somewhere east of the 1161/1195 complex. The Bravo captain found the 3d Platoon lieutenant a few wadis back of Charlie Tank's lines, and he heard a story of contradictory orders and confusion that would have brought Bravo's commander to the throat of the erring tank commander had time existed for such an outburst. In essence, Charlie Tank had been moving here and there without notifying its attachments; or, even worse, the tanker had told them to stay put and await

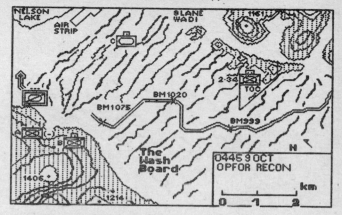

directions that never came. The other 3d Platoon track was unaccounted for, so Bravo's captain notified his XO and first sergeant to keep an eye out along the supply routes. He then issued instructions to the two befuddled squads.

Bravo's deployment was sound. The TOWs were dismounted from their carriers and dug into the east face of hill 1161, with engagement areas due south. In that way the mass of hill 1161 would protect the missile gunners from the OPFOR artillery and allow for surprise shots. Care was taken to get the TOWs far enough up to see but not so far up that they would lose range because of slope angles. The three infantry platoons were set in around the base of the hill, with 2d facing south along the low ridge that made up the south wall of the big wadi. The 1st Platoon was placed west of 2d, tied in with 2d and overlooking the wadi mouth. The 3d Platoon was out front in The Washboard wadis (the battalion had ordered this to protect Charlie Tank's M60s) to provide early warning, then to fall back to cover the Eight-Lane Wadi mouth, as a cork slamming into a bottle, when the OPFOR advanced. The infantry platoons, understrength as usual, all had Dragons and Vipers for short-range battles. The 3d, as noted earlier, was missing a squad. Company B's mortars were placed in the little bowl east of 1161, registered (theoretically, of course) to blanket the wadi entrance with high explosives. If the engineers ever arrived, they were to build a minefield to further block the vital wadi entrance.

Charlie Tank's five M60s were emplaced on the reverse

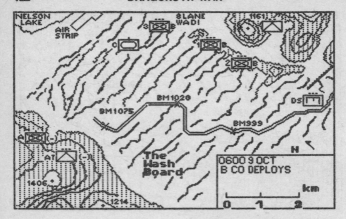

sides of the forward edge of The Washboard, on line, over-looking Nelson Lake. Team A (with the TOWs) was still on the north face of hill 1406, with the colonel's command section among its squads and mounted TOWs. Alpha and the AT Platoon (under the colonel's supervision) had made one error in positioning the TOWs. The missile tracks were so far up the hill that they could not fire over the rounded lower slopes, creating almost a kilometer of dead space right along the south wall of the Central Corridor. Nobody, however, had walked out or driven down to check out the position.

Not so in Team B. The company commander personally sited the TOWs and rifle platoons. Told not to worry about digging individual fighting positions, the antitank gunners from TOW to Viper were walking their fire lanes, shifting locations to cover dead space. Realizing ammunition would be at a pre-mium, the Bravo commander directed that nobody open fire without his permission or until enemy tanks (the main body) were sighted. That would allow the OPFOR recon to pass without giving away the Bravo emplacements and save rounds for the tanks and BMPs sure to follow. The result was that in Bravo's area, the rested troops made good use of time to es-tablish fixed range markers and good kill zones.

The scouts, far out in front of the busy task force, reported that the OPFOR were forming for attack about 1100 in the clear, blue morning. Safely squirreled into the hillsides, the scouts radioed back detailed descriptions of opposing force soldiers servicing vehicles, lining up, and dispatching their reconnaissance once again. As the enemy recon came down the valley (mounted, this time), weaving in and out of the wadis, Company B was delighted to see the GS Engineer Platoon leader finally roll up to the big wadi mouth with a dump truck full of mines. Bravo's captain left his command track to talk to the engineer lieutenant, and ordered the men of 1st Platoon to assist in laying a dense minefield on the front porch of the wadi. It was about 1145.

The OPFOR recon came nosing through, on motorcycles and in BMPs and BRDMs. Charlie Tank opened fire from all vehicles, though the enemy was well out of range. Nevertheless, as the OPFOR closed, a recon BMP was hit. Alpha and AT were bypassed in the dead ground just below them. Two motorcycles rolled right through Bravo's positions, followed by a BMP. Bravo went to ground and did not return fire. Work on the minefield continued. It was about noon.

The brigade commander, in the hill 1161 area to observe the exercise, saw the recon vehicles pass unmolested through Bravo's platoons. The brigade colonel sped to the company commander's APC. The full colonel asked in a harsh voice why the Bravo commander had not engaged the enemy. Tired, unwilling to be distracted, and sure of his plan, the captain responded curtly that he would prefer to fight the battle without interference, and ignored the colonel. The colonel drove off without further comment.[3] Already the NTC was wearing down some of the niceties of the Great Game as surely as actual combat does.

By 1215 the scouts clearly identified the main body of the motorized rifle regiment, spreading out in the open ground west of The Washboard, with the weight of the attack (two of the three columns) angling directly for the 1161 wadi. The OPFOR were picking up speed, and in Bravo Company, 3d Platoon reported massive dust clouds to its direct front. Bravo's captain radioed the TOC for permission to pull his 3d Platoon back to the wadi mouth, which the colonel jumped in and denied. The 3d would have to stay to help Charlie's five tanks fight off enemy infantry, if needed.

Bravo's commander made two quick decisions based on that guidance. First, he shifted 1st Platoon to cover the minefield and Eight-Lane Wadi doorstep. The 1st Platoon was unable to start its tracks and requested "slave" (jumper) cables (the Boeing yard electrical jury rigs striking again). The captain ordered 1st to leave the drivers with the .50-calibers, pick up all the antitank rounds and ammunition, and run down to the minefield. The platoon executed the order brilliantly under its staff sergeant platoon leader, and the net result was that the balking, lightly manned APCs formed a tenuous link to the 2d Platoon in the east.

The second decision was more critical, but it had to be made. The engineer plan had not stated who could authorize closing the lanes in the minefield on the big wadi (a detail overlooked in planning); the Bravo Company commander, faced with an imminent regimental-size assault, informed his 3d Platoon, then shut the minefield behind them. Charlie Tank would have to fight The Washboard—3d Platoon would have to battle back as best it could and fight on the front slope of 1161 proper. The Bravo captain intentionally did not inform the colonel until the minefield was closed, fearing that the tired task force commander would have waffled and left it open, as an alternative for his tanks. The dike was closed just ahead of the flood.

By 1245 the OPFOR had skirted the impotent Team A just out of TOW range and broken over Charlie Tank to strike Bravo's infantry and mines. As the enemy came to the minefield, the BMPs and T-72s milled in confusion. Where had this American force come from? The Bravo infantrymen went to work, with 1st Platoon's aggressive gunners firing at point-blank range. The 3d erupted from its hide position to join the vicious fight at the minefield, losing one APC to friendly TOW fire from Team A as it worked its way back. OPFOR casualties

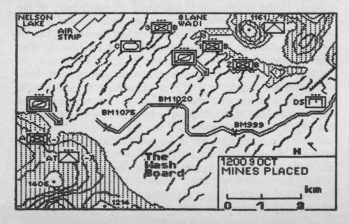

mounted in the firetrap, and attempts to flank the wadi itself along the low ridge were ripped apart by the hidden Bravo TOWs and determined infantry in 2d Platoon. The colonel, far across the valley, watched the swirling dust and listened as Bravo methodically beat back the unimaginative OPFOR bludgeons that tried to force the minefield. He was attempting to discern the OPFOR intentions and began to consider redeploying Team A and its TOWs to the east as the Bravo melee ground on.

By 1400 the OPFOR had taken quite a beating around the base of hill 1161. The single hasty minefield, the tight terrain, the OPFOR miscalculation about the wadi's defenses, and Bravo's credible fight were costing a great deal of time and had slowed momentum. Usually the MRR would have been in the American rear tearing up the trains by now. But the Dragons had proven unusually stubborn. It took almost another hour to extricate the bulk of the MRR to follow the supporting column. That motorized rifle battalion had found the blind spot below Team A. The MRR's remaining forces went pushing through the old Charlie Tank positions, staying out of range of Team Alpha to the north or inside the dead ground in the south. Bypassed, Alpha tried to pull out. The wreckage of a motorized rifle battalion was left to fix Bravo, now bottled up in its wadi as the enemy shifted to the center of the corridor. Bravo had lost seven tracks, but it had cost the OPFOR almost twenty tanks and nearly fifteen BMPs, and Bravo's position was still very solvent. Charlie Tank, opening fire at too long a range, had been blown aside, losing its last two tanks in a vain attempt to get through the Bravo minefield to the battalion rear. The Charlie Tank Company commander's APC also was "destroyed" in the friendly mines.

By 1500 Bravo had at last been bypassed, although one T-72 finally broke through the minefield in the wadi (only to be "killed" by the 3d Platoon's lost squad, which the XO had found sitting near the Barstow Road and had brought forward about 1445). The 34th defense was in disarray, with Alpha having pulled out too late. Alpha was, in fact, chasing the MRR down the Central Corridor, but the OPFOR were too fast. The TOC was ordered to join the fight to delay the enemy, a pathetic attempt that would have looked good in the movies but failed miserably at Fort Irwin. So the TOC, whose officers and men had planned and directed competently, suffered the

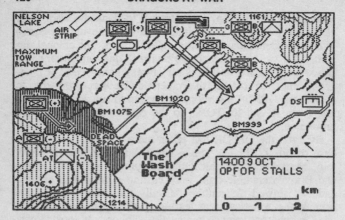

ignominy of being crushed by the OPFOR steamroller its planning had not been able to stop.

The battle ended at 1545, with the combat trains destroyed by chemical strikes and ground attack, the TOC gone, Charlie Tank written off, and Team A bypassed and out of the fight. Only Company B remained, still up in its wadi. It had been close, but in the end the task force had been soundly whipped. The remnants of the 34th were pulled back to the low hills just west of the Barstow canal.

What had gone wrong? The After Action Review that night at 2000, held in an air-conditioned trailer, did not hide the

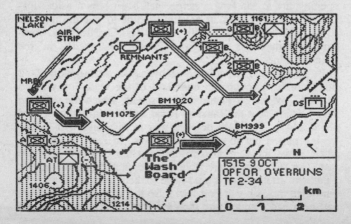

LOSSES: 9 OCTOBER 1982

	Tanks		APCs		TOW/Sagger	
	Start	Lost	Start	Lost	Start	Lost
Team A	0	0	8	8	11	8
B Company	0	0	11	7	3	0
Team C	5	5	4	4	0	0
CSC	0	0	5	0	0	0
Bn. TF	5	5	28	19	14	8
OPFOR	40	21	98	19	18	0

Source: *Take Home Package, Task Force 2-34 Infantry*, pp. III-B-1-1, IV-C-1-1.

TIMELINE: DELIBERATE ATTACK
9 OCTOBER 1982

8 OCT 82-1630:	Warning order/Leader recons
8 OCT 82-1715:	Nightfall
8 OCT 82-2130:	Battalion OPORD
8 OCT 82-2330:	Company OPORD (B Company Typical)
9 OCT 82-0500:	B Company displaces
9 OCT 82-0800:	Task organization completed (engineers reunited, tanks in Company C)
9 OCT 82-1145:	Engineers complete minefield
9 OCT 82-1215:	Scouts passed by lead elements of MRR
9 OCT 82-1230:	GS TOWs, Team A, and Tank Company attempt to engage
9 OCT 82-1300:	Enemy MRR main assault made on Company B; 3d Platoon, Company B redeploys to reinforce minefield
9 OCT 82-1400:	Enemy MRR assault blunted; weight of attack shifts to center route
9 OCT 82-1500:	One T-52 breaks through Company B; destroyed. MRR bypasses rest of TF 2-34.
9 OCT 82-1515:	2-34 Infantry TOC destroyed
9 OCT 82-1545:	TF combat trains destroyed
9 OCT 82-1645:	Company After Action Reviews; TF remnants redeploy on west bank Barstow River.
9 OCT 82-2000:	TF After Action Review (Star Wars trailer)

truth. The task force had failed to establish barriers; the only effective one was set up almost as the enemy assaulted. The engineers had dredged a huge tank ditch at the east end of the Eight-Lane Wadi that had no bearing on anything. There had been few mines or barricade materials brought forward. The fire support plan had been inadequate again, with three missions fired out of sector. Team A had played no part in the battle; the colonel was chided for misdeploying Alpha, then not moving them to react to the OPFOR's troubles in front of Bravo Company. Charlie Tank had done little to help itself. The heavy mortars had been out of the picture all day.

The good news was minimal. The OPFOR had lost two of three tank companies and most of an MRB battering at Company B. The S-2 and scouts had given clear, timely intelligence information to everyone, and it had paid off, at least in Bravo's sector. At least one company knew that the OPFOR were stoppable and that a few determined infantrymen could tear huge holes in the OPFOR formations.

Still, the most embarrassing item was kept until the end. The controllers put up a chart that delineated the myriad lost and abandoned vehicles found in the 34th sector.[4] Charlie Tank, Combat Support Company, and especially Alpha Company were the big offenders, but the resulting reprimands from the normally soft-spoken division commanding general and the irate brigade commander reddened even the sun- and wind-burned faces of the 34th's leadership. Reliefs from command were threatened, and the threats were in earnest. The shameful lists of men unfed, lost troops without water, tracks broken and abandoned, and leaders unconcerned were not the marks of a winning battalion. The 34th was beginning to feel like a lost unit, and it was displaying all the ugly indicators that accompany failing morale and exhaustion in the face of a superior enemy.

There was so much to fix and so little time. The dark night beckoned again, and the word from brigade was that the next mission would be a counterattack. The dejected Dragons gathered themselves together to try again.

Notes

1. Willi Heinrich, *The Cross of Iron,* translated by Richard and Clara Winston (1956; reprint, New York: Bantam Books, 1977), 39.

2. Department of the Army, *FM 71-2 The Tank and Mechanized Infantry Battalion Task Force* (Washington, D.C.: Headquarters, Department of the Army, 1977), 5-27 and 5-28. This 1977 manual had been superseded by an April 1982 Coordinating Draft (very similar to the Final Draft, and a companion to the *FM 71-1* company-level April 1982 Coor-

dinating Draft). The Dragons had not yet made the full mental transition after five years under the dictates of the active defense.

3. The author was not criticized for his actions, a tribute to the brigade commander's patience.

4. *Take-Home Package, Task Force 2-34 Infantry*, IV-C-13. The complete list: "Tank attached to Team B (1st Platoon) was mechanically inoperative and the crew had no food; GAMA GOAT [*sic*] was abandoned; Team A's mortar platoon M151 was inoperative for two days—the platoon leader left his platoon sergeant with only two gallons of water; Team A had an APC out of action for 2 days; the crew was left without food or water; Team A had three tanks out of action for two days." A GAMA GOAT is an M561 1¼-ton truck, nicknamed the Gamma Goat. The senior controller verbally chastised CSC's executive officer for the wandering TOW tracks as well. The tank allegedly "attached to Team B" was, in fact, the responsibility of Team Tank to recover, and the Charlie Tank captain was decent enough to interrupt the senior OC to take responsibility. The noted lost and abandoned vehicles were just the more obvious of a much larger number of similar cases.

Note: Other sources for material in this chapter include: interviews; *Take-Home Package, Task Force 2-34 Infantry;* relevant doctrinal manuals.

Chapter Eight

Counterattack

"Don't Delay: The best is the enemy of the good. By this I mean that a good plan executed violently now is better than a perfect plan next week. War is a very simple thing, and the determining characteristics are self-confidence, speed, and audacity. None of these things can ever be perfect, but they can be good."

Gen. George S. Patton, Jr., *War As I Knew It[1]*

The word that the morrow would bring a counterattack was not given until 2230 on 9 October 1982. The scattered, battered elements of the task force had regrouped in the open, scrubby flats just west of the Barstow canal while their staff and commanders had taken their verbal lumps in the After Action Review. Being overrun that afternoon had not helped matters. The controllers adjudged the task force too far gone to be reconstituted and simply ordered unit replacement. In other words, the 34th had been destroyed utterly and could not be rebuilt. The Tactical Operations Center (TOC) had been crushed in close combat with rampaging T-72s (nine vehicles were destroyed, along with eleven men "killed" and eight "wounded"). The combat trains had been doused with a barrage of persistent chemical agents then shot to pieces by penetrating OPFOR tanks and BMPs. Since the NTC is not real war, the "dead" were pulled together, fed, and fueled while the leadership suffered the criticisms of the observer controllers.

The problem of scattered, hungry troops and vehicles was nowhere nearer to solution that dark night than any other, despite the grim warnings of the brigade and division commanders. The creaking logistic lines, shortened by the withdrawal to the canal, managed to get a fairly decent amount of sustenance forward, though ammunition was running short. Fueling and feeding were just ending as the company commanders and special platoon leaders returned to their units.

The battalion commander, discomfited by yet another thrashing in front of his superiors, was convinced that the task force had to improve dramatically on the next mission, if only for the battalion's self-confidence. He and his S-3 major sat down in the ramshackle, dully illuminated M577 tent extensions at the TOC. Tired sergeants, eyes vacant from days with little sleep, mechanically moved about the dim interior of the double-decker command post APCs, answering radio messages and tying in communications wires from security posts. The colonel had very little from brigade on which to base his plans. The enemy situation was vague again, and the timing and location of the attack were not given. It was all "on order." In the meantime the Dragons would have to establish a coherent defense in the thin belt of generally open desert just west of the Barstow Road.

The colonel decided to close up into a linear defense, with Alpha to the south, Bravo in the center on the Little Black Rockpile, and Charlie Tank just above the east exit of the infamous Eight-Lane Wadi, along the southwest forward slopes of hill 910. All units tied in on their flanks, and the scouts were sent to the south to screen the gap between Alpha and the southern wall of the Central Corridor. The positional nature of the defense was necessitated by the shallow depth of the sector.

The forces had to be reorganized a little to allow for a successful attack in the morning, although the colonel applied the rule out of convenience rather than out of tactical logic. His mechanics had been able to restore three more of the M60 tanks, changing the battle calculus a bit. Company A, out in the slight depressions and creosote patches in the south of the sector, was not allocated any of the eight tanks, though its area favored long-range, high-velocity, flat-trajectory shooting. Team Bravo, in the center, would keep all of its infantry and pick up a three-tank platoon. Bravo's reliability insured its central role in the counterstroke. Team Charlie kept five tanks and Alpha's 3d Platoon of infantry. In brief, the task force disposed Company A with two infantry platoons, Team B with three infantry platoons and a tank platoon, and Charlie Tank with a tank platoon and an infantry platoon.

The massing of forces in Bravo's position was an intentional attempt to make the best use of the steady performers in Company B. However, the tank platoon that was going to Bravo was not the usual 1st Platoon, Company C, but the unfamiliar 3d Platoon, Company C. The fact that the switch would occur at night, after three trying days of simulated battle, would not ease the transition.

Charlie Tank was in even greater distress. Its infantrymen

TASK ORGANIZATION: TF 2-34 INFANTRY
10 OCTOBER 1982

Company A

Company A (−)
1 AT section

Team B

Company B
3d Platoon, Company C (3 tanks)
1 AT section (+ 1 squad)

Team C

Company C (only 5 tanks operational)
3d Platoon, Company A (all APCs broken down)

TF Control

Scouts
Heavy Mortars
GS AT Platoon (TOWs)
DS Engineer Platoon
GS Engineer Platoon

OPPOSING FORCES (OPFOR) MOTORIZED RIFLE COMPANY

1 Motorized Rifle Company (MRC) (10 BMP infantry vehicles)
1 Tank Platoon (4 T-72 tanks)

had no operational vehicles, as all three APCs were broken
down. The Charlie captain did not inform the battalion of this
condition, as he did not discover it until almost 0430, when the
attached Alpha platoon leader (the sergeant replacement for the
young lieutenant medevacked two days earlier) finally noted
that all his tracks were inoperative.

The task force operations order was given before all the
re-allocation of resources, and it was incomplete, imprecise,
and based on wishful thinking.[2] The two attached engineer
platoon leaders were not present and received no missions,
though the defense was to be continued until the counterattack
order came. The Antitank Platoon was separated from Company A but was given no real missions other than "support."

Air defense and ground radar assets promised by brigade had not arrived in sector, though both were needed. Without the antiaircraft protection of the Vulcan guns, the 34th would suffer heavily from any enemy helicopters and bombers, packed as it was into the open stretch along the Barstow Road.

Possibly the worst feature of the operations order, aside from its delivery at 0230 hours to the bleary-eyed Dragon leaders, was the imprecision of exactly what and when the Dragons would assault. The plan delineated a battalion movement back up the Central Corridor with the three maneuver units swinging on line like a mechanized push broom. The problems this formation probably would encounter in The Washboard were not explained. Because of the on-order nature of the brigade mission, it could be many hours before the operation was executed. The 34th had no real intent about how to use this "dead" time nor how to initiate a serious defensive deployment in the meantime.

Brigade's broken assurance of ground surveillance radars was merely part of an overall lack of concern in the Dragon TOC about where the enemy was and what he was doing. As noted earlier, the scouts had a security mission on the south flank, not a reconnaissance role. No company-level patrols were directed, allowing the active OPFOR infiltrators to work in quite close to the 34th's lines under cover of darkness. The lack of intelligence collection would hurt the battalion badly.

Fire support planning was inadequate once again, with only Team B updating its target lists. The battalion fire support officer did not send out the confused listings he had created, so that the various forward observers had no preplanned targets to use anyway. This artillery breakdown was all too typical, and it was robbing the 34th of its fire support. A planned target, its number and location given to the battery fire direction centers, can be fired on much quicker than an on-call target. On-call targets, given in map grid references, must be plotted at the FDC; then firing data must be computed for them. Planned target data is already computed and, for priority targets, already out to the gunners. Every time the FSO bungled the target list, the Dragons were forced to use on-call fires, with the resultant time delays.

The latenight operations order broke up at about 0330, and the commanders spent the rest of the dark hours picking up and dropping off attachments. The Bravo captain had the disquieting experience of getting lost in his own perimeter (the XO having repositioned the company while the captain was at battalion). By dawn most of the soldiers of the 34th had not slept, but they were where they belonged. And that is when the results of inadequate patrolling began to tell.

The OPFOR had slipped artillery and aircraft observers in very close to the Dragons, and dawn brought repeated barrages of artillery onto the cramped 34th positions. The situation in Team Charlie Tank was particularly bad, as its exposed vehicles and tired infantry milled about in full view of the enemy's binoculars.

The National Training Center does not adequately portray the effects of modern artillery bombardment. Sure, the OCs did insure that the guns and forward observers agreed on the target grid locations, and fires were dispassionately marked where they were called. Sometimes, careless FOs blew up friendly troops. The controllers applied the fire effects regardless and noted it for the AARs. Certainly the bursts of the little artillery simulator charges and the judicious use of the kill switch on the controller's little "god guns" did do something toward reducing the efficiency of the unit under artillery fire. The controllers would kill anyone whose head and shoulders did not pop down a vehicle hatch (and close it up tight), and they would also gradually eliminate troops on the ground who had not dug in. All of this helped to portray the artillery, and it was better than the REFORGER-style dice rolling and arbitrary decisions that usually characterize Army maneuvers.

What did not come across was the screaming, tearing, thunderous intensity of a real bombardment. Both the Soviets and Americans are big believers in artillery, and both sides have used it extensively in all recent combat experiences. The flimsy fighting position scraped out by the Dragons would do little to protect them against an actual barrage, and that was a lesson even NTC could not accurately portray. Artillery for the OPFOR and the 34th was a pale shadow of its actual self.

The morning of 10 October 1982 found the Dragons under regular bombardment from an unseen enemy force. OPFOR jets, undeterred by the still-missing Vulcans, came in low along the canal, conducting run after run against the stationary Dragons. Like other soldiers have done in real combat, the Dragons soon were firing at anything in the air, friendly or enemy, using their vehicle machine guns and small arms. The TOC, sited in a hollow east of hill 910, called brigade repeatedly to ascertain when the counterattack was scheduled. Team C lost a tank,

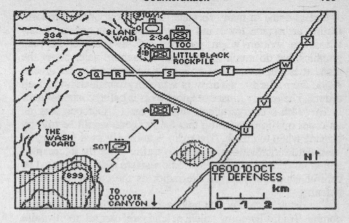

Team B lost an APC, and the combat trains took casualties when a fuel truck "exploded" under air attack. Time ticked on and on, and still the execution of the counterattack was postponed.

At this point the TOC was forced to detach a scout section of two APCs to hunt for the SD Engineer Platoon, which had called in that it was up near the 1195/1161 complex and needed to be guided into the TF 2-34 area. How the engineers had ended up way out there or why they had waited until almost 0900 to announce their presence was unexplained. The screen in the south was weakened to go forward to find the errant engineers. Unfortunately, the scouts dropped off the command radio net almost as soon as they moved forward. The TOC hoped that they had not been destroyed.

The OPFOR patrols near Team C, meanwhile, moved onto the ridge opposite the tankers and near-missed them with RPG antitank rounds. The tank commander sent his infantry forward on foot to fight off the patrol, and a confusing firefight developed in the valley between the OPFOR and Charlie Tank. The TOC never quite got the word on this infantry combat, so it made no provision to aid Team C with the static, unengaged platoons of nearby (and overstrength) Team B. The morning dragged on, and the 34th sweltered on the hot rocks, huddled into scooped-out holes or shut up in hot, buttoned-up APCs and tanks. Still, the intermittent enemy artillery came and went.

* * *

Orders come in many formats, with written orders predominating at brigade level and above. Operations orders at battalion are written when possible and always include map graphics that do much to enlighten the subordinates about the plan. It is important that orders be understood at all levels. Aside from clarity, security is a primary consideration in all orders. The enemy must not know what is being contemplated.

The 34th's counterattack mission on 10 October was an on-order mission, meaning that the Dragons would be told by brigade when to attack. The radio is normally used to transmit such battle instructions, but radio traffic is easily intercepted and monitored by enemy electronic warfare units. One must be careful what one says on the radio, as the enemy is usually listening.

The result of this is that units avoid using the radio prior to combat (radio-listening silence) and are careful to disguise their identity and intentions through the use of code words and changing call signs and frequencies. Not surprisingly, the more heavily involved a unit is in fighting, the less the radio traffic utilizes codes. In close, continuous contact, leaders talk "in the clear" over their radios, since the need to act quickly in the face of the enemy supersedes security requirements.

The 34th had codes and SOPs for its radio transmissions. Common items, like tanks and TOWs, had their own brevity codes. "I have two quarters, a dime, and three nickels" could mean that the caller had two tanks, an M901 ITV, and three APCs operational. Some actions also had substitute words, such as "thunderbolt": move the TOC forward; or "Blue Dragon": need chemical decontamination. All of this helped reduce clutter and did something to confuse the enemy, though after a few days, OPFOR electronic eavesdroppers had figured out most of the key brevity terms. The 34th, like most units, had a tendency to talk in the clear as soon as the first shot was fired. It was a sloppy habit, a costly one on 10 October.

Brigade's radio net crackled to life at 1030 hours with the long-awaited word: "Counterattack!" Brigade sent it in plain text, just like that. The 34th TOC officer, the decisive S-3-Air, elected to pass the word exactly as he had received it. He called the colonel, who was forward with Company A. Again the fateful term went out in everyday English for all the world (and the OPFOR) to hear: "Counterattack, I say again, counterattack!"

The Dragons were not slow in pulling out of their exposed

positions, but the task force's incomplete orders sent the three line companies rushing back up the Central Corridor in a virtual movement to contact. The 34th had no idea where the enemy was located, so the counterattack would be a three-abreast replay of the first morning's action in the corridor.

By doctrine, counterattacks have limited, well-defined objectives. Some counterattacks (counterattacks by fire) merely reposition friendly units to engage the enemy from a new location without close combat. But 1st Brigade, 24th Infantry Division (Mechanized), had not provided a specific objective for the Dragons. The 34th was directed to "regain forward positions," a nebulous phrase that could mean almost anything, given the dearth of knowledge about the enemy.

The OPFOR, on the other hand, could not have known more about the Dragons' intentions had they been seated in the TOC. While the Dragons had been content to while away the morning waiting for the "go" signal, the OPFOR had made excellent use of the time to gain information and to prepare a defensive setup. The enemy's aggressive infantry patrols and careful radio-listening sections had identified every 34th unit and heard the counterattack order. The forward OPFOR observers watched the Dragons pull out, and the OPFOR motorized rifle company and its attached tanks set up in a fire sack to trap Team Tank and Team B just inside The Washboard, near the Eight-Lane Wadi. A few BMPs were left forward to draw the Dragons into the trap, and one BMP was tasked to pull Alpha out of supporting range to the south. It was a simple, clever plan. It worked quite well.

The Dragons jumped off in echelon, with Alpha leading out. The rest of the Dragons followed, with Bravo and Charlie Tank turning to the west as they crossed behind the Little Black Rockpile. The TOC and colonel heard little from the roaring columns of tracks and tanks and assumed all was well. Instead, the task force began to spread out beyond mutual supporting distance. The scouts, who could have provided some help in finding the enemy, were off the radio, and, of course, some of them were searching for the wandering engineers. (They never did find them.) Brigade's intelligence assets offered no assistance as the 34th turned into the corridor once more.

Company A pushed forward swiftly, taking advantage of the open ground to make time. Its lead element spotted a BMP, and the open column rushed after the lone OPFOR vehicle into The Washboard. Alpha was pulled almost out of sector, along

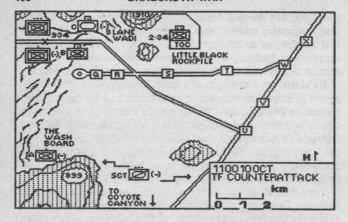

the crags on the south of the corridor. The BMP got off a lucky shot and hit the lead Alpha APC. Alpha's commander, exhausted but certain of himself, pulled his two platoons on line and dismounted his infantry in The Washboard, searching for the enemy. The Alpha captain reported contact to the TOC but did not give his precise location or the size of the enemy force. The colonel, who had been with Company A, had dropped off to follow Team B and was not sure of Alpha's position. Cautiously, Company A began to clear the wadis as it rolled slowly forward. But the enemy was gone, having moved over to deal with the tank company.

Charlie Tank's captain had made two errors that by 1100 had cost him his company team. First, he left the infantry behind since its APCs were broken down, although he could have carried the soldiers on his tank decks. Second, he ran right up the Eight-Lane Wadi at full throttle, outrunning the deploying Team B to the south and driving smack into the OPFOR's ambush. Within five minutes Charlie was destroyed by the dug-in OPFOR BMPs and tanks, with barely a peep to the listening TOC. Nobody was aware that Charlie Tank was gone, least of all Team B, which was motoring blithely into the southern half of the same fire sack.

Bravo's captain was careful to dismount as soon as his lead APC was struck by enemy tank fire, and his infantry began to clear the wadis, killing two BMPs right off. But the attached tanks, not at home with Team B, raced forward into the fire sack before the methodical infantry dispositions were complete. Bravo's intent of rolling up the enemy from his south flank was thwarted when the three tanks were hit and destroyed in an area less than fifty meters square. The Bravo captain lost his temper for the first time in the entire exercise, roundly cursing the tank platoon leader for his rashness. But the enemy had had enough and was beginning to withdraw in front of Bravo's dismounted men. The Bravo infantry killed a T-72 and a third BMP before the OPFOR pulled off their position. Bravo's soldiers inched out across two more wadis before the engagement was ended at 1215.

The colonel was furious when he discovered the fate of Team C, particularly because the Team C commander rarely monitored the colonel's battalion command net. The battalion commander was galled by the armor captain's repeated lack of reporting, and he rightly charged the tanker with causing unnecessary losses in Team B through Charlie's failures to stay "up" on the battalion radio network. The battalion commander also kicked himself for letting Alpha get off to the south. Once again the attack had been piecemeal, with Charlie then Bravo striking the enemy defenses. Alpha had not played much of a part at all, though it had lost another APC to OPFOR artillery.

The Task Force After Action Review at 1500 was briefer than usual, and for good reason. The counterattack was the final mission in the Central Corridor, and the Dragons would be taking a two-day refitting break, then moving north for the live-fire phase of training. The controllers confined their negative remarks to the usual litany: unaggressive patrolling, piecemeal attack, poor fire support (three missions on friendly units again), inadequate reporting, and utterly ineffective air defense. The gross security lapse on the radio was severely criticized, and the OPFOR leader made sure to mention the Dragons' radio indiscipline as he enumerated the factors that led to the OPFOR success. Fortunately, nobody senior to the battalion commander was present for the AAR.

Even as the leaders gathered to examine their errors at the AAR, the 34th was on the move, its various elements under way back across the Barstow Road to a battalion laager site on the lower north slope of the Tiefort massif, centered between hill 760 and the 955 ridge. The battalion's troops were tired, dirty, hungry, and much the worse for wear. The colonel watched the wheezing APCs roll by as the AAR dragged to a close, and he could not help but wonder, as he stared at his grimy men, if things would ever get better.

LOSSES: 10 OCTOBER 1982

	Tanks		APCs		TOW/Sagger	
	Start	Lost	Start	Lost	Start	Lost
Company A	0	0	8	2	2	0
Team B	3	3	11	2	3	0
Team C	5	5	0	0	0	0
CSC	0	0	5	0	9	0
Bn. TF	8	8	24	4	14	0
OPFOR	4	1	10	3	0	0

Note: Losses estimated: NTC cadre has no formal battle record of 10 Oct 82 losses
to U.S. or to OPFOR.
Sources: Interviews; *Take-Home Package, Task Force 2-34 Infantry*, pp. IV-D-2
through IV-D-9.

TIMELINE: COUNTERATTACK
10 OCTOBER 1982

9 OCT 82-2230:	Warning order/Units begin to reposition
10 OCT 82-0230:	Repositioning complete/Battalion OPORD
10 OCT 82-0430:	Task reorganization completed
10 OCT 82-0600:	Company OPORD (B Company typical)
10 OCT 82-1030:	Counterattack order issued (by radio)
10 OCT 82-1100:	Tank Company destroyed
10 OCT 82-1215:	TF assumes hasty defense
10 OCT 82-1245:	Company After Action Reviews
10 OCT 82-1500:	TF After Action Review

The Dragons had suffered four serious reverses, with only
the deliberate attack on 8 October a partial success (and that
aborted by the brigade order mixup and heavy losses in the
OPFOR counterattack). The 34th had fought long and hard but
to no avail. It had been roughly handled by the OPFOR at
every turn and overrun (albeit after a valiant stand by Company
B) by the motorized rifle regiment. Logistics had been a shameful, ineffectual nightmare. And as for command and control, it
surely seemed lacking. He hoped there would be time to sort
out all of this. Understandably, the only thing on the colonel's
mind as the AAR ended was a more primal need—sleep. At
long last, in the safety of the laager site, there would be time
for precious rest.

Notes

1. Gen. George S. Patton, Jr., *War As I Knew It* (1947; reprint, New York: Pyramid Books, 1970), 305.

2. *Take-Home Package, Task Force 2-34 Infantry,* IV-D-2; Ramsey interview; Norman interview. In Capt. Norman's words: "It was the weakest order we wrote at Irwin."

Note: Other sources for material in this chapter include: interviews; *Take-Home Package, Task Force 2-34 Infantry;* relevant doctrinal literature.

Chapter Nine

Laager

"Train in time of peace to maintain direction at night with the aid of a luminous dial compass. Train in difficult, trackless, wooded terrain. War makes extremely heavy demands on the soldier's strength and nerves. For this reason make heavy demands on your men in peacetime exercises."

Erwin Rommel, *Attacks*[1]

The men and machines of Task Force 2-34 assembled slowly on the lower north slope of Tiefort Mountain. It took well into the night hours of 10 October to sort out the stragglers and to locate all of the lost sheep. Most of the battalion settled into the thick, dreamless sleep of exhaustion. For almost all of the troops it was the first uninterrupted slumber in nearly five days.

There was work to do in the morning, aside from servicing the creaking tanks and dirty M113s. The blank adaptor devices would have to be removed from the rifles and machine guns, and the tank crews would disconnect the Hoffman simulation equipment from their main gun barrels. The missiles (TOW, Dragon) and light antitank rockets (Vipers) would remain as MILES laser systems. Every weapon would be taken to nearby ranges for zeroing (alignment of sights with bullet trajectory for maximum accuracy). Other than that, the Dragons had no prescribed requirements for 11 October 1982.

The passage from force-on-force to live-fire training also saw the 34th change its superior headquarters from its own 1st Brigade to the National Training Center's Operations Group. The chief, operations group assumed the persona of the "2d brigade commander" for the live-fire missions, and the COG was not slow in exercising his command prerogatives. The COG, an imposing, primitively powerful sort of full colonel who looked perfectly at home in bayonet combat or fisticuffs, directed the weary battalion commander to make certain that he included "retraining on unit weaknesses" during the laager period. The tired Dragon commander had his S-3 and company captains come up with training schedules, but he prudently insured that showers at the brigade trains and rest were programmed for all soldiers, including leaders. The COG promised to be there at 11 October to check the retraining efforts. The lieutenant colonel and his staff believed the implacable COG and prepared accordingly.

The live-fire training missions would be very tough. Preparation time would be minimal, and the use of every weapon, from rifle and smoke grenade to tank gun and artillery shell, would serve to complicate the problem. There were no safety sergeants or firing lanes or artificial rules, just the unit's own leaders and firing drills. The NTC staff prudently allowed sleep time before this series of missions, although the pacing of the three operations was such that fatigue would become a definite factor.

The Dragons would move north late on 12 October on a long night road march (that old bugbear once again) to the dry Drinkwater Lake valley and establish battle positions. Shortly after sunrise on the 13th, the Dragons would defend their positions, then defend the same area again just after dark. The night defense would end with orders to pull out to the south to prepare for a long movement to contact at sunrise on the 14th, implying yet another all-night battalion convoy. The final mission was the move to contact to the west, involving the reduction of several massive obstacles.

The 34th commander could sleep securely on the night of the 10th, at least so far as knowledge of the upcoming live-ammunition battles. The NTC always ran the same three missions in the live-fire area (and as a result, permitted no

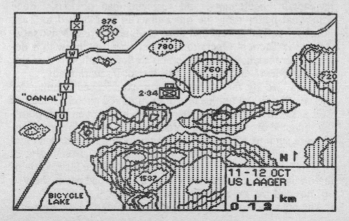

reconnoitering and released little information about the Drinkwater Lake region).[2] However, the 34th was with the second
rotation from its 24th Infantry Division (Mechanized), and the
5-32 Armor and 3-19 Infantry had briefed the Dragons' leaders
extensively on the live-fire missions they had run in August
1982. The rigid design of these operations meant that the Dragons would face the same challenges as their Fort Stewart comrades from the August excursion. The lieutenant colonel had
reviewed these three missions with his subordinates, and they
knew what to expect. He fully intended to refresh their memories in the morning.

The battalion commander might have stayed up later worrying about the first four engagements had he not been so bone
weary. The Dragons had fumbled repeatedly, and in terms of
the Great Game, the lieutenant colonel had been badly embarrassed before the brigade commander, the division commanding general, and the NTC staff. What was worse, it was all
going down on paper, with remorseless efficiency. Statistics
sent to Forces Command in Atlanta, Georgia, would record
forever that the 34th was not cutting the mustard, leading to
inferences about the battalion colonel's effectiveness. Naturally, the 34th's troubled performance was not helping the
younger gamesmen in the 34th either. The battalion XO, the
S-3, the rest of the staff, the company commanders, and
the attachments all suffered in comparison to other rotating task
forces that had visited Fort Irwin.

There were a few winners, of course. Bravo Company and
its captain, lieutenants, and sergeants had obviously done
somewhat better than the other units in or attached to Task
Force 2-34. The scouts had done creditable work. Most satis-
fying, the Tactical Operations Center was running with a degree of proficiency, lending credit to the battalion S-3 major
and his officers and NCOs. Still, the losers were many.

Alpha, led by the colonel's most experienced commander
and very much the heroes of earlier, umpired exercises such as
BOLD EAGLE and DRAGON TEAM, had proven disappointing, plagued by maintenance problems and lapses in execution.
The fire support officer and his company FIST lieutenants had
not done too well, with a few exceptions (not surprisingly, in
Bravo Company). The Heavy Mortar Platoon had done little of
importance. The air defense Vulcan Platoon had never showed
up, nor had the ground surveillance radars.

The big mistakes, the crucial errors in judgment or a general

The National Training Center at Fort Irwin occupies an area the size of Rhode Island close to the California/Nevada border. Visiting unit troops arrive at Norton Air Force Base near San Bernardino, California.

An Opposing Force (OPFOR) operations order is underway. The distinctive dark green uniforms, black berets, Soviet-style rank insignia, and black star in a circle unit emblem mark these superb soldiers. In meetings like these, OPFOR commanders create and issue the schemes that challenge and often defeat the visiting U.S. units.

A column of OPFOR tracks moves toward the maneuver area. The high, hanging dust clouds are identifiable from many miles away.

A closer view of an OPFOR column staging for an attack. The visually modified M551 Sheridan tanks reproduce a variety of Soviet equipment. The lead vehicle is a BMP (infantry carrier), followed by a ZSU 23-4 (air defense gun track) and four T-72 tanks.

Landmines are a key element of defensive barriers. Here, a U.S. infantryman buries a simulated M-21 antitank mine.

Covered by an M-60 machine-gunner, infantrymen in stifling protective masks (1-12 Infantry, Fort Carson, Colorado) employ D-handled shovels to help reduce an antitank ditch. The task is made more difficult when there isn't a proper smoke screen to obscure the efforts.

A U.S. M163A1 20-mm "Vulcan" air defense gun carrier (5-52 Air Defense Artillery, Fort Stewart, Georgia) in position. The radar-directed 20-mm Gatling-style cannon can shoot up to 3,000 rounds per minute.

A U.S. platoon leader's M113A1 Armored Personnel Carrier (3-19 Infantry, Fort Stewart, Georgia) moves into the attack. Two M-60 tanks and an APC are deployed to the rear.

Kicking up yellow dust, an M106A1 107-mm mortar carrier (24th Infantry Division (Mechanized), Fort Stewart, Georgia) rolls toward its next position. Notice the MILES Combat Vehicle Kill Indicator light on the right front of the tracked vehicle.

An OPFOR infantry squad dismounts from an actual Soviet MTLB armored personnel carrier. Going "over the side" is a typical Soviet technique, faithfully reproduced by the competent OPFOR. The MTLB is protected by a rise to its front.

OPFOR infantrymen in protective masks wait to move out. The leader to the rear is using a hand signal to overcome the muffling effect of the mask on voice communication.

A U.S. M-47 Dragon antitank guided missile gunner (left) and a grenadier with an M16A1 rifle/M203 grenade launcher dual purpose weapon (right) occupy a camouflaged fighting position. To allow for unobstructed firing of the awkward Dragon, the men have created protective shelters at either end of the emplacement.

U.S. infantry soldiers (1-61 Infantry, Fort Polk, Louisiana) defend their battle position on the south side of the Valley of Death, across from the Tiefort Mountain massif. The soldier at right center is firing a Dragon antitank missile MILES simulator. He and the other soldiers have left the protection of their fighting position; it appears that the OPFOR attack has come from an unexpected direction.

A rifleman (1-8 Infantry, Fort Carson, Colorado) engages OPFOR vehicles with the small LAW/Viper antitank rocket MILES simulator. A U.S. M113A1 APC is parked in a slight defilade position below the firer.

OPFOR BMPs snake through a wadi enroute to an attack. This sort of concentrated target group is an American artillerist's and antiarmor gunner's dream.

Two U.S. M-60 tanks establish a hasty defensive position. The tank to the left has backed into a hull-down defilade position in a little gully; the tank to the right backs toward the same low ground. By careful use of such sites, tanks can minimize vehicle exposure to enemy fire and still return fire against unprotected enemy assault units.

Spread out under a smoke screen, the OPFOR motorized rifle regiment drives relentlessly toward the U.S. positions.

A company commander and his FIST chief (3-7 Infantry, Fort Benning, Georgia) attempt to control their defense in the smoke that typifies NTC battles. Their fighting position has inadequate overhead cover (too thin) and evidently lacks a proper field of view. Given the realities of Soviet artillery effects, it would be quite dangerous to expose oneself in this way.

A rifleman (1-22 Infantry, Fort Carson, Colorado) stands in the breach made by infantry and engineer squads under the cover of dense smoke. His job is to direct the following elements along the cleared path.

Two OPFOR T-72s and a BMP lead their regiment into the battalion task force rear area. The lead T-72 is making smoke. While a few vehicles turn to brush aside frantic U.S. resistance, the rest continue toward the rear areas to destroy logistics units. An observer-controller is on the far left. The seated man to his right is "dead," and another soldier rushes to take his LAW/Viper tube. The fact that these troops are fighting out in the open indicates they were taken by surprise.

One of the most powerful men on the battlefield: a Forward Observer (soldier with radio handset) (1-35 Field Artillery, Fort Stewart. Georgia). He can request and control a variety of fire support, ranging from mortars to huge artillery barrages and even air strikes. His APC carries a few extra aerials to allow him to talk on several radio nets.

An AH-1S Cobra attack helicopter (24th Combat Aviation Battalion, Fort Stewart, Georgia) ready to fire simulated TOW antitank missiles into massed OPFOR tanks and personnel carriers. The two-man craft also has a 20-mm antitank Gatling gun in the nose.

A pair of USAF A-10 ground attack planes (nicknamed "Warthogs") work over the OPFOR units with simulated 30-mm cannon fire and munitions. A terrific "tank-buster," the A-10 mounts a massive seven-barrel 30-mm Gatling gun that fires depleted uranium slugs capable of punching holes in any tank. It can also carry a variety of bombs and air-to-surface missiles.

Two M109A2 self-propelled 155-mm howitzers await calls for fire under the cover of camouflage nets. These cannons provide the majority of a battalion's artillery fire support.

The self-propelled howitzer delivers an artillery round on a distant target. Three of the 155-mm projectiles can be seen in the lower right hand corner. The cannon will move after every few fire missions to avoid enemy counterbattery fires.

A U.S. M220/M113A1 TOW Carrier (3-19 Infantry, Fort Stewart, Georgia) at a halt. Although this older model antitank missile vehicle has been largely replaced by the M901, at NTC the M220 is used to make up shortages in the equipment yard.

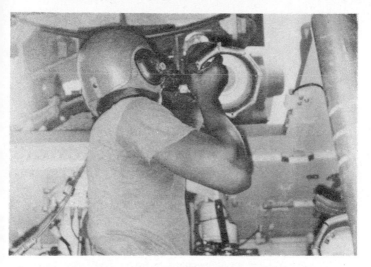

Some like it hot, but not this U.S. M901 Improved TOW Vehicle crewmen. In desert heat, crews often strip to shirt-sleeves, though this risks
burn injuries in event of on-board fires. The track's unique cantilever turret allows the crew to reload the TOW launcher tubes without leaving
the armor protection.

Two Parrumph irregular snipers take aim at U.S. positions. The guerrillas augment the OPFOR effort at Fort Irwin. They represent anti-U.S.
partisan forces likely to operate in many foreign combat contingencies.

Near the base of a live-fire target board, a "smoky SAM" replicates the launch of an AT-3 Sagger Soviet antitank missile. The styrofoam smoky SAMs enable static targets in the live-fire area to "return fire." Even if the projectiles strike, they are too light to harm a person or vehicle.

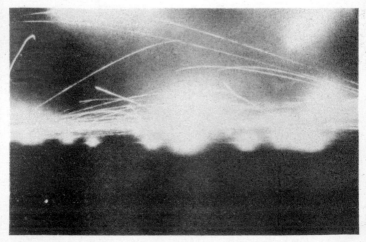

Tracers and illumination flares brighten the live-fire night defense.

inadequacy in organization, the kinds of things that make a battalion's officers a cellar team in the Great Game: these serious failures could be traced to four elements. One, the tank company headquarters was not up to the demands of the NTC, though its individual tanks and platoons were often quite good. Two, the TOW platoon had contributed nothing, especially damning in light of the TOW's importance to the mechanized infantry's antiarmor firepower. (The three TOWs with Company B had made a substantial dent in the MRR's strength on 9 October, so it *could* be done.) Three, the engineers, particularly the DS platoon, had been unaggressive and had given poor assistance on both offense and defense; conversely, the task force had not helped them much with logistic and labor support. Finally, the combat service support platoons were using the "pull" concept (line units ask to receive) instead of the doctrinal "push" idea (line units receive standard items such as fuel and ammo, and CSS leaders recon forward as they deliver to anticipate needs). Reputations in these four crucial task force units were on the line—they had much to prove to redeem themselves.

Still, the Army is not just the Great Game. The other imperative (prepare for war) was also important to the colonel and the Dragon subordinates, though in varying degrees. To do well and reverse the skid in the career column, one had to go beyond mere assessments of who "looked" good or bad. The battalion commander knew that his analysis of the task force's errors and how he ordered them corrected would determine the 34th's future at NTC, not to mention his own.

The Seven Operating Systems provide a convenient organizational structure for examining the performance of TF 2-34 during its first force-on-force training period. In a less pedantic fashion, the leaders of the Dragon battalion and its supporting attachments considered their methods and took steps to preserve the good and upgrade the inadequate. The 34th leadership concentrated only on the critical areas, letting some other factors slip by through neglect, conscious or not.

The *command and control* system of the battalion task force was under the closest scrutiny of all, since the National Training Center was designed to provide real-battle experiences with an emphasis on stressing leadership to the maximum extent. It was no accident that observer controllers rode with and concentrated on the actions of those in charge. Almost every event, for good or ill, was a direct result of the Dragon leadership's actions or inactions. Fortunately, positive troop initiative could be relied upon to help the issue at many sticky points. Even this quality, in a sense, could be attributed to the sergeants and officers who had trained the soldiers.

Command and control thus far had been a mixed bag. Viewed solely as an information flow and coordination procedure (tactics aside and doctrinal issues in abeyance), things were fair at best. The passing of battle orders from TOC and colonel to foxhole and tank makes up troop-leading procedures. There are eight doctrinal steps, and the 34th applied them with unequal emphasis.

The first procedure was to receive the mission. Brigade had usually issued its plans as early as possible, and the Dragon S-3 and commander were careful to generate orders quickly, habitually using one-third or less of the time available between mission receipt and mission execution. (This notion of using one-third of available time at your level and giving two-thirds to subordinates is called, not surprisingly, the one-third–two-thirds rule.) The second procedure was to issue a warning order, which was routinely done as early as possible. Among the subordinate commands and platoons, Bravo and scouts followed the one-third–two-thirds rule and issued warning orders swiftly. Alpha sometimes did and sometimes did not do so. The tank company was even less consistent, with the initial warning order often sufficing for the entire operations order. Engineers and antitank were hindered by internal disorganization. Significantly, orders to TF 2-34 logistics personnel were never given in either combat or field trains, though the companies usually briefed their own supply and maintenance troops.

The formulation of a tentative plan was the next troop-leading procedure, and the 34th's colonel and TOC crew did this quite well. The problem here was that initial impressions and good map reconnaissance were not modified by experience, patrolling results, or personal terrain study. The tentative plan quickly became the "final" plan as the dictates of time (remember, one-third–two-thirds) pressed down in the TOC. In the companies the quick formulation of a tentative plan was also typical, with Bravo issuing it as a complete order, usually immediately upon return from battalion headquarters. Alpha did not issue a tentative plan but gave formal orders to all later. Charlie Tank issued the tentative plan late and labeled it the operations order. Bravo's shortcut was proved successful in the first four engagements, though like battalion, it did not allow for patrolling results or personal recons. Unlike battalion, Company B's captain was not adverse to modifying his orders as the situation changed (as he did throughout the 9 October defense).

Initiation of necessary movement came next, and there was not any trouble with moving out on time. March plans, however, were weak throughout the task force, with all companies and platoons subject to scatter and straggle in supposedly simple point-to-point road moves. The task force concentrated on combat plans, and, thus, such "housekeeping" tasks as moving from here to there were designed as slapdash afterthoughts. Bravo and part of CSC had provided the most glaring example of this failing on the night of 6 October.

Reconnoitering, preferably personal, was not very good. Orders were not issued in daylight on commanding terrain (though part of this was due to the time missions arrived at the TOC), and personal reconnaissance was rare. One case where personal recon was tried and helped was in Bravo's 9 October deployment in the defense. A case where it was not tried, with ill effects, was on Team Tank's 10 October counterattack into the teeth of an OPFOR ambush.

Completion of the plan and issuance of the order were the next two measures. Considering that the battalion plan was all too often a well-written, graphically correct portrayal of the colonel's and S-3's initial musings, the operations staff could be proud that it regularly got the word out in suitable format. Though the ground maneuver plan was generally logical (though not always tactically or doctrinally sound), the TOC officers and NCOs often forgot to get input from the various attachments or the CSS people (S-1/S-4/motor officer). On 9 October this came out in the form of a beautiful plan to defend the Central Corridor predicated on barrier material that would not arrive and engineer priorities seemingly set at random. The plans, though adequate, were not quickly modified in response to dangerous battlefield developments. The tendency to stick with the plan was marked at battalion level.

Of the subordinate elements, Bravo Company issued complete, five-paragraph format operations orders with map symbology for all four missions. Alpha did so for the first mission and issued fragmentary orders for the other three missions. Charlie Tank did not use either the OPORD or FRAGORD framework, issuing instead general guidance and some map markings in lieu of an order and justifying it on the basis that "tankers move too fast to give operations orders."[3] Interestingly enough, the effectiveness of the three companies directly related to how much information was going downward to the soldiers. The more the men knew, the better their innate imagination and drive assisted the overall mission.

The final troop-leading procedure, and the one most often overcome by events, was the supervision of preparations. Supervision was lacking at all levels and in all units, leaving the troops and junior leaders to do what they thought (or knew) to be best. A well-trained unit (such as the scouts), took up the slack. A poorly organized unit (such as the DS Engineer Platoon) just sat in place and marked time. One should not get the impression that the Dragons' officers and sergeants were relaxing instead of out "riding the circuit." Their supervision time was eaten away driving to and from orders; listening to plans; attending AARs; moving their units; picking up and dropping off attachments (who usually needed a commander to brief them on their new role, as XOs and first sergeants were usually busy in the CSS "war"); directing patrols; issuing company, platoon, or squad orders; eating; sleeping (on occasion, which was very necessary); checking maintenance; maintaining one's self and weaponry; and simply thinking about what to do next and how to do it. The battalion-level leaders had brigade to appease, written operations orders and maps to crank out (an impending OPORD would see the whole TOC, less the colonel and the guards but including the S-3 major, penning copy after copy of map overlay diagrams), and a seemingly endless series of bewildered attached units to orient and lead to the proper places. Still, it is critical to go up and look at the men and check them out. The colonel had not really done this. Bravo's captain had done it best on 9 October (and gotten a good payoff). Alpha's captain had checked things out on 8 October, and his unit had done well in the early going, though both the Alpha and Bravo captains did nothing to inspect precautions for the OPFOR counterattack on 8 October, with dire results. The tank company commander did not supervise at all in any of the first four missions, busying himself around his command track when lacking for more pressing duties. It is an old Army truism that the unit does well only those things that the commander checks. Leaders in the 34th were not checking much, leaving all the considered OPORDs to fate and the ingenuity of some tired privates. Even at Irwin the headquarters tracks were powerful magnets for tired, harried commanders.

Other than troop-leading procedures, the command and control system also had to do with the physical layout and functioning of the TOC and command group. The TOC was a beacon of steadiness in the NTC's shifting situations, and its changeless, regular setup (in accord with the colonel's express direction) proved itself quite efficient. The TOC had two weaknesses that it shared with much of the task force: it was poorly secured, and it was unable to move rapidly from place to place. As for the command group that rode with the commander and the operations officer, it was with the wrong unit when action developed three out of four times. On 7 October the command group followed Team A and got pinned down. On 8 October it stayed with the overwatch element and missed most of the battle. On 9 October the colonel was bypassed early on, with the main fight well off to the northeast. On 10 October the colonel was correct in his guessing and followed Team B up the middle on the main effort.

The alternate command post (CSC headquarters) had never been used, though admittedly it was tough to use it with its captain on emergency leave. The alternate CP would have been a great place to coordinate the polyglot of wandering engineers and ADA guns, but the gaunt CSC executive officer had his hands full just trying to inform, feed, and supply his farflung platoons. The attachments were out of control, as the TOC was unable to keep an eye on them. Like the average private rifleman, they were left to their own devices when time grew short.

Communications and electronics, the final part of the command and control system, were marginal in every way. The force used FM radio for everything, disdaining wire communications in assembly areas and the defense. Only Bravo used flags and hand and arm signals with regularity, as it had a company SOP for visual signals. Radio-listening silence was rare (since there was no wire to fall back on when the radios shut down and there was plenty of routine traffic).[4] Only the scouts, Bravo, and CSC headquarters stayed on the battalion command net throughout all four missions. Alpha came and went, and Charlie Tank was notorious for not monitoring the battalion radio network. Radio codes and brevity patterns were not used with consistency, with much information being passed clear text, even when well out of enemy contact. The company and platoon nets were much worse, often sounding like a party-line telephone conversation during the mock battles.

The 34th commander dictated immediate action in three command-and-control-system areas to his subordinates. He vowed better, more personal supervision efforts and strongly enjoined the same to all his officers, even to the detriment of some planning. The colonel directed that task force–level attachments be controlled by the HHC commander, pending the return of the CSC captain. So the headquarters commandant became the "attachment daddy." Finally, the colonel demanded that all his special platoons and companies stay on the battalion command radio frequency at all times. He could not correct the typical American radio sloppiness overnight, but he would not tolerate continued hibernation apart from his command net.

The second operating system, *maneuver*, related to the tactical employment of the 34th's men and machines in ground combat. This area was shaky, as evidenced by the four drubbings administered by the cocky OPFOR units. MILES was designed to fully train the activities in this area, emphasizing direct fire and movement in the face of the enemy. The 34th's experiences in the refereed road races that often permeated big field exercises did nothing to train the squads and platoons in the drills needed to move against a determined, firing enemy force.

The first element in the area of maneuver is to observe and understand the battlefield. Though everyone at battalion and below could understand general missions (attack, defend, move), the details on how one moves to contact or defend in a wide sector were quite hazy among men trained in the pine woods of Fort Stewart, Georgia. In other words, the Dragons knew what to do, but not precisely how to do it. Nothing could be assumed; orders had to spell out things. Everybody now had a good taste for the speed and nature of the OPFOR in attack or defense. As for terrain, the 34th could find good terrain to attack through or defend from, but too many decisions were based on map inspections, not ground inspections by patrols or leader reconnaissance. Bravo and the scouts had shown a fine mastery of terrain on 9 October's defense, with the scout tracks particularly well hidden in their observation posts.

The use of the various arms that made up the task force was uneven. The 34th did not fight as a combined-arms organization. Infantry in all the companies initially tended to run around in their aluminum APCs long after enemy antitank guns and missiles began to pick the 34th columns apart. The aggressive use of dismounted infantry, not "rat patrol" mounted tactics or Israeli-style tank sweeps, dominated this rocky desert. It was a great hidden lesson of NTC that the Soviets, stuck in their little BMPs and ordered to assault mounted, are terribly vulnerable to American foot soldiers. The first four engagements were learning experiences for the Alpha and Bravo infantrymen, with an edge to Bravo's ground troops because of better platoon leaders, better pre-Irwin training, and a positive experience against massed OPFOR units on 9 October.

The TOW crews' contributions had been disappointing, but a certain amount of their behavior could be dismissed as owing to the confusion in the Antitank Platoon, which resulted from the late draw at the Boeing yard and the platoon's disintegration of 7 October. The three missile crews attached to Bravo had done yeoman work against the MRR during the defend-in-sector mission, so there was a hint that things could be different for the TOWs.

As for the mighty M60 tanks, they had proven unequal to the pace of operations (there were many maintenance casualties) and were overpowered by the rills and gullies of The Washboard. The tankers could shoot and move as platoons and individual vehicles, but under the Charlie Tank headquarters, they generated not shock action but shocking ineffectiveness. The weakness of the tank company as a whole was a major crippling deficiency in the task force.

Concentration of combat power was planned for in only two of the four operations: the 7 October movement to contact spread the task force too thin; the 10 October counterattack had no real focus. Mutual support was ignored, with teams fighting independent actions until whittled down to nothing. The challenge of establishing effective overwatch[5] in the rolling Washboard was never solved, though both Alpha and Bravo had learned by 10 October that dismounted infantry were certainly a key. Actions on contact were too often reactions, as all three companies experienced the humiliation of being picked apart while trying to figure out what to do about it (Alpha on 7 October, Bravo on 8 October, Tank on 10 October).

As for using the defenders' advantage, the 34th had fought only one defense, and only Bravo Company had succeeded in welding ground and weapons to halt and destroy the enemy.

The main lessons in Bravo's case were careful examination of the ground and commander involvement in weapons placement (which rippled down to troop level, of course—that supervision element once again). The Dragons had made no use of obstacles at far ranges to support tank and TOW fires and to stall the enemy attacks. As for the abortive, long-delayed counterattack, it was merely another example of offensive shortcomings.[6]

NBC defense measures were not widely put to the test, though the whole task force suffered the burden of wearing the thick, velvety, charcoal-impregnated chemical suits throughout the force-on-force period. The combat trains suffered the ignominy of a persistent liquid chemical attack, and only one soldier had been able to mask in time to "survive." The colonel dismissed the torpid reaction of the trains sections as another case of noninfantrymen cracking under stress. But the other parts of the TF 2-34 would have done little better. This area was a troubled one throughout the battalion, though it had yet to be tested in earnest.

The colonel decided that decisive actions on contact and more widespread use of dismounted infantry in the attack were related subjects that could solve many problems in the maneuver area. The Washboard (and the OPFOR's use of it in defense) had to be cracked, and a solution was discussed on 11 October that would be trained then tested. The TOWs and infantry would have no choice but to take up the battle for the troubled tank company. TOW crewmen were ordered to confer with Bravo's TOW attachments to find out how to beat the OPFOR.

The third operating system was *fire support,* and it had not been very supportive to the task force. Stuck with a preplanned map overlay designed at Fort Stewart (and firing batteries that wanted to stick with it), the fire support officer and his artillery observers labored to please the Dragons (who needed a plan for each mission) and the gun batteries (who hoped for minimal changes). The compromises and late-delivered plans were not of much worth in the four missions.

Artillery fires were not timely, and coordination errors abounded. Duplicate target numbers, late overlays to companies (or more typically, no overlays), fires out of zone, fires atop friendly companies, and long delays in getting fire suppression were all evident. Without artillery the 34th was fighting with one hand behind its back, and the FSO had to correct this disconnection. The battery FDCs (Fire Detection Centers) would have to accept unique plans tailored to each operation, and the FSO would have to get completed target listings back to his company FISTs a lot faster.

Mortars at company level were providing most of the Company A and B fire support, filling in for the absent artillery. Real mortar rounds from 81-mm tubes would be too light to influence the battles, but at least the infantry companies had something. The tankers, hobbled enough already by their weak organization, had no mortars to rely on. The battalion mortars (107-mm) were being lost in the shuffle, through both lack of initiative and FSO neglect.

The colonel had some guidance here as well: the FSO was told that he would get fire plans back down to scouts, AT, and the companies, and there would be no excuses. Company commanders were admonished to help their FISTs plan fires and to insist that indirect fires were used; letting the FIST handle it was a no-go. Last, the Heavy Mortar Platoon leader was told to get vocal and to insure that the TOC and FSO used the big barrels. The artillerists in 1-35 Field Artillery, facing the live shooting on 13 and 14 October, were anxious to solve this knot of fire support problems.

As far as the essential *intelligence system*, the Dragons had gone about halfway toward knowing the land and their foes. It was not unusual for the 34th TOC or its companies (or both) to have gathered information (sometimes at cost) vital to an upcoming or ongoing engagement then flatly ignore the implications of the data. This problem related to the idea of sticking to the plan.

Intelligence collection was directed rather well by the eccentric S-2 and his more conventional BICC (Battlefield Intelligence Coordination Center). The two officers did a good job of figuring out just what the colonel needed to know and often picked out crucial terrain and enemy data requirements from the S-3's tentative planning guidance. The strict adherence to one-third–two-thirds in the TOC often forced the S-2 into the difficult position of bringing in intelligence that threatened a plan about to be disseminated. Like Cassandra, the S-2 was right, but his views went unheeded.

The actual collection was well executed but poorly supervised. The S-2 did not go forward on the first four missions to debrief patrols, relying instead on the company commanders to send in ''anything hot.'' The active captains, more concerned with their units than seemingly arcane requests from the TOC, rarely sent back anything from their patrols. The S-2 allowed it through his inaction.[7]

The scouts, if not being employed by the S-3 for a security role, were fine gatherers of reconnaissance data. In-action spot reports were as bad as the scouts were good; though as expected, Bravo was a bit on top of "down" in sending information to the TOC. The result was that the S-2's picture grew murkier, not clearer, as the battles progressed. Brigade S-2 and air recon were asked repeatedly for help, but the strictures of NTC limited the role of these valuable higher assets.

Intelligence was processed and evaluated quite well, although, as noted, the Dragons rarely reacted to the changing picture that flowed in through the S-2. The intelligence officer and his assistants had humble status in the peacetime garrison environment (the fact that he was usually a military intelligence branch officer, not infantry, rarely helped; the 34th had an infantryman S-2). At Stewart the S-2 worried himself with barracks key control and putting up Russian vehicle recognition posters, hardly real staff work by any S-1, -3, or -4's standards. In field training in Georgia, S-2 was the other, skimpier half of the TOC, and it was hard to start listening suddenly to guys who until a week ago were good only for the weather forecast. The Dragon S-2 was very much a prophet without honor in his own TOC.

The colonel elected to make one change in the intelligence area, but it was as important for its image as its substance. He required the S-2 to go forward to debrief patrols and to help with the collecting of prisoners of war, and even gave the S-2 himself a permanent spot in the battalion command APC. In this way the S-2 was guaranteed the colonel's ear outside the shadow of the benevolent but overworked S-3 major, and the intelligence officer was able to more actively supervise collection patrols.

The fifth operating system, *air defense,* had been heavily pressured just once so far, on 10 October while the Dragons waited to start the counterattack. The Redeye gunners were with the companies, as per doctrine. And the 34th soldiers shot at everything that flew over, as per the history of troops new to hostile air situations. Passive air defense was limited by the open terrain, though the battalion did little to use shadows or camouflage nets; Bravo Company had not even brought its nets to the field. The Vulcans attached for the 13 October operation would offer the colonel and his staff the first chance to supervise major antiaircraft assets. For now, this was not an issue.

The sixth system, *mobility/countermobility*, involved engineer activity in the reduction and construction of minefields and obstacles. Breaching was not yet tested, though the 34th could rest assured that its infantry companies (especially Bravo) were well schooled in punching through barriers, with or without engineers. On 11 October the Bravo commander gave an impromptu half-hour class to the assembled commanders and special platoon leaders to reinforce this skill. The colonel directed that breaching, likely to be needed on the 14 October move to contact, be refreshed on 11 and 12 October in the laager site training. Wirecutters, grappling hooks, ropes, and explosives were to be inventoried and readied for the upcoming missions.

Countermobility, as seen in 9 October's defense, was hurt by the logistics shortcomings of the battalion and the less-than-energetic engineers. Coordination was poor for the engineer barrier plan between the S-3, the companies, and the trains (for mines and barbed-wire supplies). Vital earth-moving blades spent much time waiting for fuel or digging positions far to the rear of the 34th sector. The engineer lieutenant seemed personally unwilling or unable to find missions for his men, and his troops were seldom worked up to their potential. The battalion commander hoped that his assignment of the HHC captain (and later, the CSC commander)[8] to supervise attachments (especially the important engineers) would give him some leverage over these specialists in construction and destruction.

The seventh system, and the most inadequate of the Dragons' task force, was *Combat Service Support*. The stability of the laager site and the competent demeanor of the battalion executive officer led the colonel to wash away once again the dull but insidious failings of his service support platoons. The battalion XO, a thoughtful major who did not need the colonel to tell him what was wrong, tried mightily to untangle the maintenance and supply mess.

The Dragons' combat trains were too large, time consuming to move, poorly secured, and uncontrolled by the Administration-Logistics Operations Center (ALOC). The ALOC was just a place to monitor radios. The S-1 and S-4 were not involved in operations orders at the TOC (with results such as the barrier-materials fiasco on 9 October). Additionally, the trains soldiers were not fully briefed on the tactical plan or any logistics plans. In effect, the logistics plan was always the same: get close to the front and wait for someone to call back or come back for help or supplies.

Vehicle recovery was ineffective. Further investigation of the infamous list of straggler vehicles (from the 9 October AAR) revealed that the battalion motor officer (BMO) and his aides knew where half of them were exactly but "had not gotten around to them yet." There was no urgency to fix forward; on the contrary, everything went to the combat trains for repair. Alpha and Charlie Tank had some operator maintenance troubles exacerbated by the old Boeing-yard equipment, and the Dragon maintenance effort plodded along in its "motor-pool" mentality. The average mechanic had no idea what was going on at the "front." Between the old equipment and the "fix-in-the-rear" concept, the BMO had to exert prodigious effort just to break even in the world of maintenance and recovery. There were better ways, but it was too far along to change over.

Supply was piecemeal, with fuel, food, and ammunition arriving at all sorts of times, but only if someone from the line unit went back to pick them up. The haphazard resupply efforts were not really coordinated, except by the companies. In fact, while the support platoon's fuel and ammunition trucks rolled all over the post like unguided missiles, the platoon leader was wrapped up in drawing, inventorying, and turning in three mountains of ammunition (one set of blanks for each FFT and combat rounds for the live fire) that removed him from the trains for many hours at a time. No logisticians jumped in to replace the absent support platoon leader in controlling the supply flow.[9]

The evacuation of simulated casualties was poor in all units, with particular problems on the night of 7 October in B and A companies. The adjutant and his S-1 section had trouble figuring out just who was in which company team, and the S-3 did not send task organization changes to the ALOC. As a consequence, loss reports were inaccurate. Coupled with the poor treatment of simulated casualties, the 34th was doing very little to keep up its soldier strength.

The major, like any battalion XO, knew that he was being judged in the Great Game based on the battalion's logistics and administration. The colonel insisted that barrier material be moved immediately when a defensive mission came up (as on 13 October), and the XO talked to his men about how to do this. It was hardly gratifying to see broken tanks, hungry soldiers, and confused support troops. The XO made his decision: he would personally supervise resupply and trains operations. And, with the S-3's hearty agreement, the adjutant and supply officers would have a role in every order formulated at the TOC. The mechanics and supplymen would have to work harder. There was no time to change the whole system.

So much for the Dragons and their internal troubles in each of the Seven Operating Systems. Yet there was another culprit in the difficulties: brigade. Far from helping, brigade headquarters had been neutral at best and inadvertently malicious at worst. The outright foulups (such as the misrouted stop order on 8 October and the later counterattack directive given in clear text on 10 October) were bad enough. What were more harmful were the failures to aid the 34th. Engineer, ADA, and GSR units were sent into unfamiliar wadis at night with map coordinates, rather than guided by men from brigade who knew the way. The natural outcomes were long-lost attachments and missing combat power. Brigade logistics staffers did nothing to help the 34th get the desperately needed barrier materials on the night of 8 October, though brigade controlled helicopters and ten-ton trucks aplenty right near the engineer supply yards. Finally, brigade seemed to have a hands-off attitude, typified by the comment that the NTC was, after all, a "battalion-level exercise." The battalion commander could not really buck his boss, particularly with the 34th's stock at rock bottom in the Great Game. But it was a gnawing annoyance all the same, outside the purview of the observer controllers and their dispassionate oversight.

The colonel's decisions and his commanders' thoughts were all discussed on the morning of 11 October at the TOC, which was erected in the center of the spread-out laager site. The colonel, refreshed by his night's sleep, tried to be optimistic and upbeat. He longed for a week back at Stewart, a week to systematically work through and correct the 34th's problems, but, of course, that would not occur. Instead, the Dragons had a day or so to shake off their fatigue, clean up and fix up, and learn a few tricks to beat the wadis and the impending obstacle belts of 14 October. The colonel was hardly happy with how things had gone. He blamed himself, and vowed against his own nature to get more personally involved and to be more visible.

The XO mused in the corner, trying to figure out a solution to the problem of pushing supplies forward through the inertia of the traditional Dragon logistics network. Next to him, the operations officer hung on the colonel's words, convinced that with some sleep his TOC troops would soon be churning out greater OPORDs than ever. The S-2 wondered how his new arrangement with the battalion commander would work out and hoped he could find a crucial snatch of data that would win an engagement.

The Alpha commander sat hunched, irritated at his mistakes and determined to do better, starting with some retraining of his riflemen that very afternoon. Bravo's captain had just finished explaining the intricacies of blowing through mines and barbed-wire aprons, and he sat uncomfortably, picking at his scabrous lips and chapped hands. The Charlie Tank Company commander stared out the side of the TOC, his grimy bandage askew on his head. His head ached, and he wondered why his company was having such a rough time. He was tired of being criticized in the AARs.

Out around the crowded TOC, with its engineer lieutenant and FISTs and CSC special platoon leaders and humming radios, the Dragon soldiery worked in the sunlight. Cleaning out .50-caliber barrels, singing along with smuggled transistors, or cranking open C-rations, the young men were rested, and happy for the break in the action. On them, as in a true war, would rest the burden of their commanders' choices. So while the leaders cogitated, the troops relaxed as best they could. There would be tough work for everyone soon enough.

Notes

1. Erwin Rommel, *Attacks* (Vienna, Va.: Athena Press, 1979), 8.

2. FORSCOM *Circular 350-83-10 Rotational Unit Training at the National Training Center* (Fort McPherson, Ga.: U.S. Armed Forces Command, 15 March 1983), 5. On the July 1982 terrain-exploration trip by 1st Brigade, 24th Infantry Division (Mechanized), all officers and NCOs were notified that the Live-Fire Training Area was off limits, though nobody was shooting there at the time.

3. This attitude that tank leaders need not give proper orders is a perversion of the sensible armor school belief that mobile forces do not have time for elaborate, set-piece plans. The Army fragmentary order (FRAGORD) offers a way to get the message out and still touch all the important bases.

4. *Take-Home Package, 2-34 Infantry*, III-E-1-3. "Numerous instances of transmission security violations were noted, especially in the area of clear-text messages which compromised the task force mission, locations, and unit strengths."

5. *Take-Home Package, 2-34 Infantry*, III-E-1-5. Overwatch in the task force was rated "initially poor."

6. *Take-Home Package, 2-34 Infantry*, III-E-1-7. "The TF counterattack was poor. Units were out of mutual support and failed to coordinate indirect fires, which caused the attack to stall after the task force advanced only a short distance."

7. *Take-Home Package, 2-34 Infantry*, III-E-1-11. The NTC controllers noted that "the task force's supervision and control of collection assets was accomplished in a sporadic manner."

8. The reason the HHC commander took over the engineers was twofold. First, it gave the colonel a reliable handle down in the construction platoon. Second, it spared the overworked CSC XO from one more duty, as the CSC commander was not yet back. The TOC grew less organized with the departure of the HHC commander, normally in charge of TOC security and displacement.

9. Interview with 1st Lt. Ralph G. Newton, 16 July 1983. First Lieutenant Newton's stories of tangling with the civilians at the Fort Irwin Ammunition Supply Point are classics of red tape and petty bureaucracy. *Take-Home Package, Task Force 2-34 Infantry*, III-L-20, notes that because of a signature-card error, certain mines were unavailable on 9 October 1982.

Note: Other sources for material in this chapter include: interviews; *Take-Home Package, Task Force 2-34 Infantry*.

Chapter Ten

Defend a Battle Position
(Day/Night)

"Less than a minute later, a single shell came whistling in over his head. Despite himself, he was startled by how quickly it was over him and how loud it sounded—like a freight train roaring through a narrow canyon. A moment later it exploded. A white puff rose out in the valley. Almost right on, he thought; a bit too high, though. Excited, sweating on his hill, he pressed the button again, with the guns working unseen miles behind him, doing whatever he asked. He felt somehow as if he were conjuring up the Devil."

Ronald J. Glasser, *365 Days*[1]

At 1900 on 11 October 1982, the company commanders, special platoon leaders, and attached outfit leaders were gathered in the bright enclosure of the Task Force 2-34 Tactical Operations Center. The officers and sergeants were clean, fed, and rested, regarding the silent observer controllers with the sullen gaze of grade school pupils looking at teachers early in September. The colonel came in and took his center seat in the rusty folding chair reserved for him. In front of them all, the map of Fort Irwin was plotted with the mission for 13 October: defend a battle position. The operations officer, after a nod from the battalion commander, began to speak.

The mission of defending a battle position (BP) is the middle ground between the fluid defense in sector and the absolute, rigid restriction of a strongpoint. The battle position could be used for platoons, companies, or even a whole battalion. The commander establishing a BP for his subordinate unit normally reserves the right to order a withdrawal from the site. The unit in the BP may maneuver freely inside the area assigned but cannot leave without its superior's permission. Battalion BPs are usually subdivided into company positions, and company battle positions are split down to platoon locations. Battle positions are improved as much as time and resources permit and are placed on advantageous terrain whenever possible. A battle position implies a relatively static defensive concept, with strict controls by the higher headquarters, though units would often prepare and reconnoiter several successive BPs. In the heyday of the 1976 *Operations Field Manual* and its active defense theories, unit planning maps often were spotted with battle positions as thick as pepperoni on a good pizza. Defenses seemed to consist of driving from position to position, piling out for a skirmish, then packing up and running to the next post. By 1982 a few BPs anchored on solid terrain were more the rule. Movement between the defensive localities was less capricious and better planned, and preparations were heavily emphasized.

The 34th warning order and tentative plan on 11 October focused on the retention of a key chokepoint at the east end of the Drinkwater Lake valley region. The floor of the basin narrowed at the lakebed, then ended abruptly a few kilometers eastward in the jumbled, basaltic rocks of the 1203/1134 hills and the 1172 massif. The chokepoint aspect came in because there were only two exits from this wide "box" canyon, both leading onto the gravel Silver Lake Road and heading southeast. (The Barstow Road, also a way out, was still playing the part of a canal and hence was not a factor in the live-fire training.) The northern exit went between hill 1134 (topped by the electronic paraphernalia that ran the target boxes) and Unnamed Ridge to the northwest. The southern exit, around hill 1049 and across benchmark 1047, was a bit more circuitous. Each outlet traced directly to benchmark 1086, the center of a narrow (less than 100 meters wide) rock gate formed by the hulks of 1161 to the north and 1283 to the south. An old cemetery was at roadside just west of the pass as a landmark. The NTC chief of the operations group, in the role of the brigade colonel, designated the horseshoe of hills west of Cemetery Pass as the battalion battle position for TF 2-34. When the OPFOR attacked (this time as unmanned target boards), they would be aiming to seize those hills and capture the pass to free them for a push south. The Dragons would be there to block the OPFOR.

It was a frighteningly realistic mission for more reasons than live bullets. If the Dragons ever deployed overseas with the Rapid Deployment Force into some high, craggy desert like Afghanistan, Pakistan, Iran, or Iraq, the soldiers might well face their first true Russian foemen in a similar stand at the base of a twisting canyon. Of course, the situation there would be tinged with an air of desperation and portent that Fort Irwin could never re-create. But the circumstances, if not the emotions, were faithfully duplicated, right down to the heavy odds against the 34th.

The Dragons went into this one with four big advantages. First, they had rested, refitted, and retrained (especially in infantry dismounted tactics), which put the battalion task force at full strength for its assigned objective. Second, there was enough planning and preparation time to design and build a cohesive defense through the considered application of weapons to ground. Third, the Dragons were defending on a good piece of dominant terrain. The OPFOR had nowhere to hide in the valley. This alone was a major difference from the dead space in the cuts and berms of the Central Corridor, which had required dense troop concentrations to hold small sectors. Fourth, and most important, the 34th had already experienced the desert, the tenacious OPFOR defense, the feeling of undergoing a big enemy assault, and the vigilant attention of the observer controllers. The NTC was still a formidable challenge, but no longer a great mystery.

The colonel and his S-3 planned this battle with assistance from the logisticians (S-4 and motor officer), the adjutant (S-1), the engineer, the ground radar leader, the Vulcan lieutenant, and all the subordinate maneuver units. The three teams were organized with two infantry and a tank platoon in each element, as infantry was the best arm to hold ground. The task force retained control of its Antitank Platoon, scouts, heavy mortars, Vulcans, and the engineer company (−). Ground surveillance radars and Chaparral air defense missile carriers were also under the TOC's supervision. The battalion was strongly organized, freshly resupplied with a multitude of capable munitions, and allotted plenty of precious time to work out its designs.

The 34th scheme was simple, devised to take maximum benefit from the time available and the excellent terrain in the battalion battle position. The hills that blocked egress from the valley formed a wide-mouthed U lying on its side, open end toward the west. Drinkwater Lake was in the south center, an oblong patch almost 3 kilometers long by 600 meters wide on an east-to-west axis. It was designated by the COG as heavily contaminated by persistent chemicals and untraversable by the OPFOR vehicles. The lieutenant colonel's plan placed Team B on the north leg of the U, Team Alpha on the curve along the western base of hill 1134, and Team C on the south arm of the

U. The Antitank Platoon was directed to set up just behind Alpha, allowing the TOWs to fire out to their full 3,000 meters of range down the canyon floor. The missile gunners would use crossfire techniques (gunners to the north shooting enemy tanks in the south, gunners to the south cutting across to hit OPFOR in the north) to cut down on difficult head-on shots. As for the scouts, they would deploy in a frontal screen about 4 kilometers west of the baked lake bottom, pulling back once they had identified the lead enemy units inbound. The heavy mortars, air defense, and radars would be set up to cover the whole battle position and the big engagement area to its front. The engineers, with the aid of the GS platoon (which had laid that helpful minefield in Bravo's sector on 9 October), and under the command of their own engineer company captain, would lace the basin with ditches, wire, and mines that locked into the 34th fire plans. Artillery and Air Force jets would be on call, with preplanned targets ranging from far up the valley to directly in front of the Dragons' emplacements.

Time, as always, was the crucial resource, but for this task the Dragons would make good use of it. The issuance of the warning order and tentative scheme of maneuver of 11 October prescribed a leader's reconnaissance/quartering party that would depart the laager location for the BP at 0800 on 12 October. Brigade restricted the size of this party (after all, the Drinkwater Lake region was stated to be under enemy surveillance) and denied the 34th permission to move up any main-body units until after nightfall. It would seem that this alone would put the battalion back in the familiar old time crunch, with only a dark desert night to ready itself for the battle expected after sunrise on 13 October. But the battalion commander was shrewd in his thinking and solved this puzzle rather neatly.

The reconnaissance element that left at 0800 would consist of the company commanders and their platoon leaders, the special and attached platoon leaders, the S-3 and his key players with one TOC vehicle and materials to produce a final order up at the BP, the fire support officer and all company FIST lieutenants, the S-2 with parts of his bag of tricks, and even the previously ignored S-1 and S-4. Everyone would go in APCs, with a single scout track for security. The battle position would be reconned tactically, as if the enemy were really watching.[2] Company and platoon positions would be evaluated, finalized, and marked with captains and platoon leaders together picking

out the positions of tanks, TOWs, and obstacles. The platoon
leaders would go on to set up their platoon areas (machine guns
and Dragons), spotting each track position in the process, to
include alternate sites. Luminous symbols would be used, so
that when the troops arrived that night under the XOs and
platoon sergeants, they could be picked up by their leaders
(doubling as quartering parties), guided to the laid-out positions, and set directly to work digging in and building barriers.

The colonel would go through the proposed company emplacements with the company commanders, correcting as
needed to meet overall TF 2-34 needs. The battalion commander
set 1500 on the 12th as the time for the final OPORD, confirmed
by the on-the-ground inspection of the terrain. The colonel fully
intended that the scouts, heavy mortars, artillery observers, and
especially the engineers be as ready to start work as the tankers,
TOWs, and infantry once the main body rolled in. The 1500
order would tie it all together, integrate the plan with all the key
leaders, and still allow some daylight to correct any errors. All
that would remain was the actual execution.

The colonel's major concern was the timely arrival of three
particular assets. First, he needed the scouts early on so that the
limited security of the recon party could be augmented to the
front. Second, he needed the fullest possible allocation of
barbed wire, mines, steel plates (foxhole overhead covers),
timbers, and sandbags, and he needed them forward before the
mass of the battalion. Third, and related to the barriers, he
ordered the engineers to lead the march up to the BP, so that
they could rush forward to the previously surveyed obstacle
sites. The battalion commander and S-3 were relieved when the
NTC chief of the operations group, fascinated by the alacrity of
the battalion's efforts, allowed the engineer platoon leader to
bring forward one squad as early as 1500 on the 12th.

The battalion commander's upbeat mood and professionalism were infectious in the TOC the night of the 11th. The
Dragons had placed a few mines, sandbags, timbers, some
wire, and steel plates on every vehicle so that each squad
would have its own supply as soon as it stopped.[3] The second
in command in each unit would break out the live bullets while
the leaders crept about placing the weapon stakes and checking
ranges up to the north. Then at 1900 the Dragons would drive
up the gravel tank trail to meet their leaders and begin building
on the blueprint so painstakingly created. The prevailing atmosphere breathed purpose and conviction, and as the leaders

TASK ORGANIZATION: TF 2-34 INFANTRY
13 OCTOBER 1982

Team A

Company A (–)
3d Platoon, Company C (tanks)
2 AT sections

Team B

Company B (–)
1st Platoon, Company C (tanks)
1 AT section (+ squad)

Team C

Company C (–)
3d Platoon, Company B
3d Platoon, Company A

TF Control

Scouts
AT Platoon (–)
Heavy Mortars
DS Engineer Platoon
GS Engineer Platoon
GSR teams (4), B Company, 124th MI.
Vulcan Platoon, A Battery, 5-52 ADA Battalion
Chaparral Platoon, A Battery, 5-52 ADA Battalion

OPPOSING FORCES (OPFOR) MOTORIZED RIFLE
REGIMENT (–)

2 Motorized Rifle Battalions (MRB) (31 BMP infantry vehicles each, 62
total)

1 Tank Company (13 T-72 tanks)

returned to their units to enjoy the last night of undisturbed
sleep for a while, it looked, sounded, and felt as if the Dragons
might have gained back a measure of confidence.

The leaders' reconnaissance pulled into the hollow just west
of Cemetery Pass, spreading out the vehicles and dismounting

cautiously, on guard, in accord with the colonel's forceful guidance that this was to be no terrain walk. The forbidding figure of the COG waited there to greet the soldiers. The battalion colonel set the example as he followed the flinty "brigade commander" to the summit of hill 1134, crawling on chest and stomach over the hot rocks and creosote vegetation behind the hulking, slithering full colonel, who played his role to the hilt. It took only a few minutes to examine the lay of the ground with the COG, squinting through binoculars; the battalion commander was amazed to see that, indeed, this box canyon resembled the map and conformed to the stories told by 5-32 Armor and 3-19 Infantry.

It did not take the sweating lieutenant colonel long to clamber back down the hill and motion his commanders and special platoon leaders to him behind his M113A2. Watchful platoon lieutenants and NCO platoon leaders from the companies remained on security, fulfilling the duties of riflemen with the easy attitude of experience. The battalion commander was not long in his commentary. Everyone knew what to do.

The only man he asked to remain with him for a few minutes was the Charlie Tank commander. It was not the captain anymore, but the tall, calm executive officer. The tank first lieutenant was the acting commander, his sorely disappointed commander having been ordered to the brigade trains field dispensary for rest and recuperation from the throbbing head wound sustained on 7 October. The tank XO was competent, having been coached well by the previous Charlie Tank captain, a tremendous trainer. The colonel wondered if the temporary change of command would improve the tank unit's performance, but the battalion commander was certain that the armor captain needed some peace and quiet to restore himself.

Fanning out across their hills, the captains, lieutenants, and sergeants methodically arrayed their fighting positions, walking off final machine-gun protective lines and using the little laser range finders of the FIST lieutenants to check distances. A fixed defense (and even the most mobile defense has some elements holding while others move) is rather simple to create, given some open ground and a good spot to situate it (a slope will do, and usually does). In many ways siting weapons to ground is an exercise in geometry, in which straight lines of fire must be placed to fire down the long axes of likely enemy assault lines as the foes debouch out of approach avenues.

Recalling that all military forces move in column and fight on line, it is a matter of knowing where the enemy is likely to come on line to know where the defense must concentrate its fires to break the attack. TF 2-34 was blessed with an enemy who liked to play by the numbers (even when not represented by wooden target silhouettes). The OPFOR, copying the Soviets, switch from regimental column to a line of battalion columns at eight to twelve kilometers. The battalions swing into a line of company columns four to six kilometers out. The MRCs move to platoon columns on line around 3,000 meters. The BMPs and tanks move to an assault line at about 1,000 meters.[4] Conveniently, the TOW could fire out to break up the shift to platoon columns, and the less effective Dragon AT missile could pick apart the spreading assault line as it formed. Since the 34th's enemy would move mounted to within a kilometer, the defenders would need to fight three battles: the long-range battle against the enemy vehicle columns in the battalion security area (3,000 meters out to the limit of scout artillery observation), the midrange battle against the mix of enemy lines and columns of tanks and BMPs between one and three kilometers, and the close-in fight against the opposing infantrymen and their combat vehicles in close support. Each of these engagements was important in the overall task of defeating the enemy attack.

The long-range struggle in the battalion security area was the province of the scouts. In a large-scale war the Scout Platoon would tie in to the back end of the Division Covering Force Area, though this was not the case at NTC (and may not be, because of force shortages, the case in combat). Though capable of direct-fire self-defense, the scouts would try to use artillery fires, heavy mortars, airstrikes (if available), engineer barriers, and some terrain depth to slow the enemy, working the security area until the battalion commander was convinced the enemy had committed his major elements. West of dry Drinkwater Lake, the 34th scouts would establish a thin crust of observation posts. As for obstacle work, some was planned, but it was third in priority after the engineer efforts in the middle and close areas. The main job of the Scout Platoon was to identify the enemy attack as far as strength, direction, and composition and, secondarily, to slow it and pick it apart with indirect fires.

With the Battalion Security Area providing early warning, the tank and TOW gunners would fight the middle-range battle.

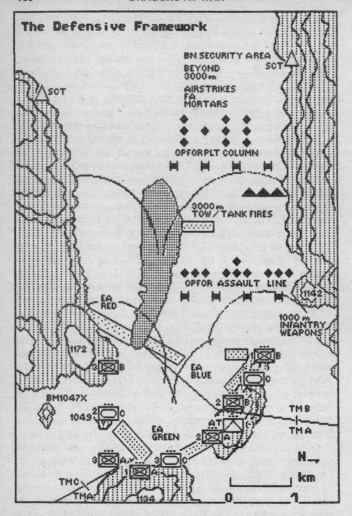

The Defensive Framework

BN SECURITY AREA
SCT
BEYOND
3000 m

AIRSTRIKES
FA
MORTARS

OPFOR PLT COLUMN

3000 m
TOW / TANK FIRES

OPFOR ASSAULT LINE

1142

1000 m
INFANTRY
WEAPONS

EA
RED

1172

EA
BLUE

B

C

BM1047X

1049

C

EA
GREEN

B

AT

TM B

TM A

A

N

A

C

km

TMC

TMA

1134

0   1

This engagement would be fought around the Drinkwater scrabble bed, and to control it, the colonel split the area into three engagement areas (EAs), coded by color. North of the lake bed was EA Blue, extending to the border of Alpha and Bravo. South of the Drinkwater Lake was EA Red. East of the hardpan was EA Green, in the bowl of the big horseshoe. The main killing was to be done in EAs Blue and Red, with TOWs firing out to 3,000 meters and tanks from 2,000 meters in. To insure flank shots and the advantageous effects of an interlocking lattice of high-velocity tank shots and low-velocity, powerful missile warheads, battalion orders gave the AT Platoon EA Blue, Bravo's tanks and TOWs EA Red, Team C's tanks EA Blue, and Team A TOWs EA Red. The enemy's destruction in these EAs would be aided by the construction of a series of AT minefields and ditches north and south of the lake bottom to slow the OPFOR momentum and to trap the enemy in the open. These barriers had top priority. Artillery and mortar targets were plotted in each EA to further disrupt the enemy. The 34th commander hoped to break the OPFOR here, as they struggled to shift to company lines of platoon columns, with the Dragons' missiles beating on their vehicle flanks and the big 105-mm guns of the M60 tanks raking the stalled BMPs and tanks.

The close-in battle would, it was hoped, be limited to the elimination of OPFOR stragglers, but the colonel could take no chances. To lose the infantry fight at less than 1,000 meters was to lose the battle position; it could not be held if the enemy could close in force and wrest the hills from the grasp of the 34th. Here the colonel had stacked the deck by assigning two platoons of infantry to each team. The fighting here would be won by machine guns, grenade launchers, Viper antiarmor rockets, and rifles. The infantry would have tanks and TOWs to help them with the antivehicle duels, but it was quite possible that the close- and middle-range clashes would be in progress simultaneously. The Dragon missiles and Vipers were each given EAs to shoot into, with Bravo handling EA Blue, Alpha EA Green, and Charlie EA Green as well. EA Green had to be controlled by fire to keep the hills and protect Cemetery Pass, so two of three teams would "do or die" there. Artillery and mortars would be lashed together with the interlaced machine guns to create final protective fires (FPF), indirect fire reinforcement for the chattering MG final protective lines. The machine guns would be placed low on the hills, on the corners of platoon positions, cracking across the platoon fronts to rip along the long axis of enemy infantry assault lines from both sides. Finally, the colonel stressed that infantrymen would build the obstacles in the close-in engagement areas,[5] helped if possible by the engineers, though it was but second priority to them.

So the Dragons' leaders went about their business systematically, surveying firing lanes and tank positions like consulting engineers involved in a new water project, yet all the time mindful to stay in the shadows and off the ridgetops. It gave a powerful feeling that all was for real and that this time all would work out well. The OPORD confirmed the solid preparations, and as the S-1 and S-4 returned down Silver Lake Road to brief the trains soldiers and the engineer squad rolled through Cemetery Pass right on time, the colonel thought that the remaining phases were bound to be eased by the fine groundwork laid so far. Radio reports indicated that all was going well back at the laager. The colonel and S-3 shared some C-rations and settled down to await the battalion. The Dragons were expected about 2030 at the latest.

Something was wrong on the road march; the forward TOC knew that much by 1900 when word filtered in that the tanks were still loading ammunition. The company commanders and platoon leaders were up at the march-release point in the gloom, gathered around crackling radios, listening as the XOs tried to implement the task organization as tanks rolled one by one into the column. The engineers were already under way, crunching slowly along, well under the proposed march speed. The fine white dust was as thick as a fog, and a passing convoy of artillery ammunition trucks raised even more of the choking clouds. There was discussion about an injury in the AT Platoon, but it died down as the last of the tanks fell in. By 1910 Bravo was on the road, the XO leading, with the mortar section right behind him, followed by the rest of the company. The other units were forming right behind, and the battalion XO speculated that perhaps the ammo foulups might delay the column only about fifteen minutes. The colonel asked about the trucks of barrier materials and was reassured to hear that the two ten-ton tractor trailers were moving with the engineers without problems.

The white dust and black night shrouded Bravo, and the drivers needed no urging to keep their speed slow. The company XO was carefully scanning for the left turn that would be Silver Lake Road, no easy task in the spiderweb of tread and tire ruts leading off the trail as the moving vehicles approached the turnoff. He halted Team Bravo to dismount, surprised to hear the whistling bursts of nearby artillery simulators to the near north. Probably some firing battery under observer

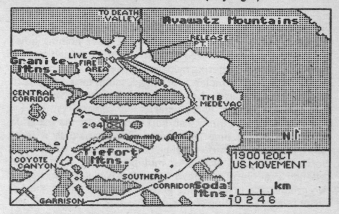

controller–delivered "counterbattery," thought the first lieutenant. He was aligning his compass with the turn for verification when he heard two more whistle/cracks of simulators and whiffed the telltale odor of CS irritant gas in the still air.

The clanging of hatches and the throaty roar of diesels sounded behind him, and in the settling dust he saw the second mortar track, hatches buttoned in the face of the "incoming," swing sharply off the trail to the right. Then, to his horror, the Bravo XO saw the M125A1 tilt and drop out of sight, followed with sickening speed by the attached medical M113A1 that took the same ill-fated path. Thunderous crashes of metal on basalt rock, shouts and curses, engines still rumbling, soldiers running up from the rest of the column: the XO heard it all as he ran to the lip of the previously unseen cliff. Almost twenty feet down he saw the two APCs, both on their sides, engines whining, without any sign of life.[6]

The radios up at the BP came to life with the grim news, and the Bravo captain was shocked to hear the initial casualty assessment: unconsciousness, broken knees and arms, skull fractures, and multiple lacerations. The Bravo XO wasted no time in calling for a medical-evacuation helicopter, and for a half hour, the battalion XO, the battalion commander, and both parts of the TOC fought to gather information, guide in the helicopters, and get the injured men out. Bravo's unruffled first sergeant arrived to take charge as the first helicopter landed in a blaze of floodlights. Bravo's mortar section was left to help, and an M88 recovery vehicle was detached from the trains to aid in the eventual recovery of the stricken tracks. The battalion executive officer ordered the Bravo first lieutenant back on the road (standing there worrying would solve nothing now) and energized the paralyzed battalion column, which pushed slowly around the fluttering medevac helicopters. The road was choked with OC vehicles and brigade staff men coming to help, so it was no easy job to get around the mess. Five soldiers seemed to be injured, two severely.

The accident did more than hurt men; it cost the battalion hours of valuable time. The convoy decelerated to a mere crawl, drivers skittish after seeing the accident site. Rather than closing by 2030, it was after midnight before most of the battalion came in. The Bravo Company vehicles came up in two groups, the tanks having gotten separated during the accident and the following confusion. The captain of Team B was gravely concerned, but it was better to work than to worry. So like the rest of the task force, the Bravo soldiers were taken to their assigned sites and spent the rest of the warm, black night chipping into the rocky hillsides, stringing barbed wire, and laying mines. Time had been lost, and worse, troops had been hurt. Nobody could rectify either situation.

The sunrise on 13 October revealed a network of stout barricades out on the open basin floor, installed in darkness by the engineers and infantry of TF 2-34. The enemy did not come at dawn, though the scouts were waiting, so the rest of the 34th kept right on digging fighting positions and planting mines, an insidious form of victory gardening that can win wars.

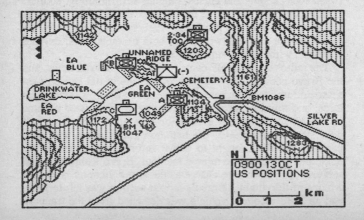

The battalion communications platoon had outdone itself, spinning out miles of tough WD1-TT communications wire to every company command post, linking the subordinate units to the TOC. The AT crews had walked out to the obstacles that served as the target reference points, checking distances and marking their range cards accordingly, accountants of destruction lining out their ledgers. Camouflaged positions were chopped out of the slopes around the big U, though overhead cover was lacking on all but a few machine-gun bunkers thus far. Breakfast C-rations were scooped between shoveling and mining.

In Bravo Company the missing mortar section and the previous night's injuries had not hurt the unit's desire to succeed. And 1st Platoon was so far along that it detached a squad (at task force TOC's request) to go forward to help the engineers build a minefield in EA Blue. Working without the 81-mm mortars left a gap in the tactical plan, but at least word had come in from the post hospital that the injuries reported had been greatly exaggerated. In fact, all but one of the soldiers would be back for duty later that day.[7] The Bravo captain spread the welcome word as the sun climbed in the sky and he traversed the fighting positions once again, checking and talking.

The colonel was quite happy that the battalion had lost only time in the frightening wreck. The motor officer had called to say that the APCs involved in the accident would be back in action by noon and would follow the Bravo first sergeant and the rest of the mortar section up to the battle position. The TOC had reports that every element was on the radio and land-line networks, and the battalion commander waited for word from the scouts.

The use of actual artillery was tricky with the scouts out front, though the 34th had a decent, well-disseminated fire plan for the first time in its NTC battles. The scouts would call in the first missions, then as they pulled back, they would cover their backsides with shellfire. Besides the scouts, the 34th had the engineers still toiling on their barriers, ready to close holes once the scout sections withdrew through. The NTC had no formal range regulation by regular Army standards, but there was no indirect fire permitted within one kilometer of friendly units, and there were other restrictions on the shells and fuses available to the gunners (airbursting VT fuses were out for sure).[8] The scouts and engineers would have to be back in and accounted for before the heavy artillery barrages and direct fires could engage the enemy with impunity.

It was about 0930 when the scouts first spotted the consecutive erection of rows of target boards, presumably the enemy recon. Dragon soldiers looked up as the big 155-mm shells sighed overhead, popping far out to the west in dirty little mushroom clouds with delayed, muttering explosions. The scouts knew instantly it was the real thing. (After all, how clever can wooden targets be?) The TOC sent out the word to stand to, and those engineers and infantrymen not engaged in holding open gaps for the returning scout APCs pulled back to their fighting positions. Soldiers in emplacements and tanks readied their ammunition and peered through their sights, waiting for targets.

There was a momentary scare when the Bravo squad track helping the engineers in EA Blue died in place, its engine fatally damaged, oil spewing everywhere. Team B's 1st Platoon rushed another track out to pull its broken stablemate back in, just ahead of the scouts.

The enemy array was visible to all now, and the word that scouts were in (and the gaps closed behind them) accompanied the command to fire when the enemy came into range. There were a lot of black dots out there, "rolling" relentlessly as target belts rose and fell in succession. Where was the artillery, the long-range disrupter? Delayed, late, came the answer. There was some sort of problem with the Fire Direction Centers at the batteries verifying that they were not shooting friendlies. It hardly mattered by now; the target lines were almost in direct-fire range. As almost an insult, huge blossoms of artillery fire opened far behind the advancing OPFOR, and the big guns kept firing aimlessly behind the moving target array for some time.

The OCs opened up with their little airburst simulators, and across the task force soldiers in open foxholes and open vehicles ignored the loud thuds. Most of the M113s and tanks slammed their hatches, but rear ramps were down on tracks in all companies (though the soldiers, less drivers and machine gunners, were outside in their own holes). In Team Alpha, .50-caliber gunners tore at camouflage nets that blocked their weapons traverse. Both A and B teams should have ground-mounted some of the big M2HB machine guns from the APCs, but Bravo had left its tripods at Stewart and Alpha had simply chosen not to do so. So tracks had to creep up to shoot when the time came.

The wooden enemy was "'firing'" back as he came up to the lake bed. The TOWs fired their MILES systems as the OPFOR silhouettes hung up on the outermost obstacles, stopping a few that smoked a black, oily pillar as they sat in place, leaving a hole in the next line to spring up to mark their destruction. The tankers were just opening fire when the desultory OC-inspired barrage of enemy "artillery" turned heavy and, without warning, began to include CS irritant gas in great, choking clouds that hung around the positions. The Dragons, already laboring in their tanks, ITVs, and foxholes, added stifling protective masks to their sweat-soaked chemical suits. The Bravo commander choked and gagged in his CP track. Unable to hear or talk effectively on the bulky field phones, the colonel told his commanders to shift to radio. The enemy moved on, holes in his ranks, pausing momentarily at the obstacles to simulate breaching attempts.

The tanks were doing most of the damage in EAS Red and Blue, with TOWs helping out. Every time the OPFOR array halted at the barricades, black target BMPs and tanks halted and smoked, and the half-suffocated antitank gunners and tank crews squinted through the smoke, mistakenly rekilling more than one dead vehicle. Careful plans about shooting into this or that Engagement Area swiftly degenerated as the targets filled the three EAs and smoke and CS drifted everywhere. The infantry weapons stuck to their assigned sectors (they had insufficient range to do otherwise), but the TOWs and tank guns fired all over the place, piling shot after shot into the fleeing targets. The enemy appeared to turn into each company position, "dismount" man-size silhouettes, and struggle slowly through the protective minefields and murderous trajectories of M60 squad machine guns. The human-form silhouettes were swiftly dispatched. Then all targets went down, a few more artillery shells dropped west of Drinkwater, and the call came: "Cease fire!"

Had they won or lost? The Bravo commander could not believe that the strings of static silhouette targets were all there was to this allegedly mighty OPFOR live-fire array. After seeing the NTC's OPFOR regiment, the target rows were less than impressive, despite a superb pyrotechnic display from both firing targets and dead targets. The CS had been a nasty surprise, the first intentional use of gas other than that one strike of the combat trains.

For the TOC, it had been a deadly surprise, with confusion at the height of the OPFOR assault, multiplied by misplaced protective masks (TOC soldiers inside seldom wore full uniform) and missing chemical-detection kits (so nobody knew when the gas had dissipated enough to unmask). This incident also had something to do with the switch from wire to FM radio, as the colonel was forward on hill 1134 and could not raise the choking TOC troops on the wireline, so he immediately turned to (and stuck with) the radio. The TOC had been ineffective during the last half of the enemy attack.

It was hard to tell if the 34th had done well or not in all the smoke and confusion, though the AAR at 1300 cleared it up and cheered up everyone. Yes, the Dragons were taken to task for fouling up and shooting in the wrong EAs as the battle

GUNNERY: DAY DEFENSE, 13 OCT 82

U.S. Weapon	Rounds Fired	Hits	Vehicle Kills
Tank cannon	264	61	22
TOW/Dragon/Viper	Unknown	24	14
Accumulative	264 plus	85	36
Army Average	682	62	26

Sources: Brig. Gen. E. S. Leland, Jr., "NTC Training Observations" (Fort McPherson, Ga.: U.S. Army Forces Command, 18 November 1982), 1; *Take-Home Package, 2-34 Infantry*, III-C-1-1.

TIMELINE: DEFEND A BATTLE POSITION
13 OCTOBER 1982

11 OCT 82-1900:	Warning order
12 OCT 82-0800:	Leader recons/Quartering party sets up
12 OCT 82-1500:	Battalion OPORD
12 OCT 82-1630:	Final company OPORD issued (B Company typical)
12 OCT 82-1900:	Movement of TF begins
12 OCT 82-1930:	Major vehicular accident blocks column
13 OCT 82-0100:	Final elements of TF 2-34 infantry close on positions
13 OCT 82-0930:	Scouts engage lead enemy elements
13 OCT 82-1015:	Enemy MRR withdraws
13 OCT 82-1045:	Company After Action Reviews
13 OCT 82-1300:	TF After Action Review

closed. The artillery battalion commander, resentful that coordination measures to avoid shooting friendlies had slowed his response rate to a snail's pace, engaged in a brief (and unsuccessful) verbal tirade against the chief battalion controller. The senior OC seemed to think that the battalion commander should have left two tank platoons with Team Charlie Tank and made Bravo infantry pure, but that did not account for the inexperience of Team C's commander (who had done a respectable job, staying on the radio and closely controlling his company team). The road-march delays were discussed in scathing detail, with the battalion XO taken to heel for not pushing on sooner and faster after the accident. The TOC's embarrassing reaction under chemical attack was brought out. The OCs correctly criticized the 34th's maneuver units because the tanks did not displace after they fired a few rounds. Finally, the engineers took a lot of flak for building weak obstacles; and, of course, the slow pace and confusion of the road march had retarded the arrival of the trailers of barrier materials, which had not helped.

But the good news was very good. The TOWs had awakened from their long slumber and contributed almost a third of the TF 2-34 kills. The task force had made good use of time, and despite some mistakes in execution, the sound planning and good preparation had paid off. Whereas the average unit at NTC gets sixty-two hits and twenty-six kills against the OPFOR array of seventy-five vehicles, the men of TF 2-34 had hit eighty-five times, killing thirty-six of the enemy vehicles. As of 13 October 1982, that was the best shooting of any infantry task force.

Unfortunately, the excitement over the accurate firing was damped by the assistant division commander for training, who spoke up near the end of the AAR to berate the Dragon leaders for not using proper fire-control techniques. The dour full colonel turned off most of the Dragons by starting his comments with "Hey, girls." The battalion commander was rightly incensed to be publicly insulted (along with his officers), but he saw a Great Game implication here and did not retort. The ADC-T was a powerful man, outranking all in the 24th Infantry Division (Mechanized) but the other ADC and the division commander, so his critical remarks were suffered in silence. The lieutenant colonel resolved to do something to win over this influential character to preclude any similar outbursts.

* * *

There was another, literally darker, side to the defense of the battle position, as the AAR ended with congratulations from the brigade commander and word of a nighttime attack to repulse. Everybody knew it was coming, and some preparations were taken before the AAR, but position improvement came to a near halt as the leaders left for their meeting. Units refueled and fed and swapped ammunition around among the squads and tanks to even up the stockage that would have to last through the 14th. Bravo's mortars and medic track returned with their soldiers, though one aidman hurt in the crackup remained hospitalized for observation. Soldiers relaxed too much, confident that they had won in the morning and could win again that night (rumors of the gunnery record moved through the ranks with lightning speed). It was almost 1700 and nightfall when the company commanders returned to their men, having attended a fragmentary order covering a more pressing problem: another night road march, this one to get in position for the movement to contact on the 14th. The night defense was dismissed under the old "improve your positions" line. The TF 2-34 fire support officer was queried about illumination and promised that the artillery would not fail that night.

The engineer platoons had cleaned equipment and eaten during the AAR, and only some lackadaisical attempts were made to strengthen the obstacles or to build the next set. One squad, far out front stringing wire, was told to return at nightfall but was not in radio contact. The air defense and ground radar units spent most of the late afternoon trying to get fuel and food, the Vulcans having been used as ground weapons to cut down the infantry silhouettes in EA Green that morning. Around the TOC everyone was working on the order for the big movement to contact the next morning. The night defense was allowed to take care of itself.

As usual, it did not. There are definite steps to convert a day defense to a night defense. Weapons are repositioned closer to their target areas. Night-vision devices are checked out and distributed. Movement, noise, and light are restricted. Security elements are closer to the main force. Finally, illumination is adjusted at last light so that parachute flares can be used to light the engagement area if necessary.

All of those actions are in addition to normal defensive improvements. Most of the 34th fighting positions lacked overhead cover (though materials were available). No attempt was made to fix this serious deficiency; airbursting artillery could wreak havoc on open holes.[9] The scouts had come in to eat a hot meal, which was great for their morale, yet they left the entire task force front unsecured except for a few inattentive close-in company listening posts. The scouts ended up only about halfway out to their screen line by 1900, and that engineer squad was not accounted for as yet, but the inanimate enemy did not wait.

The colonel was alarmed to hear that the enemy was already moving against him, but he had no reason to fear any reverses. After all, hadn't the Dragons just set the infantry gunnery scoring mark for NTC? With a few artillery and mortar flares, they could repeat the performance, then move on to bigger things the next day. He did not realize where his scouts were and told the FSO to start opening illumination rounds out in front.

But there was a big problem. The controller with the scouts called the OC with the artillery batteries and told him not to allow live fires (illumination or high explosive) until the scouts, TOC, and artillery FDCs agreed on the scouts' exact location. The OCs knew, but they were not to help the gunners or the infantrymen sort this one out. The OPFOR targets started their inexorable advance.

Fifteen minutes went by as the FDC, TOC, and OCs argued about whether to fire the cannons. The silhouette files pushed forward, rising and falling until they were near the scouts' hasty, short-distance OPs. Hearing this, and realizing the artillery had failed again (though this time it was the fault of the scouts and engineers), the colonel called on the radio, not even bothering with the landline. The scouts were ordered in immediately, and in their rush back they came upon the engineer track and brought it in too.

The target array was up to the lake, in range, and all was dark. If the ITVs and M60 tanks had brought their thermal sights from Stewart, the battle could have been joined right then as the flat, black wooden targets entered engagement range. But MILES had no thermal capability and relied upon the flowering, bright yellow light provided by mortar and artillery illumination.

The colonel was in his forward command post when Bravo Company's mortars finally spat a few flares up into the night air, but the rounds were wild, unaimed. (Bravo's captain had

GUNNERY: NIGHT DEFENSE, 13 OCT 82

U.S. Weapon	Rounds Fired	Hits	Vehicle Kills
Tank cannon	64	0	0
TOW/Dragon/Viper	34	9	2
Accumulative	98	9	2
Army Average	199	27	19

Sources: Brig. Gen. E. S. Leland, Jr., "NTC Training Observations" (Fort McPherson, Ga.: U.S. Army Forces Command, 18 November 1982), 1; *Take-Home Package, Task Force 2-34 Infantry*, III-C-1-2.

TIMELINE: DEFEND A BATTLE POSITION (NIGHT)
13 OCTOBER 1982

13 OCT 82-1300: Units warned to prepare for night defense
13 OCT 82-1900: Enemy forces engage scouts

---

told them to just fire the FPF data, set for high-explosive 81-mm rounds, with illumination cranked to burst as high as possible.) It was pathetic and sporadic, but it was some light, and a few tanks and machine guns fired nervously at the half-seen enemy.

Bravo's mortars pumped up more light, adjusting it down to a useful height. Artillery illumination began to bloom at last, lighting up the whole valley to reveal the enemy in EA Green, almost unmolested. The colonel saw only one vehicle target panel smoking, down near Bravo's infantry sites. The sky filled with flares, and it was as bright as an electric day, shadows washed out as mortars and artillery banged away. But it was far too late. The Dragons' direct-fire shooting was ragged and of short duration. In minutes the targets were down, and the cease fire went forth on the net. The last few parachute illumination shells burst and swayed far above, then drifted, darkened, and died.

The 34th would not find out until the AAR on 15 October just how badly they had done in the night defense. Well, they had not put their hearts into it, and they had paid for their sloppiness. The Dragon leadership would discover on 15 October that they had also set a gunnery record (admittedly not one to boast about) on the night defense with a paltry nine hits and two kills.

Notes

1. Ronald J. Glasser, M.D., *365 Days* (New York: Bantam Books, 1971), 58.

2. Department of the Army, "Information Paper Live-Fire Training (LFT)" (Fort Irwin, Calif.: National Training Center Operations Group, 1 September 1982), 2. There was no requirement for a tactical reconnaissance effort, but one look at the chief of the operations group indicated that such a method was wise.

3. Based on the 2-34 operations, this particular "basic load" of materials was standardized for Task Force 2-19 Infantry, the next unit to go to Irwin from Fort Stewart.

4. Department of the Army, *Soviet Army Operations* (Arlington Hall Station: U.S. Army Intelligence Threat Analysis Center, April 1978), 3–31.

5. Department of the Army, *FM 71-2 The Tank and Mechanized Infantry Battalion Task Force, Final Draft* (Fort Benning, Ga. and Fort Knox, Ken.: U.S. Army Infantry School and U.S. Army Armor School, June 1982), 7-33 and D-6. The use of infantry to handle a major part of the engineer work is doctrinal.

6. Finley interview; Norman interview. The author reviewed the complete accident report and examined the site personally. Capt. Finley offered the belief that a nearby artillery battery controller, while "barraging" his unit, may have inadvertently caused the "turnoff" reactions that initiated the accident.

7. An HHC medic was the only soldier who did not return immediately. That young man came back later in the exercise.

8. Finley interview. Capt. Finley pointed out that the OCs experienced the highest percentage of actual injuries on the live fires and during night operations of any type.

9. Sayers interview; Morin interview. In the author's unit only half of the positions had overhead cover.

Note: Other sources for material in this chapter include: interviews, *Take-Home Package, Task Force 2-34 Infantry*; relevant doctrinal literature.

Chapter Eleven

Movement to Contact (II)

"Your business is to do your duty, like a soldier in the breach."
                                              Marcus Aurelius, *Meditations*[1]

After the impotent flailings of the night defense, the Dragons turned to what they had been reckoning as their major task of the evening: moving the task force south to the assembly area for the morrow's movement to contact. The fiasco of the poorly adjusted illumination was shrugged off. There was simply no time to worry about it, and not much inclination. Fatigued from a night without sleep (but certainly not yet exhausted), the soldiers turned to the difficult operation of pulling off their battle positions and heading through Cemetery Pass.

The 2d Brigade commander (the COG) had been careful to construct a plausible scenario to drive the 34th's retrograde motion. He briefed the battalion commander that the Dragons would be conducting a night retirement to allow the division commander (notional, in this case) to explode a fission demolition to close Cemetery Pass and to cut off any OPFOR pursuit. Then, with the task force rear secured, the Dragons would establish an assembly area just east of Silver Lake Road and jump off at 0800 in the valley directly south of Drinkwater Lake, pressing to exploit the effects of the nuclear device. All of this had been translated into a march order before dusk on 13 October, and as the swaying flares of the night live fire flickered out, the task force awaited word to start its retirement.

A retirement is a movement away from the enemy when that enemy is not in contact with the departing unit. It is the easiest type of retrograde operation, and distinct from the withdrawal (where contact must be broken, by stealth or violence) and the delay (where a unit pulls back, fighting and in contact all the way to slow and destroy the enemy). For the Dragons, the retirement would kick off with the scouts leading off, followed by Alpha, then Charlie Tank, then Bravo. The combat trains were already in the assembly area (the logistics sections were quite close to the position they had used to support the defense of the Drinkwater battle position). The TOC would move in a split section, with half of it following the scouts and the other half following Team Charlie. Though the route was painfully obvious (Silver Lake Road, then left at benchmark 1017 to Arrowhead Hill), the colonel told the battalion XO to have his trains personnel along the route as guides.

The only potential difficulty related to the pullout looked to be the collection of the task force attachments. With the HHC commander leading the DS engineers by the nose (they would follow the scouts and first half of the TOC), the colonel parceled out the other attachments to the companies to bring down the pike. Alpha was given the Chaparral ADA missile platoon and the Antitank Platoon to mind. Bravo took responsibility for the GSR section and the Vulcans. The 107-mm mortars were to move with Charlie Tank. Once the assembly area was reached, the special platoons would revert to TF 2-34 control. Fortunately, the movement-to-contact mission was well supported by the current task organization, so the nightmare of swapping platoons in the dark scrub fields was avoided. The Dragons had to leave the GS Engineer Platoon to the engineer company, for they had more pressing duties in the Task Force 2-70 area far to the south. But other than that deletion and the temporary march assignments, the order of battle remained constant from 13 October.

The pullback of TF 2-34 would facilitate (and be covered by) the explosion of a low-yield nuclear mine in Cemetery Pass at 0030 on 14 October. As the road distance (even at creeping speed) was short, the TOC planners calculated the whole battalion would be in the new laager site almost an hour before the atomic detonation, and safe from the local radiation and blast. Of course, the National Training Center controllers had a wonderful simulation munition set to blow up on schedule in the pass. It would provide a credible approximation of a fission explosion.[2]

Nuclear weapons, like the related, though infinitely less potent, chemical weapons, are devices of mass destruction. In Army terms, atomic artillery shells, missile warheads, or atomic demolition munitions (ADMs) (nuclear, command-detonated land mines, like the simulator employed in Cemetery Pass) are "government-classified high explosives." In a military sense (and in the United States, soldiers do not get involved, save as advisors, in political decisions), once the

TASK ORGANIZATION: TF 2-34 INFANTRY
14 OCTOBER 1982

Team A

Company A (−)
3d Platoon, Company C (tanks)
2 AT sections

Team B

Company B (−)
1st Platoon, Company C (tanks)
1 AT section (+1 squad)

Team C

Company C (−)
3d Platoon, Company B
3d Platoon, Company A

TF Control

Scouts
AT Platoon (−)
Heavy Mortar
DS Engineer Platoon
GSR Teams (4), B, Company, 124th MI
Vulcan Platoon, A Battery, 5-52 ADA Battalion
Chaparral Platoon, A Battery, 5-52 ADA Battalion

OPPOSING FORCES (OPFOR) MOTORIZED RIFLE REGT. (−)

2 Motorized Rifle Battalions (MRB) (31 BMP infantry vehicles each, total 62)
1 Tank Company (13 T-72 tanks)

decision has been made to use nuclear weapons, the only questions become which type, how many, and where. If it is time for the Apocalypse, the Minutemen and Tridents will fly and the actions of units like TF 2-34 would soon be eclipsed in the general mayhem of thermonuclear war. But it is more likely that the situation will be less drastic: outnumbered Americans, far from home, menaced by enemy forces (probably Soviet) and at the end of the rope as far as conventional strength, trapped in a modern Dunkirk. Their corps commander may ask for, and get, nuclear release from the President. This request procedure is tortuous and full of checks and double-checks, and without getting into classified areas, laden with codes and countercodes to prevent any local artillery colonel from chucking a few unauthorized Big Ones into the opposition's knickers.

Assuming (as the NTC staff did) that nuclear release was granted, soldiers at the battalion level would have little to do with planning or firing these weapons. The Dragons' main job would be to get the hell out of the way of both U.S. and adversary bursts. All nuclear systems produce certain dramatic effects upon detonation, not all of which are militarily significant. The power released by an atomic warhead is divided into five effects: blast (as in any explosion, though more intense and wider in area), thermal (fires and blindness caused by heat and light), electromagnetic pulse (EMP—a weird jolt of raw electrical energy that burns out solid-state radio and weapons circuitry for miles around ground zero), prompt radiation (killing neutrons that destroy organic life), and residual radiation (hot spots at ground zero and windborne fallout). American nuclear calculators consider only the effects of blast and prompt radiation for battlefield weapons, since it is relatively easy to avoid fallout and hot spots, and thermal and EMP effects are included in the blast-effect radius. In military terms, fires, burns, blindness, fried radios and computers, contamination, and tree blowdown are termed "bonus" effects; TOC officers cannot count on them, because weather and terrain influence these phenomena too greatly.

The average APC or tank provides decent radiation protection (a foxhole with overhead cover is even better) and good blast shielding from all but the largest weapons, so that it would take fission devices of well over ten kilotons (10,000 pounds of TNT) to create more than local damage to a deployed battalion.[3] Popular visions of square kilometers turned into smoking, glassy craters are not true for tactical weapons, which are usually employed in airbursts to maximize blast and prompt radiation. In any case, the nuclear battlefield will probably be harder to deal with psychologically than physically, since the weapons are unknown, their appearance is terrifying, and everyone keeps getting told how once the first nuke goes off, Armageddon will shortly ensue. The NTC operations group integrated the atomic weapon situation into the training to familiarize American soldiers with these frightening, but understandable, inventions.

The confusion generated by the night attack on the BP had died down by 2030, allowing the scouts to begin the eight-kilometer march down to the new assembly area. The battalion S-4 had called to confirm that he had positioned guides along Silver Lake Road and had men to lead each company and special platoon into position. The night was as coal black as any so far, with a light breeze stirring across the hills as the Dragons began packing equipment and checking people and weapons to insure that all were present. Ammunition was towed away, and cannons, machine guns, and rifles were inspected to insure they were unloaded. By 2100 the NTC "2d Brigade" authorized the 34th to begin displacing to the south. The first scout APC nosed past the cemetery moments later, following the other blacked-out M113s of its platoon. Behind them came the first part of the TOC, a hulking M577 and two M113s, with the engineer platoon tagging obediently behind. The pass was tighter than usual, because the ten-ton trailers, still half-filled with lumber, sandbags, and wire, were parked along the north wall, awaiting the return of their tractors from brigade.

It took awhile for the initial block of units to thread the pass, with the battalion commander trailing them in his APC. By the colonel's estimation it would take less than two hours to clear the battalion off of the BP. The colonel looked behind him for

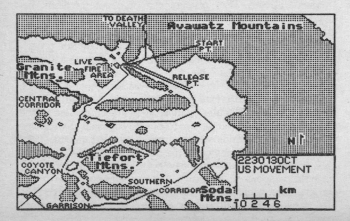

Team Alpha, but already the dust was rising and barring all but
the most immediate images.

Alpha was not right behind; worse, both Alpha and Charlie
Tank had broken down their ends of the defensive field telephone wire layout and had dropped off the FM radio as well.
The TOC called again and again when the time reached 2130
and there was still no Team Alpha up near the pass (the second
half of the TOC having pulled up near the two truckless trailers
to count heads as the battalion filed through). There was a
plethora of rumbling diesels and winking red-filtered flashlights over behind hill 1134, but Alpha was not on the radio,
even on its internal net. Charlie Tank was reached on its internal frequency, but the answering radio operator had no idea
where the first lieutenant in command had gone.

The Alpha and Charlie Team commanders had gone into the
twisted ravine behind hill 1134, between benchmarks 1034 and
1056. Charlie Tank had jumped the gun and gotten intermixed
with Team Alpha, not to mention the heavy mortars and the big
Antitank Platoon, who had bumbled into each other trying to
line up with Charlie and Alpha, respectively. The cramped
corridor was swollen with APCs, ITVs, tanks, jeeps, trucks,
and dismounted soldiers and sergeants trying to sort things out.
Since part of Team C was almost at the opening near the
cemetery, the two company commanders wisely elected to let
Charlie go first. It was almost 2230 before the tank team finally
started to inch through the pass, its acting commander sheep-
ishly coming on the radio (urged by a messenger from the rear

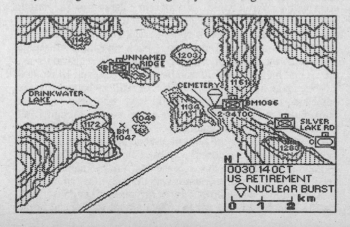

half of the TOC) to the deserved tongue-lashing of the frustrated battalion colonel.[4] The Heavy Mortar Platoon, disoriented in the traffic jam below 1134, fell out of the column to wait for what the platoon leader thought was Team C (but was really Team A, the two units having swapped positions without telling anyone). It took nearly an hour of stopping and starting to get all of Charlie through the pass, with sleepy drivers nodding in their hatches and missing the motion of tracks and tanks to their front.

Alpha, its captain irritated by the unnecessary delays, fell in with good order and cleared Cemetery Pass by about 0015, slowed by the poking tank units to its front. Bravo's soldiers, their vehicles already lined up, squatted in their security sites along Unnamed Ridge, discussing what in the world could be taking so long. The Bravo captain was told by radio to insure he picked up all the ADA when he pulled off, so that the team commander had to make another circuit of the dark hills, reeling in an errant Chaparral track in the process. Bravo's captain had just reached his track (having zipped off in a jeep to sweep up the straggler) when he saw the pass light up. He checked his watch dial: 0030. It was the ADM simulator.

In the confined space of Cemetery Pass, the other half of the TOC was just passing through when the thing went off. The S-3-Air, his head out of the track commander's hatch on the M577 as he talked on the radio, was talking to Team Charlie at the time of detonation: "Roger, understand you are at Charlie Papa Four and have—WHOA! What the hell is that?" The controller's pyrotechnic contraption flared in a bright magnesium-flare light, then choked up a dirty orange, glowing mushroom cloud, all with a rolling crack and rumble that fascinated the watching Bravo troops back on Unnamed Ridge and shocked the TOC in the pass.[5] Speaking in scenario terms, the second half of the TOC had been atomized, and Bravo and its appendage units were all cut off. An artillery battery just the other side of Cemetery Pass would have also been baked in immediate neutron radiation. For some reason, though it all was noted and would definitely be meat for the 15 October AAR, the controllers did not kill anyone and allowed Bravo to move through the supposedly "closed" pass. It probably had something to do with the expense and unique nature of the upcoming live-fire attack, but it was the only time an artificial "resurrection" was allowed to occur on the Dragons' NTC rotation. Such arbitrary twists of fate are all too typical in the usual refereed exercises like BOLD EAGLE or REFORGER.

Anyway, Bravo was as sluggish as Charlie had been in departing, its captain taking extra (and probably excessive) pains to collect all attachments. The Heavy Mortar Platoon and the shrunken CSC headquarters left about 0100, passing the smoldering remains of the atomic simulator on the way south. Bravo would not clear the pass until almost 0200, its column swollen by a lost ITV in the process. The Bravo captain, already wary of night navigation and feeling the effects of a second sleepless night, led the column at a torpid pace. Twice the company commander wandered off onto side paths from the main tank trail, and the convoy experienced two major breaks in contact when an artillery battery passed them, also heading south. At the TOC (finally, though poorly, erected in the laager area) the colonel kept setting back the operations order as he waited on Bravo, the heavy mortar lieutenant, and the Vulcan platoon leader.

It was just before dawn (about 0500) when Team Bravo finally dragged into the perimeter. The S-4 had given directions to the disheveled company team, and its bleary-eyed captain put them in a tiny wash in a mad jumble and struck out to find the TOC, instructing his company XO to gather the leaders, redistribute ammo, and be ready for a fragmentary order when he returned.

At the TOC the OPORD for the big movement to contact (over thirty kilometers long) was being given, though the Team B commander, Vulcan platoon leader, and heavy mortar lieutenant were missing. Meanwhile, Bravo's captain was bouncing around the darkened perimeter in his jeep, searching for the TOC. There were no instructions that he could get over the radio; the TOC was in the middle of a nondescript field in a small hollow and not readily observable. So the Bravo jeep circled on and on as the sky finally began to gray to the east.

Aside form the Bravo Company commander's poor night navigation and the rumpled state of the 34th TOC, the colonel was satisfied that the task force could do its job well on this operation. The line of departure was Silver Lake Road. There were three march objectives designated, with the first, Objective GO, being a narrow mountain pass leading to a huge valley. Objective GO was five kilometers due west of the line of departure. It was heavily mined and known to be defended.

The commander of 5-32 Armor had told the Dragon lieutenant colonel that it had taken him until 1100 to begin passing through Objective GO. It was that tough.

Beyond GO, fifteen kilometers west and a jink to the north past the big hill 1517 mass, lay Objective INDIAN. It was the edge of an escarpment that led down to the far west end of the Drinkwater Lake valley, and it, too, was reportedly heavily mined and defended. Past INDIAN was hill 1141, Objective COWBOY. The colonel had never heard anything about COWBOY because nobody ever made it that far.

The TF 2-34 plan was based on two principles: breaching holes in obstacles quickly and keeping the teams close together (within two kilometers) for mutual support. The S-3 and colonel had concocted a scheme that had the scouts lead to GO to check out the obstacle, with Team B and the engineers to breach. Team C would overwatch, and Team A would exploit the breach and pick up the engineers. Once Alpha broke through, Bravo would come up, echeloned to the south; and Charlie Tank would come through and angle off to the north, forming a task force wedge. With the scouts leading, the wedge would hit INDIAN; then Alpha would breach, overwatched by Bravo, with Charlie to push through. The battalion would come on line in the Drinkwater valley and push for COWBOY, with Charlie in the north, Bravo in the center, and Alpha (leaving INDIAN last) in the south. The plan was simple, but it addressed every phase of the mission. The colonel was determined to get to COWBOY.

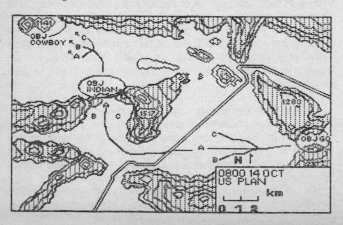

Needless to say, the battalion commander was gladdened to see the Bravo captain finally appear as the sun started to peek over the horizon. It took the colonel only minutes to acquaint the young captain with the mission; after all, they had talked this one through many times back at Stewart, and if there was one thing Team Bravo was good at, it was breaching obstacles. It had better be good, thought the colonel, because there was no time left to plan or prepare. For Bravo it would be more a rote drill than a fancy operation.

Breaching a defended obstacle is an ancient part of warfare, though castles and fortresses have given way to tank traps and pressure mines. The techniques are unsubtle and direct, the purest application of irresistible force against an immovable object. The 34th had gotten the word early that opening barriers was a big part of NTC and had trained hard during DESERT FORGE to master this task. Interestingly enough, Bravo (and, to a lesser extent, Alpha) trained to punch through without engineer support, working with hand tools rather than mine plows or demolition guns. Learning to do it the hardest possible way was the best means to learn the drill.

The letters SOSR summarize obstacle-breaching tactics. The first *S* stands for *suppression* of the enemy weapons around the obstacle and the elimination of OPFOR on the near side. The *O* is for *obscuration*, which means the use of smoke grenades, smoke pots, artillery smoke shells, and white phosphorous mortar rounds to curtain off the obstacle from enemy view and degrade the foe's ability to engage the breaching team. The second *S* stands for *secure* the far side, using quickly cleared footpaths to put riflemen, Dragon gunners, and M60 machine gunners out onto the far side to protect the teams clearing paths for tanks and tracks. The final letter, *R*, is for *reduction* of the obstacle, which means the actual removal of mines, wire, tank spikes, or the filling of ditches to create multiple lanes for vehicles. The most common error is to start reducing the obstacle before the far side is secured—a dangerous practice, since the enemy will likely send his defending infantry to find out what is transpiring as soon as the smoke cuts off his view. If there are not security teams across the barricade, the OPFOR could quickly move right up to hold the minefield, slaughtering the prematurely committed mine-clearing teams.

A company team preparing to run the SOSR drill would typically have two infantry platoons and one tank platoon, dividing itself into two breach platoons of infantry and a supporting fire platoon of tanks. If another company was not available to quickly push through the lanes created, the tank platoon might double as the exploitation force. Upon identifying an obstacle that could not be bypassed, the company would go to full MOPP (mission oriented protective posture; in other words, protective masks and full, zipped-up suits). This precluded danger from any bursting chemical mines. The tanks and TOWs would provide suppressive fires (the support element) while each of the two platoons secured, cleared, and marked a lane (breach element). The company commander's FIST would call in continuous smoke to screen the action. If engineers were present, they would aid the infantry by actually reducing the minefield through demolition charges. Without engineers (the way Bravo and Alpha's infantry had trained) the riflemen had to manually probe (with blunt sticks) and mark the mines, then dispose of them, usually with explosives. It was tedious, tiring work even in training. In wartime it would be bloody and frightening to boot.

There was one other rule, not covered in the SOSR sequence but mentioned in every description of barrier breaking. The breaching force had to be certain to reconnoiter vigorously for any available bypass or, at least, a weak spot in the obstacle. Even a successful obstacle reduction was likely to cost so many casualties that any way to avoid the whole exercise had to be used.

The breach was unavoidable at GO, and that much was evident almost within minutes of the 0800 LD time. The scouts reported that the obstacle consisted of almost 100 meters of antitank and antipersonnel mines, but no wire. The mines had thin triplines on them, lacing across the whole field, and several BMP silhouettes had risen on the nearby cliff abutments to challenge the Dragon efforts. Bravo was almost a half hour late crossing the Silver Lake Road, though the captain had the colonel's approval to use the extra time to complete his preparations. The early morning light clearly showed GO, and the distant pops of the scout .50-calibers told the task force it would not be easy. Bravo's commander had wasted too much time on the road march, and now he was delaying the operation.

The colonel toyed with the idea of letting Alpha breach with the engineers, but that idea was scratched when he noticed the

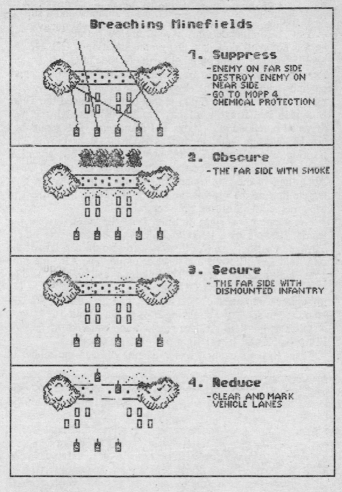

Breaching Minefields

1. Suppress
- ENEMY ON FAR SIDE
- DESTROY ENEMY ON NEAR SIDE
- GO TO MOPP 4 CHEMICAL PROTECTION

2. Obscure
- THE FAR SIDE WITH SMOKE

3. Secure
- THE FAR SIDE WITH DISMOUNTED INFANTRY

4. Reduce
- CLEAR AND MARK VEHICLE LANES

ridiculous sight of the M728 Combat Engineer Vehicle and engineer APCs lined up like docile baby ducks behind a diesel fuel truck along Silver Lake Road. It was too much; the engineer lieutenant was conveniently not on the radio to absorb the colonel's scalding remarks. Alpha and Charlie were potting the BMPs on the cliffs, and by 0830 Bravo was under way and Air

Force F-4 Phantoms were due to be on station at 0855. So he let it ride.

Bravo's commander may have been slow getting started, but he was not at all slow in sizing up the situation at GO. He had his FIST officer begin pummeling the far side of GO and asked for white phosphorus to be readied, so that the smokescreen could be laid on call. The news over the radio that the engineer platoon had elected to refuel at this time convinced the Team B captain that Bravo's infantry would push through the way they had practiced with sticks and manpower. The scouts had sized things up well, so that as Bravo's tracks moved into position, the dismounting infantry clumsy in full chemical garb, the infantrymen had the right tools for the task at hand. About half of the rifle squads spread out to fire at any enemy targets that might appear; the others plunged into the nest of tripwires and half-buried blue ceramic mines.

Fire support was right on time, from the two overwatching teams, Bravo's own tanks and TOWs, and from the timely barrage of artillery smoke that crashed into the far side of the minefield and billowed into a white cloud. The APC machine guns, tank cannons, and TOWs clattered and cracked as they swept the clifftops above GO, allowing Team B to work the big mine patch unmolested. The colonel and task force FSO collaborated to send two streaking F-4s to pound hill 1517 in the distance as the field artillery smoked and battered the far side of the barricade. It was right out of the textbook.

Team Bravo's captain was wheezing through the rubber of

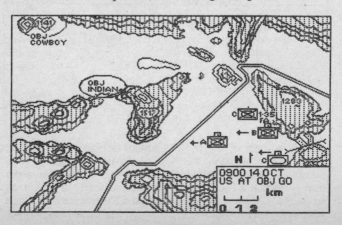

his protective mask, out on the ground with his men. While they were biting into the minefield, trying to work a footpath through, the captain was looking for a weak spot. The steep slopes on either side of the mines insured that there would be no bypass, but the captain knew the breaching game (as far as one can from textbooks and common sense) and figured that there was a lane somewhere in the pattern. There usually was, since barriers are often left open to let security forces through them then later sealed off, sometimes hastily. At NTC the captain was sure that a gap had been opened and closed to let range personnel service the targets, then patched over when the range detail moved on.

A few unlucky Bravo troops had tripped the tension wires strung between the mines, and smoke grenades buried beneath the ceramic models pumped purple smoke and CS gas into the air. The OCs "killed" the soldiers involved with their controller guns, and the rifle platoons pushed replacement probers forward. But the Bravo Company commander, moving behind his 2d Platoon on the southernmost lane, spied what looked like a gap to his left. In fact, there were only tripwires, not mines, in a six- or seven-meter pathway that ran the depth of the mine belts. It was a little sloped, but passable, so the captain directed the 2d Platoon leader to concentrate on clearing the wires. The captain cut and marked a few himself for good measure.

The colonel was elated at 0930 to discover that he had a hole in the mines, and he ordered Bravo to secure the far side and notify him when that was done. The Team B leader came back immediately to say that it was already done, and the colonel directed Team A to exploit the breach. Bravo's captain asked if the colonel still wanted two lanes (as 1st Platoon was still crunching along, losing men as it chewed into the thick mines in front of it). The colonel said to forget the second lane for now.[6] With his men laying white engineer tape to mark the cleared way, the Bravo commander waved Alpha's lead tanks forward. By 0940 the task force was moving through the opening.

It took Team A about fifteen minutes to clear the aperture, and the TOC called up Team C to rush them through. But there were other units that wanted out, and the Alpha commander was amazed when his tailing mortars and TOWs were cut off by a racing column of self-propelled 155-mm guns and their ammunition tracks. It was an artillery battery moving to provide fire support past Objective GO, but the artillerymen were not on anybody's frequency in TF 2-34 (except, sort of, on the FSO's fire direction net, usually reserved for actual calls for fire). The big guns slowed Alpha, blocked Charlie Tank; then, with an oblivious nod to the waving Bravo guides, the second of the big M109 howitzers edged off of the white engineer tape and struck a mine. Now there was real trouble, as the straight-backed, turreted 155 completely filled the lane, blocking further movement. The colonel (and a lot of other soldiers) cursed.

It took about twenty minutes to drag the "damaged" (OC ruling) gun track out of the lane. The artillery battery commander prudently pulled it to the enemy side of the lane with the use of the first M109 to get through. It was 1020 before the rest of the artillery battery eased through the lane, and, in the meantime, the colonel ordered a reluctant Bravo team commander to start probing again with his 1st Platoon. By 1035 Charlie Tank was passing through, the dogged infantrymen of Team B's 1st Platoon had pried open a second lane (at a cost), and the CSC commander had rolled up to assume traffic control duties at the busy pass.

The actual CSC commander was back from Georgia. The senior captain quickly took charge at the gap, freeing the weary Bravo soldiers to remount their M113s and push out toward INDIAN. The failure to have him, or some similar traffic czar, forward had tied Bravo to its breach and slowed task force momentum. One cannot afford to leave a third of one's combat strength immobile after the breach is completed.

The action at GO had been pretty good, and the colonel watched as Bravo and Charlie slowly deployed on either flank of Team A. Bravo ended up to the north, the tank team to the south, a reversal of the plan. Even the perversely slow engineers had rolled in, and by 1200 the whole wedge was well under way toward INDIAN, blasting away at BMP and T-72 target boards among the rocky hill bases. The big artillery cannons (less their "wrecked" mate) were already pounding INDIAN as the 34th moved out in the huge valley.

By doctrine there are only two battalion formations.[7] The first, a familiar one, is the column. The second, with at least two companies abreast, is the line. The Dragons were using a wedge because it made sense, but one could not find it in the doctrine, because the doctrine did not envision complex formations at the task force level. The Dragons swept up the valley, stopping now and then to shoot. It looked almost like a naval fleet from the dreadnought era, swinging here and there to engage targets or avoid rocks and small knolls.

The sense of "steaming up the basin" permeated the battalion, and Alpha soon began to pull out and away from the trailing teams. Worse, the colonel and his forward command post track were moving farther and farther west from the TOC, still disposed in its unkempt little hollow way back in the assembly area. The TOC was a hovel by its normal standards, with maps unposted and communications to brigade and the companies rendered spotty by the hills around GO. The fact that the headquarters company commander, who normally moved and secured the TOC, had once again been forced to babysit the engineers probably had a lot to do with the fact that the TOC just sat in place and gradually lost touch with the battle.

Alpha reached INDIAN about 1245, and it was nearly 1315 before Charlie and Bravo came up behind. One Bravo platoon (the badly depleted 1st) was dragging far behind, nursing a weak-engined APC toward INDIAN. It would have plenty of time to catch up, for the barrier at INDIAN made Objective GO look like tissue paper. This one would not be at all easy.

The day had grown hot by the time the tired infantrymen had dismounted, pulling on their stinking protective masks and zipping up their sweaty MOPP suits as they prepared for more of the same. As luck would have it, Team B had driven right up to the only obvious route down off INDIAN onto the Drinkwater valley floor, though the path looked more suitable for mountain goats than for armored vehicles. Team A was just west of Bravo, scrabbling about on some other skimpy trails. Charlie was behind Team A, and the scouts were reconnoitering farther west. The colonel and S-3 had pulled up behind Bravo as the breach teams once more moved forward.

INDIAN was a geological obstacle even without the help of the barrier materials feastooning it. Its anchors, hill 1184 to the west and hill 1338 looming to the east, flanked the crooked center road in front of Team B. Water runoff gullies writhed through the big, jagged rocks of the escarpment, and Alpha was trying to find a way through the dry stream network just west of the 1184 feature. The scouts were poking farther up the spine of the Granite Mountains, to which INDIAN connected.

The man-made work at the objective completed the natural hazards to movement. Every wadi, every footpath, was choked with piles of staked-out concertina wire and carpets of trip-

fused blue training mines. The top edge of INDIAN was traced
by a deep tank ditch, its trough filled with mines and iron
triangles. On the "main" thoroughfare, alternate bundles of
wire entanglements and strings of land mines covered the path,
with a succession of iron antivehicle triangles staggered at each
switchback and curve. At the last major curve near the bottom,
two old target tank hulls dating back to the 1950s had been
dragged onto the trail to block it. Then, more mines and wire
completed the picture.[8]

It was 1330, and the colonel seriously wondered if anyone
could bull through this tangle of barricades, let alone his Dragons. To add to his travails, he was "wounded" and declared
immobile by the OCs, a victim of the omnipresent tripwires all
around the tank ditch. The battalion commander sat on a big
rock and watched as Bravo's infantrymen worked the tortuous
trail; he had the S-3 contact the HHC captain to get the CEV up
to bulldoze the tank hulks and to fill in the ditch once the
infantry cleared the mines.

With 1st Platoon still dragging, Bravo's commander committed his 2d Platoon and called for the long-lost engineers.
Amazingly, the next thing he saw was the DS engineer lieutenant and the famous bulk of the combat engineer vehicle. By
1335 1st Platoon was up, and Bravo and Alpha, huffing in their
greasy green chemical suits, began to open a way off the elevation.

The engineers moved with languor and without urgency behind the diligent Bravo infantry of 2d Platoon.[9] The big CEV

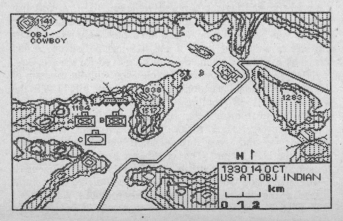

was perfect for pushing wire and iron AT triangles off the roadway. Two engineer squads were unaccounted for, the platoon leader having lost them between GO and INDIAN, but the colonel forbade him to go back to search for the missing APCs. The field destructors were finally doing something, and the battalion colonel would not stop them. Alpha was making minimal progress on its steep gorge. Completing the picture, the colonel began to get needling calls from the 2d Brigade commander, demanding that he get the battalion down off INDIAN. "I want COWBOY!" said the gravel-voiced COG. The battalion commander wanted it too, but it would take awhile longer to get to the valley floor.

The afternoon passed slowly, with recon teams returning disappointed in searches for alternative routes down. Bravo had a squad from 1st Platoon scouring the wadis around hill 1338, but the rest of the platoon was relieving the weary 2d Platoon probers on the twisting major trace. The colonel called Bravo and Alpha repeatedly, but the answer was always the same: progress slow.

At 1530 the colonel, seated in his M113 dozing, was shaken awake by the S-3. "It's clear," said the S-3 major, shouting through his gas mask. The colonel jumped up and began talking coolly on the radio. Bravo would go down first, then Charlie Tank, then Alpha. The HHC commander, his APC full of tank rounds he was cross-loading from "damaged" tanks to fully capable M60s, was told to insure the engineers collected themselves and went down below quickly.[10] The colonel suspected that COWBOY would also have barriers.

It took only a brief time to align the battalion on the plain below, with the teams arrayed Bravo, Charlie Tank, and Alpha, north to south. By 1600 the mass of tired soldiers and vehicles started to roll up the valley. It was a tactical washout, a frontal cavalry charge, and a sorry example of how to attack. The artillery pounded a bit, then lifted, and Bravo's 81-mm section provided some excitement by opening a few high-explosive shots within a hundred meters of its own 1st Platoon.[11] The S-3 and colonel, gladdened to finally snake through INDIAN, had left the TOW platoon at the top without orders. When the AT lieutenant saw the formation move, he started to move down behind the dust cloud that marked the moving battalion. Far to the rear the TOC was finally moving, passing GO almost as the colonel kicked off the assault on COWBOY.

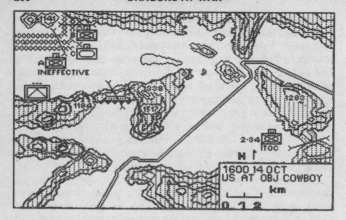

On they came, across five kilometers of open ground, unscreened by a shred of smoke. OPFOR targets appeared on the southern valley wall and showered Alpha with little styrofoam rockets, simulating Sagger ATGMs.[12] The OCs began dispassionately "attriting" Team A. Bravo slipped in behind a roll of a rocky hill, and part of Team C followed Bravo into the dead ground. Then Bravo was up against a single fence of wire and a thin band of mines; this, at last, was COWBOY. OCs whittled down the thin ranks of Team B's breach teams as the troops used grappling hooks and rope to tear chunks out of the weak barrier. To the south, Team A was down to two APCs and a tank and unable to do much about the Sagger barrage it was absorbing. Team Tank followed Bravo's 2d Platoon, and Bravo's captain followed his 1st, as OCs began to pick off tracks and tanks with their controller guns. Smoke grenades were all the Dragons had now to cover their breaches, and the rest of the B and C teams raced forward to tear down the next set of wire and mines.

The colonel's track was "'destroyed," then the S-3 was eliminated in the Sagger fusillade. They sat in the valley, watching the shrunken pieces of Teams B and C breast the second fence of concertina wire against the dark bulk of hill 1141 and the reddening sunset. The headquarters company commander, working with his driver and a set of grappling lines, was tearing open the third wire net. He would be first on COWBOY. Unfortunately, the attack was not supported by any overwatch elements.

Bravo's captain and a track from his 2d Platoon were next to break into the objective. A few scattered ITVs and a scout track followed. Everyone else was "destroyed," their yellow kill-indicator lights turning in clusters across the big basin, all the way back to INDIAN. It was starting to get dark when the order came: "Cease fire!" It had not been pretty, but a tiny part of the 34th had reached COWBOY.

There are three postscripts to this wild race from GO to COWBOY, each important in its own way. The cease-fire order ended the tactical phase of live-fire training, and the battalion was allowed to coil up just outside the first COWBOY wire fence, similar to the way it had at the laager at Tiefort's base. As the battered M60 tanks and M113s pulled into their company areas in the gathering gloom, the darkening western sky pulsed with a green-blue dot that gradually expanded to a great, glowing green cloud. It was never discovered what caused that unusual phenomenon. Speculation on the strange cloud centered on a sounding rocket from several nearby research ranges.

Second, the TOC, combat trains, and company supply sections had to work their way through the wreckage of INDIAN in the pitch blackness. It took extensive direct efforts by the tired infantrymen on the valley floor to guide the trucks down to the battalion laager. Bravo's commander and XO had some nervous moments when the 1st Platoon M113 that had broken down at the BP (and had been pulled in just before the day defense) twisted on its tow bar and nearly slipped off the narrow path at INDIAN. It was 0100 before every task force unit was in the assembly area, fed, and fueled. It was all right, though. The battalion would not move back to fight the live OPFOR until afternoon on the 15th, so everyone got some deserved sleep.

Third, the AAR at 0700 on 15 October was almost pleasant, though the review of the night defense started the proceedings on a sour note. It was not dwelt upon. The senior controller went on to discuss the live-fire movement to contact. The first part, particularly the assault on GO and the artillery and air-strike coordination, came in for outright praise. Of course, the sloppy TOC setup and the engineers' slothful behavior were noted and criticized. Team Bravo's slow movement down from Drinkwater had increased fatigue among the leaders and limited the information flow by making the OPORD occur later,

GUNNERY: MOVE TO CONTACT, 14 OCT 82

U.S. Weapon	Rounds Fired	Hits	Vehicle Kills
Tank cannon	234	29	17
TOW/Dragon/Viper	123	37	17
Accumulative	357	66	34
Army Average	761	Unknown	32

Sources: Brig. Gen. E. S. Leland, Jr., "NTC Training Observations" (Fort McPherson, Ga.: U.S.Army Forces Command, 18 November 1982), 1; *Task Force Take-Home Package, 2-34 Infantry*, III-D-1-1.

TIMELINE: MOVEMENT TO CONTACT
14 October 1982

13 OCT 82-1600:	Warning order for night retirement issued
13 OCT 82-2030:	Enemy assault ends
13 OCT 82-2100:	Movement order implemented (by radio)
13 OCT 82-2230:	First element (Team C) departs
14 OCT 82-0030:	Nuclear warhead detonated
14 OCT 82-0200:	Trail elements (Team B) depart
14 OCT 82-0500:	Battalion OPORD/Team B arrives at assembly area
14 OCT 82-0645:	All unit leaders receive OPORD by this time
14 OCT 82-0715:	Team B OPORD issued (final company-level OPORD issued)
14 OCT 82-0800:	Line of departure/time of attack
14 OCT 82-0900:	Team B begins breaching Objective GO
14 OCT 82-1100:	TF clears Objective GO
14 OCT 82-1330:	TF begins to clear Objective INDIAN
14 OCT 82-1600:	Objective INDIAN clear; TF deployed to assault Objective COWBOY
14 OCT 82-1700:	TF remnants reach Objective COWBOY

which showed in increasingly dull reactions as the day wore on. The COWBOY attack was pilloried as unimaginative, foolhardy, and lazy, with little use of overwatch or supporting artillery.

Still, the good news outweighed the bad. The aggressive infantry barrier breaking was rightly lauded, with Team B gaining special plaudits. The Dragons had breached INDIAN and even put a few units on COWBOY, a rare feat in the first year of NTC rotations. The 34th had killed thirty-four enemy vehicles, just under half of the targets shown, and they had done it with 357 total rounds (Viper, Dragon, TOW, tank cannons). The average rotational unit killed thirty-two vehicles, but used 761 rounds to do it, so the Dragons had excelled on daylight shooting, at least by comparison to other FORSCOM mechanized infantry units. The general impression was that the 34th had done well on the live-fire missions, and the 1st Brigade commander congratulated the 34th colonel once again. In the Great Game, or in any game, two out of three ain't bad.

Notes

1. Marcus Aurelius, *Meditations*, translated by Maxwell Staniforth (Baltimore, Md.: Penguin Books, 1976), 106.

2. The atomic simulator is a standard piece of Army training ammunition, though rarely used.

3. Department of the Army, *FM 71-100 Brigade and Division Operations (Armor/Mechanized)* (Fort Leavenworth, Kan.: Combined Arms Center, May 1977), 6-3. Dug-in units 2,000 meters from ground zero of a ten-kiloton weapon will suffer no ill effects from blast or immediate radiation. The table shows that smaller weapons are even less effective on dispersed, dug-in units and/or men in tanks and APCs. Incidentally, ten kilotons is a pretty big tactical nuclear yield. The Hiroshima bomb was about twenty kilotons.

4. The acting tank company commander had been quite good about staying on the command frequency, both before and after that one incident.

5. Norman interview. Captain Norman had forgotten all about the atomic demolition munition in the press of coordinating the night march.

6. The TOC was still coordinating the battle at this point. The TOC lost communications with the forward elements as they neared Objective INDIAN.

7. Department of the Army, *TT 71-2J The Mechanized Infantry Battalion Task Force* (Fort Benning, Ga.: U.S. Army Infantry School, 1983), 4-59. This doctrine has not changed, though Task Force Wedge and Vee are mentioned in the 1982 draft of *FM 71-2*. They are considered "modifications" of the two basic formations.

8. Sfc. Michael Brown, "Learning the Hard Way," *Soldiers*, February 1984, 19.

9. *Take-Home Package, Task Force 2-34 Infantry*, IV-G-13. The controllers' words were harsh. "The engineers had no sense of urgency and organization in breaching the barrier" [*sic*].

10. The HHC commander took charge of the ammunition transfer when he wasn't shepherding the engineers around.

11. Safety rules at NTC prohibit overhead fire by mortars. It is an

aberration to place mortars on the flanks, though that was the correct solution. The mission fired by the Bravo 81-mm section was the only mortar mission all day. The heavy mortars received no missions at all.

12. These little missiles, called Smoky SAMs, are an adaptation of a Red Flag training aid developed by the U.S. Air Force for its Nellis Air Force Base exercises. The USAF uses them to depict surface-to-air missile engagements, hence, their name. At NTC they depict AT-3 Sagger anti-tank missiles.

Note: Other sources for materials in this chapter include: interviews; *Take-Home Package, Task Force 2-34 Infantry;* relevant doctrinal manuals.

Chapter Twelve

Movement to Contact (III)

"When the line wheeled and charged across the clearing, the enemy bullets whining past them, wheeled and charged almost with drill field precision, an ache as profound as the ache of orgasm passed through me. And perhaps that is why some officers make careers of the infantry, why they endure the petty regulations, the discomforts and degradations, the dull years of peacetime duty in dreary posts: just to experience a single moment when a group of soldiers under your command and in the extreme stress of combat do exactly what you want them to do, as if they are extensions of yourself."

Philip Caputo, A Rumor of War[1]

At the same time the captains and special platoon lieutenants were listening to the After Action Review, the sergeants and soldiers in the laager were going about the housekeeping tasks that had to precede the march south to face the human OPFOR again. Live ammunition was turned in and inventoried, tracks and tanks were serviced, and weapons were cleaned again and again to remove the clinging thin white dust coats they had accumulated. That afternoon the task force would be moving to the Southern Corridor, south of the great Tiefort Mountain. It would be moving in daylight, a fact that pleased everyone from colonel to private. The rumor was that the first mission down there would be yet another movement to contact.

The live-fire training had been exciting and grueling, but it had lacked some of the realism of tangling with a thinking opponent. For one thing, though the targets did "return fire" with styrofoam projectiles and display flashing bursts to show cannon shots, the OCs had not been uniformly harsh in assessing casualties in the Dragons' ranks. There were no replacement requests to send back to the S-1 or S-4; everybody came back to life after the cease-fires on each mission. As noted earlier, the fact that a third of the task force was trapped on the wrong side of a nuclear burst was not allowed to affect the next mission; everybody arrived and participated. The long barrier-cracking drill at Objective INDIAN had been conducted over a few hours in broad daylight with only minimal losses levied by the controllers. Though the 34th gunnery had been adequate, there was little guarantee that the Dragons' tactical maneuvers would succeed against a live opponent.

The cleanup and turn-in of combat shells and bullets was routine and uneventful, and for a change so was the long motor march to the Southern Corridor. The companies moved in their pure, garrison configurations, having swapped back all attachments on the night of 14 October. The fifty-kilometer route was the longest distance the Dragons had to move at NTC, and the march was completed without a single incident, on time and well before sundown. It augured well for the impending mission of 16 October.

The night of rest had refreshed the colonel and S-3, and they regarded the orders from 1st Brigade with clear minds as the road march began at 1430. The return to control of their parent brigade meant that this was the last period of training, the final series of force-on-force missions. It seemed they had been at NTC forever, but it had been less than ten days. The Dragons had scores to settle with the OPFOR. Reputations hung in the balance.

The mission for 16 October 1982 was the battalion's third movement-to-contact operation in eight tasks to date. The terrain was different again, resembling neither the basin/washboard of 7 October nor the succession of barricaded passes that characterized the live-fire attack on the 14th. This opening mission stretched the entire thirty-kilometer length of the Southern Corridor. The line of departure was in the east near dry Red Pass Lake (nine kilometers due south of the infamous

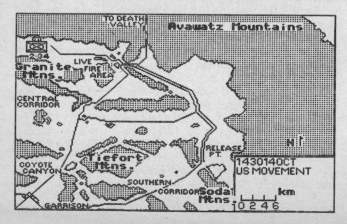

hill 720 that was so hard to find on the night of 6 October). The TF 2-34 zone ran west through a huge open area, gently sloping to the north and cut by shallow wadis. To the south lay the reservation boundary, Bitter Springs, and the gray-black ovoid ridge called The Whale. West of The Whale the ground funneled into a great valley, rising slightly as one went west. The north side of the valley was formed by Tiefort Mountain; the south side by the lower, yellower 801/831/842 feature nicknamed Furlong Ridge (after one of the OPFOR unit commanders). At the west end of the valley, the funnel narrowed and abruptly stopped at a slanting, rocky cliff face topped by three hills (839, 785, and 826, north to south), allowing three exit routes. There was a small flat spot along the escarpment called The Shelf. The whole valley had been the scene of many OPFOR victories and was called the Valley of Death.

The 1st Brigade's instructions to the task force were maddeningly vague: locate and, if possible, destroy the enemy in zone. The battalion commander studied the ground with his S-2 and S-3 at his side, recalling his July visit to the same Southern Corridor. The 34th staff and commanders had already seen and walked this ground on that July weekend. The marked, abrupt, clear-cut features were familiar to these leaders. Two of these terrain distinctions caught the attention of the intelligence officer as the three leaders analyzed the brigade mission and the terrain.

The S-2 pointed out to his colonel that there were three key spots in the Zone of Action. One, The Shelf, was already designated by brigade as a march objective. The two that concerned the young lieutenant were farther to the east: the small gap where Furlong Ridge ended and The Whale began, and a roll in the valley floor about six kilometers west of the pass. The roll in the basin grounded out in Furlong Ridge in a series of wadis and rills not unlike the hated Washboard of Central Corridor memory. This mini-washboard was most pronounced there, though it was present all along the base of Furlong Ridge. The sheer slab sides of hulking Tiefort offered far too few useful crevasses.

The reason the S-2 was so interested in these two pieces of territory was that he strongly anticipated that the Dragons would face more than the usual motorized rifle company in the morning. As an intelligence staffer, he was worried that the enemy would slip through the pass, and he saw possibilities in the small gully lattice for a Dragon hasty defense in the face of an onrushing MRR. The first lieutenant explained his theories about a regimental attack to his commander and the operations major. First, TF 2-70 had just departed the Southern Corridor to go up for its live-fire training, freeing the OPFOR regiment to concentrate on TF 2-34. Second, the Dragons had already done two movements to contact without striking a superior moving force, though that was a strong possibility on any move to contact. The NTC operations group would no doubt want to train on that task. Third, Soviet doctrine and training stressed the meeting engagement as the most common form of clash in modern war, and the 34th had yet to fight such an encounter battle. Fourth, terrain supported an OPFOR regimental attack, as the enemy could demonstrate in the Valley of Death to draw the 34th west, then cave in the Dragons' flank from Furlong/Whale Pass. This combination of frontal and flank attacks was also a favorite Soviet regimental tactic. Finally, the S-2 speculated that the 34th's decent showing in live-fire training may have encouraged the NTC controllers to order a regimental assault to reindoctrinate the task force in handling a live OPFOR and to dispel any misplaced confidence.

The colonel and S-3 were impressed with this logic and vowed to structure their plan with this OPFOR course of action in mind. If the enemy was not out in strength, TF 2-34's scheme of maneuver could easily account for a lesser adversary if it was prepared for a regiment. The task force order of battle would need a few alterations to account for changes on 15 October. For one thing, the bulk of the engineer platoon had to be detached to its parent company to clean construction materials off the Drinkwater battle position before TF 2-70 got up there. For another, the return of the experienced CSC commander meant that the special platoons would get better supply support (as the CSC XO was free to work) and the colonel could depend on his CSC captain as an alternate TOC and director of attachments. This permitted the HHC commander to return to duty at the TOC to improve its abysmal security and displacement standards. Additionally, the old Charlie Tank captain was declared fit for duty again and had returned to resume command of his outfit. The colonel ruefully figured that the tanks had done better under their XO and resolved to be circumspect about counting too heavily on Charlie Company at the outset. Also, major maintenance failures were chipping away at the strength of the battalion. Three tanks and three TOWs were out of action with engine and transmission malfunctions, and one infantry platoon in each rifle company was down to two APCs. Finally, the ammunition for the 16 October mission had yet to be distributed, and the colonel had learned the hard way that such matters grew increasingly more difficult to accomplish as time grew short.

Given these factors and the likelihood that the 34th might well go head to head with the regiment in the Valley of Death, the colonel and S-3 designed a task organization to meet the contingency and to optimize the situation in the tank company. Alpha was organized as a reinforced team, adding TOWs and a tank platoon to its three rifle platoons. This reflected renewed confidence in the Alpha captain, who had been alert and cogent throughout the live-fire engagements. Bravo went with its usual, giving up 3d Platoon in exchange for Charlie Tank's 1st Platoon. Team C was understrength, with one infantry platoon and its own 2d Platoon. The colonel had plans for the 3d Platoon, Company B, besides simply cross-attachment to the tankers, and he gave them a TOW squad to facilitate their special mission. Scouts, antitank (−), heavy mortars, air defense (Vulcan and Chaparral), the few engineers, and the ground surveillance radars were kept under task force control.

The OPORD briefed to the TF 2-34 leaders at 1845 on 15 October laid out the colonel's intentions. The Dragons would kick off operations that night with a reinforced combat patrol (3d Platoon, Company B, and its TOW squad, attached to Team C but under TOC direction for this particular job). Departing at 2300, the platoon would move mounted to The Whale and establish a small minefield and an ambush to seal off the Furlong/Whale gap. The S-3 agreed with the S-2 that leaving this opening unwatched invited OPFOR flank attack in the morning. The ambush patrol would insure that any adversary recon units snooping around the pass would be eliminated. The scouts, meanwhile, were posted up near the foldover to watch the main valley.

The movement to contact proper would start at 0630, with Team A leading out. Team C would fall in to the north and rear, Team B to the south and rear to complete the task force wedge. Alpha would guide on the tank trail that spanned the open arena between Red Pass Lake and The Whale, and the Dragons' wedge would roll up the valley. The colonel stood up and forcefully emphasized that the teams would stay within two kilometers for mutual support. On passing the ambush site at Furlong/Whale Pass, Team C would reassume control of its infantry platoon. The task force would maintain this formation until the enemy appeared or The Shelf was reached.

The S-3 fully explained actions in the event of contingencies. If the task force banged into a small enemy element, Team Alpha would fix it and one of the trail teams (probably

TASK ORGANIZATION: TF 2-34 INFANTRY
16 OCTOBER 1982

Team A

Company A
3d Platoon, Company C (tanks)
2 AT sections

Team B

Company B (–)
1st Platoon, Company C (tanks)
1 AT section (+ 1 squad)

Team C

Company C (–)
3d Platoon, Company B (OPCON to TF 2-34 for ambush)
1 AT squad (OPCON to TF 2-34 for ambush)

TF Control

Scouts
AT Platoon (–)
Heavy Mortars
DS Engineer Platoon (–)
GSR teams (4), B Company, 124th MI.
Vulcan Platoon, A Battery, 5-52 ADA Battalion
Chaparral Platoon, A Battery, 5-52 ADA Battalion

OPPOSING FORCES (OPFOR) MOTORIZED RIFLE REGIMENT

3 Motorized Rifle Battalions (MRB) (31 BMPs each, plus 2 in HQ—95 total)
1 Tank Battalion (40 T-72 tanks)
1 SP Artillery Battalion (18×122-mm SP howitzers)
1 Recon Company (3 BMPs, 9 BRDM2s, 5 motorcycles)
1 Antitank Battery (9 BRDM2s)
1 Antiaircraft Battery ($4 \times$ ZSU-23-4s, $4 \times$ SA-9s)

B) would destroy the enemy. Every attempt would be made to pin the enemy against the valley walls to cut off escape routes. If the 34th made it to The Shelf, Alpha and Bravo would assault abreast (Team A to the north) with Charlie Tank in support. Then he asked the S-2 to stand up.

Normally the S-2 briefs first, giving the usual data about weather, enemy strength, and any recent sightings of opposing units. The intelligence officer had let his BICC lieutenant handle that duty, reserving his comments for this time, during the explanation of the ground maneuver plan. The first lieutenant explained that the Dragons would most probably face the motorized rifle regiment in an encounter battle, and he explained his reasoning to the listening leaders. The S-2 emphasized that the MRR outgunned the 34th by a wide margin and that the battalion was the sure loser in any running shootout. Furthermore, he pointed out that if the Furlong/Whale aperture was left unwatched, the battalion could expect a heavy flank attack from that area, probably while the Dragons were fully engaged farther west from their front. Gesturing forcefully, the S-2 pointed at the pass and then at the gully complex near the valley rollover. The task force must block the pass and move quickly to get into the wadis on Furlong Ridge. If TF 2-34 could do that, the OPFOR would be forced to try to clean the Dragons out of the wadis without dismounted infantry and without the shock effects of a flank assault.

The colonel stood up as the S-2 finished, touching the map at the same two points and explaining the 34th's plan. Team A would be used to block the pass if the enemy flanking threat materialized (that was why Alpha was beefed up). Teams B and C would speed to the little washboard and establish a hasty defense if the MRR appeared. The enemy would have only two alternatives: dig the 34th out without dismounted men (very costly), or withdraw. In either case, victory would go to the 34th.

There is a danger in assuming the enemy's actions will go a certain way, but the Dragon TOC had covered its bets by preparing for the worst possible case. As any intelligence type would agree, if the unit is ready for the height of enemy capability, it could always deal with lesser actions. The real crux of the battle (if the S-2 was right and the MRR descended) would be the race for the defensible ground and the blockage of the pass. If the Dragons were sluggish, they would be pursued and wiped out on the sloping, bush-dotted plain.

The commanders and special platoon leaders returned to their units, dismayed in most cases to discover that the supply system had broken down again. Tank simulator ammunition was short in Teams A and B, and fueling was limited by dry diesel tankers at battalion (the long road march had recreated the situation of 7 October). The S-1 and S-4 had nothing to do with the otherwise excellent operations order, and the combat trains that had so capably supported the live fire had slipped back to their old, slovenly ways. There were no food/fuel/ ammo push packages, which had worked so well up north with engineer materials.

The lack of fuel and tank ammunition was serious. Diesel tanks were at a quarter or less in most M113s and down to a half in the guzzling tanks. The empty fuel pods on the fuel trucks could not be refilled until early the next morning, but by then the attack would be underway. It was almost 0500 before Team B got its tank ammunition; Team A had to make do with cross-leveling its meager supplies, leaving less than a dozen shots for each Alpha tank.

Part of the problem was the absence of the hard-charging support platoon leader, off inventorying live ammunition for turn-in. The troubles were across the board, however, and the battalion XO's diligence could go only so far to correct things. The S-4 had written a sketchy logistics order, but only a few of his subordinates were briefed. Part of the combat trains had strayed for two hours on the march down from Drinkwater, which did little to help matters. As for the M577 Administration-Logistics Operations Center (ALOC), there was not even a posting of the 34th's OPORD graphics, let alone an attempt to monitor the battle situation. Once more, it was all left up to XOs and first sergeants to extract the teams' and special platoons' fuel and food from the muddle of the 34th CSS organization. The trains sat in a barren, open stretch near Red Pass Lake, camouflage nets unerected, security positions indifferently manned. The colonel had forgotten about his logistics troubles for a day, and like untended weeds, they had grown up again.

The reports from the scout OPs and the 3d Platoon (Bravo) ambush at the time of attack convinced the S-2 that he had guessed correctly. OPFOR reconnaissance BMPs and motor-cyclists had probed each site, though a lack of OPFOR controllers (or inoperative OPFOR MILES detectors) allowed the enemy to escape without losses. The ambush patrol's lieutenant at the gap was certain he had stopped the enemy recon unit before it could detect the two rows of half-buried mines between The Whale and Furlong, though the OPFOR knew someone was there. Like cautious rats, the enemy BMPs had sniffed the trap and backed off. Up on the rollover the scouts stayed hidden and saw BMPs and motorbikes examining the tank trails. The total count of intruding vehicles reported was four BMPs and three motorcycles, close enough to convince the S-2 it was a regimental recon company. The regiment would be sure to follow.

At 0630 the colonel was in his APC, waiting to fall in behind Team A as it turned the corner to lead the battalion attack. Team A was right on the money, spread out in a wide column with tanks leading. The colonel turned around to look for Team B, but it was not there. Nor were the tanks. Bravo's captain was on the radio, reporting he would be late crossing the LD. The colonel was enraged, asking why Team B was tardy. The Bravo captain gave no excuses, but said he would be under way by 0640. Team C was not even on the radio net. The colonel swore and ordered the TOC to go down on Charlie's internal frequency and try to find out what was going on.

There was a reason in Team B, though it was pretty embarrassing. The task force had set "stand-to" at 0500, which meant all men up, all weapons manned, and all tracks and tanks started. Team B's soldiers did not even wake up until 0530, an outright screwup. Because of the patched-up electrical wiring on most of the Boeing-yard tracks, there was a

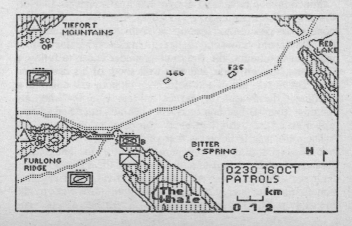

time-consuming struggle with the heavy jumper cables as APC after APC refused to start. Had Bravo's commander insured his men awoke at 0430 for the 0500 battalion "stand-to," these problems would have been solved long before LD time, and the battalion TOC would have at least been aware of them. Missing an LD time is a serious failing, as it throws off the fire support plan and disrupts the maneuver scheme. Missing an LD because of oversleeping was inexcusable.

Team B's late start left the battalion commander with two choices. He could give up mutual support and cut Alpha loose, or mark time and await the dilatory Bravo Team. His decision was heavily influenced by the clear sight of huge dust clouds near The Shelf and, more ominously, a report from the ambush location that there was a big dust cloud south of Furlong Ridge as well. The scouts confirmed the moving clouds both north and south of Furlong Ridge from an observation team near the summit. Now the colonel was in a quandary, with two teams ineffective and strong evidence that the enemy was bearing down on his task force.

The TOC was unable to contact anyone on any of Team C's radio frequencies, and the colonel wasted no more time when the patrol at the pass reported it could see vehicles in front of the dust clouds. The colonel ordered his senior maneuver company commander to take the pass and be ready to hold it against a motorized rifle battalion reinforced with tanks. The Alpha captain affirmed the command and spurred his unit toward the critical pass.

The welcome news that Bravo had finally met its LD followed the colonel's message to Team A at 0640. The Bravo captain was ordered to close up on Team A and move north of the pass toward the wadi complex. In his second major error in less than two hours, the Bravo commander chose to follow a wadi that, though wide, led him well south of his designated path. Bravo was out of action for over an hour and a half as it negotiated the treacherous curves and tangles of the wadi. By the time Team B had emerged from behind Bitter Spring near The Whale, the battle had been won essentially, though nobody in the task force knew that yet.

The advantage in the engagement went to the Dragons as soon as Alpha reached and deployed on the Furlong/Whale Pass about 0715. It was Alpha's swift arrival at the key pass that derailed the enemy plans, coupled with quick work by the fire support officer in guiding in two U.S. Air Force F-4s.[2] The

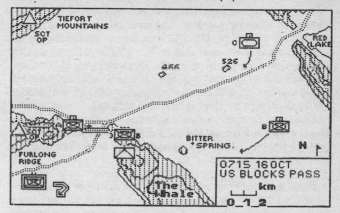

scout OPs were directing the effective artillery barrages and airstrikes on the OPFOR just east of The Shelf and south of Furlong Ridge. The regiment's dust settled as it applied the brakes under American aircraft and howitzer fire and started to pull back, outmaneuvered by a task force fighting with only one effective company team. But the OPFOR were not finished yet, though their game plan was in a shambles. The battalion commander's risky move had paid off. However, it was the disrupted OPFOR, not the Dragons, that sent its lead MRB and tank company to wedge into the mini-washboard to await the Dragons' attacks. The scouts saw it all transpire, and, with good reports from Team A and the ambush patrol, the colonel and the TOC knew what to expect.

By 0815 Bravo had crawled back into the main arena, and the lethargic Charlie Tank, only rarely on the battalion radio frequency, had also closed up. The colonel had been talking to Team B the whole time, and the chagrined captain was determined to get into the fight as he swung north of Team A and moved toward the scuttling OPFOR BMPs. The colonel allowed Team C to continue up the valley to draw fire, urging it to go carefully. Piling force into the Bravo attack, and knowing it would take a lot of infantry to break through the enemy's washboard defense, the colonel gave back to Team B its 3d Platoon and directed Alpha to send a platoon down the top of Furlong Ridge in support.

It was about this time, as Bravo doggedly spread out to begin cleaning the washes and cuts along Furlong Ridge, that the

Dragons lost their Chaparrals, Vulcans, and part of their heavy mortars in a bizarre accident. The three platoons came roaring up, hot on the tail of Team C, and turned south through the Furlong/Whale Pass minefield for some unknown reason. OCs were unable to stop them to assess losses from the U.S. mines. The OPFOR solved that problem. The U.S. vehicles were too close together in addition to being misoriented, and hidden BMPs picked them apart within five minutes. It was another unexplained Dragon miscue. Naturally, as soon as the air defense weapons were destroyed, the OPFOR called in their air power, and two little A-7s streaked in to begin bombing the pass area.

Beating the OPFOR in their washboard defense was the one thing the Dragons had not done in the Central Corridor, and it should be recalled that the colonel had directed some specific retraining on 11 October to develop a technique to beat this enemy method. Not surprisingly, the enthusiastic Team B commander had gone the farthest toward developing the discussed procedure, and he was given a perfect opportunity to test this new desert drill about 0900 on 16 October.

The purpose of the wadi-clearing tactic was to flush the enemy tanks and BMPs up from the wadi corridors onto the berms between the washes, where the supporting fires would destroy the OPFOR as they crested the rills. It was merely a variation on bounding overwatch. Dismounted infantry, heavily armed with Viper rocket launchers and Dragon missile

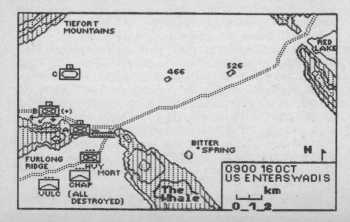

launchers, would descend to the streambeds and move stealthily to engage the enemy armored vehicles. As the enemy was
expecting APCs or tanks in his fire lanes, not riflemen, the
aggressive ground troops could usually get off the first shot.
About a third of the time, a pair of Viper hits or a Dragon
impact would kill the OPFOR combat vehicle, which was fine.
But the other two-thirds of the time, like a bull stung by bees,
the OPFOR track would take a near-miss and try to get away
from its tormentors by climbing out of the wadi (since infantry
in rocks are hard to hit and vehicles are not, driving in forward
or reverse left the OPFOR in the American infantry sights).
When the OPFOR element surfaced, the attacking American
unit would meet it with three layers of direct-fire overwatch.
APC M2HB .50-caliber machine guns would fire from defilade
spots on the reverse slopes of the nearest friendly berm, directly supporting their squads. Tanks would be hull down, one
or two fingers back, TOWs farther back still. Artillery and
mortar shells would be used to cut off the enemy escape. This
method forced the OPFOR to come up to meet the American
overwatch (whereas an American mounted attack across the
grain allowed the enemy to pick off U.S. vehicles one by one
unmolested). It put the OPFOR on the unexpected defensive,
rather than in chosen ambush. Most important, it took advantage of the biggest weakness of the washboard defense (lack of
mutual support from wadi to wadi, BMP to BMP) by systematically isolating and destroying enemy vehicles one at a time.

Team Bravo went after the enemy with vengeance, unload-
ing all three infantry platoons in the first three wadis. The
tanks, APCs, and TOWs disposed themselves to shoot the

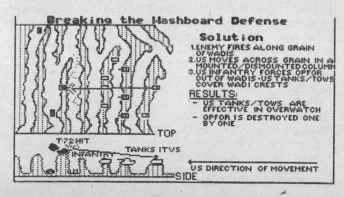

Breaking the Washboard Defense

Solution
1. ENEMY FIRES ALONG GRAIN OF WADIS
2. US MOVES ACROSS GRAIN IN A MOUNTED/DISMOUNTED COLUMN
3. US INFANTRY FORCES OPFOR OUT OF WADIS-US TANKS/TOWS COVER WADI CRESTS

RESULTS:
- US TANKS/TOWS ARE EFFECTIVE IN OVERWATCH
- OPFOR IS DESTROYED ONE BY ONE

TOP

T-72 HIT   TANKS ITVS
INFANTRY

US DIRECTION OF MOVEMENT

SIDE

enemy as he came up, and it was only a few minutes before the Bravo soldiers saw just how effective the new method was. Two BMPs were dispatched one after another, and the infantrymen, their blood up, moved smoothly forward, leapfrogging abreast to clear each crack. Sometimes the stalking Viper men bagged the T-72s in the washes. More often the enemy roared up and took TOW and tank hits from the overwatch element. Up on the crest of the ridge, Alpha's infantry shot down to squeeze the trapped OPFOR vehicles from their flank. Pressure by the four infantry platoons and tanks and TOWs moved the frontline forward slowly but surely, and the OPFOR commander was forced to dig deeper into his combat support assets to help him disengage from the relentless infantry.

The OPFOR response took a few forms. First, the OPFOR began a gunnery duel with the tiny (one platoon) Team C, shrewdly using BMP Sagger missiles (range, 3,000 meters) against the tanks (range, 2,000 meters). The Team C commander, anxious to do his part, ordered his platoon to fire at the enemy missile tracks.[3] By 0930 Team C had been annihilated. But it had done its duty, drawing attention from Alpha and Bravo's infantry.

The OPFOR also made great use of airstrikes. Having destroyed the task force air defense platoons by a lucky fluke, the enemy rotated pairs of A-7s in and out of the Valley of Death, concentrating on team B's potent overwatch tanks and TOWs. The aircraft managed to destroy two antitank missile carriers and a tank in Team B, and a fleeing T-72 got another tank. The jets also pounded Team A back at the pass, knocking out three tanks and two squad tracks. The Antitank Platoon lost four ITVs driving up to the pass (and a fifth later). The 34th passive air defense was weak—after all, they were engaged along their front, and it was hard to camouflage moving troops. Most of the 34th ammunition was needed to kill the ground enemy, so machine-gun and rifle antiaircraft fire was scattered. The Redeye gunners were out of the squad tracks they rode with but got no kills.

The OPFOR also resorted to electronic warfare for the first time on the NTC rotation, jamming the 34th command net at approximately 1000 hours. The Dragons had an easy solution to this problem, an old standard procedure familiar to the scouts, Alpha, Bravo, TOC, and antitank units and, coincidentally, mentioned in the previous evening's operations order. When the command net went blank, all stations switched immediately to an alternate (sometimes called A/J for antijam). Had the alternate been jammed as well, the units would drop to the ground radar frequency, then to the administration-logistics net. It took only seconds to work through the frequencies, and the 34th voices were familiar to everyone by now, so one could tell when he was "home." The sequential switch happened quickly on 16 October, and the OPFOR jammers were not effective.

A BMP shot got the colonel's APC about 1025, and a stray OPFOR tank knocked out the S-3 a minute later. The CSC commander, who manned the alternate command post, had been eliminated in the initial enemy airstrikes back near Furlong/Whale Pass. Task force command devolved onto the Team A commander. Enjoying his best day at Irwin so far, the Alpha captain took charge. He talked to Team B, which was still dutifully working along Furlong, killing tanks and BMPs. His force and vigor kept the attack going, and he began to maneuver the rest of Alpha off of the pass to support the successful Bravo assault. The acting task force commander told the remnants of the TOW platoon to replace Team A at the pass (just in case the OPFOR came back that way). The scouts called in to announce that the OPFOR were pulling back, over The Shelf. Bravo reported that they were out of targets. The fire support officer was gone ("killed" with the colonel), so the Alpha FIST directed some parting barrages onto the retreating OPFOR. The Alpha captain gave brigade the situation and received orders to assume a hasty defense. The brigade S-3 added a "well done."

The company After Action Reviews were positive in Alpha and Bravo, a precursor of things to come at the task force After Action Review. The task force AAR was extremely upbeat. Negative remarks were made about the confused start-off, with a sheepish Team B captain having to explain why he could not start his APCs on time, and the Charlie Tank commander was criticized for being off the radio again. However, this was balanced by the senior controller's remark that the colonel's risky deployment of Team Alpha had gained a positional advantage and ruined the OPFOR plans.[4] This was confirmed by the OPFOR commander, who agreed that he was taken aback by Alpha's excellent speed then chewed to pieces by the Bravo-led infantry assault into the wadis. Task force air defense had been almost nonexistent, with the loss of the air defense platoons and the weak small-arms engagement of the potent A-7s. The enemy air had dealt almost as much damage to the 34th as the enemy ground fire in this engagement. Combat Service Support failures in fueling and arming were brought out, and once again attributed to the noninvolvement of the logistical leaders in the battle plan. It was noted that the task force had not yet recovered from the live fire as far as service support was concerned.[5]

But these problems had been eclipsed by a good calculated risk based on a sound intelligence estimate. Praise was given to task force orders and graphics. The effective counterjamming and change-of-command processes were mentioned favorably. Fire support had been well designed and well executed and had hurt the OPFOR badly. Airstrikes had done much to delay the MRR attack as Alpha raced for the pass. Naturally, the infantry in Team Bravo was noted for its violent, grinding wadi-clearance tactics. The biggest commendation went to the Dragon TOC staff, special platoon leaders, and commanders who had planned and fought a coordinated, difficult battle and overcome problems; command and control was described as "excellent" at all levels. Reporting and crosstalk between units had been especially good.

The colonel could not have been much happier because he had the satisfaction of winning a big one in front of the division commanding general and the brigade commander. He had won it by making the right choices at the right times, and he could thank the S-2, S-3, FSO, Alpha commander, scouts, ambush-patrol leader, and the Bravo commander for the success. The colonel's reputation took a major jump, for he had outthought and outwrestled the OPFOR regiment.

There were some disquieting items, to be sure. Team B had done a great job clearing the crevasse network, but the captain there had been slow getting started on the last two missions (though as reliable as ever once committed). Based on his good performance up until now, the colonel wrote it off to a mistake. As for Team C, the commander had been late and off the radio a lot and had lost his tanks by opening fire before the enemy was within range. The colonel chose to keep Team C small for now.

In the Great Game the Alpha commander's stock took a needed boost. He had been sorely disappointed by his early mistakes at NTC, and now he felt he was performing up to standard. His company seemed to have come together. The battalion commander was confident that he could count on Alpha as well as Bravo from this point forward.

LOSSES:16 OCTOBER 1982

	Tanks		APCs		TOW/Sagger	
	Start	Lost	Start	Lost	Start	Lost
Team A	4	3	11	3	4	0
Team B	3	2	13	5	3	2
Team C	4	4	7	1	1	0
CSC	0	0	5	2	6	5
Bn. TF	11	9	36	11	14	7
OPFOR	40	18	98	9	18	0

Source: *Take-Home Package, Task Force 2-34 Infantry*, pp. III-A-1-1, IV-H-1-1.

TIMELINE: MOVEMENT TO CONTACT
16 OCTOBER 1982

15 OCT 82-0700:	TF After Action Review (Night defense/Movement to contact)
15 OCT 82-1430:	Movement to assembly areas begins
15 OCT 82-1845:	Battalion OPORD
15 OCT 82-2000:	Company OPORD (B Company typical)
15 OCT 82-2300:	Team C ambush departs
16 OCT 82-0615:	Dawn
16 OCT 82-0630:	Line of departure/Time of attack
16 OCT 82-0640:	Team B line of departure time
16 OCT 82-0655:	Team C line of departure time
16 OCT 82-0715:	Team A seizes the pass; enemy MRR attack grinds to a halt
16 OCT 82-0900:	Team B and part of Team A begin clearing Furlong Ridge
16 OCT 82-1100:	TF assumes hasty defense
16 OCT 82-1130:	Company After Action Reviews
16 OCT 82-1400:	TF After Action Review

Notes

1. Philip Caputo, *A Rumor of War* (New York: Holt, Rinehart & Winston, 1977), 268.

2. *Take-Home Package, Task Force 2-34 Infantry*, IV-H-9. The FSO did a particularly fine job, considering the Air Force liaison officer was not present.

3. Norman interview. The author observed the exchanges of MILES shots at the time but did not know what it signified or why it occurred.

4. *Take-Home Package, Task Force 2-34 Infantry*, IV-H-7. The lack of mutual support was still criticized, however.

5. *Take-Home Package, Task Force 2-34 Infantry*, IV-L-30. Page IV-L-28 explains how two Team B tracks were refueled during the actual battle. One was the author's command APC.

Note. Other sources for material in this chapter include: interviews: *Take-Home Package, Task Force 2-34 Infantry*; relevant doctrinal manuals.

Chapter Thirteen

Deliberate Attack (Night)

"A good plan, then, and unexpected good luck to go with it; and yet, as that wet black night unrolls its story, one gets the impression of a queer, uncertain fumbling, as if there mysteriously existed in the army a gap between conception and execution which could never quite be bridged."

Bruce Catton, **A Stillness at Appomattox**[1]

Task Force 2-34 Infantry was back on track, having outsmarted the OPFOR and curtailed the swell of a regimental onslaught in midstride. In the general air of good feeling following the AAR, the S-3 from brigade pulled his battalion counterpart aside and, with a few company commanders listening, issued the brigade fragmentary order for 17 October. The background given was that the 1st Brigade would be going over to the defensive soon, and the Dragons were told to conduct a limited attack very early the next morning to gain control of The Shelf. A motorized rifle company was dug in up there. By seizing this objective, the 34th would control the entire Valley of Death when the task force went over to defense. The colonel arrived late in the briefing, just after a pep talk from the brigade commander. The mission looked easy: a five-kilometer punch to take the most obvious land feature in the valley.

Still, there were two items that mitigated against an easy Dragon victory. The first was the time of attack, 0200 on 17 October 1982. So far everything the battalion had done at night had been marred by navigation trouble and confusion.[2] The other concern was that the 34th had fumbled badly on the night live-fire defense after a very satisfactory showing on the day defense. The conditions here were disturbingly similar: a seemingly simple night followup to a praiseworthy daytime performance. Overconfidence during a military operation is no virtue.

The colonel turned from the brigade S-3's concluding remarks to face the grinning 1st Brigade commander. The full colonel mentioned that Task Force 2-70 had utterly destroyed an OPFOR MRC in a night attack on The Whale a few days prior. The intriguing thing was that the tank task force attacked *mounted*. He suggested slyly that the battalion commander think about forgoing the usual foot infantry night-attack tactics and trying something unorthodox.

The S-3 and Team B commander were already conversing about the best routes for an unilluminated infiltration of The Shelf. This was the usual means of conducting a short-distance offensive in the dark. The Dragon infantry would advance along the bases of Tiefort and Furlong, with the rumbling tanks and the squad M113s moving up to drown out the trudging boots and to provide fire support. The little 692 knob jutting out of Furlong Ridge two and a half kilometers east of The Shelf would be a good spot to halt the tank and APC base of fire. The little knoll would protect the vulnerable vehicles and yet permit them to move to the forward west slope to pummel The Shelf when needed. The S-3 major estimated it would take nearly until dawn to get the walking infantry onto the objective, but he was sure that the combination of predawn gloom and the OPFOR's known shortage of dismounted troops would work in the Dragon's favor. Just to maintain continuity with the original movement-to-contact plan, Team A would strike in the north on line with Team B in the south. Charlie Tank would resume control of Bravo's 3d Rifle Platoon and, with the AT Platoon, provide supporting fires for the two marching companies.

A night infiltration is especially effective against an enemy without strong security postings, and the OPFOR's ground troop shortage certainly made that a likely circumstance. The infantry conducting a night attack dismounted follow a prescribed sequence of actions developed by doctrine writers to minimize the confusion that is possible under limited visibility. The company of infantry forms in an assembly area as usual; then moves forward to the line of departure. The foot soldiers may halt in a covered attack position just short of the LD, normally to await the coordination of other units, to make certain all forces cross on line. Each company files out of a manned point of departure (usually run by the APC teams of the departing company) to assure that everybody leaves together and that units do not wander into each other at the LD. The troops walk up a specific route, guided by pace counts and compass bearings. About a kilometer and a half out from the objective terrain (barring OPFOR interference), the company commanders release their platoons from the march column to come on line under their own leaders. About 800 meters away the platoons release their rifle squads to swing on line and establish a probable line of deployment (PLD) on a recognizable road or streambed designated in the OPORD. Whenever possible, the attacking companies will try to slip out early patrols to secure their PLDs long before the actual attack. In either case, secured or not, the PLD is the start of the assault and as near to the enemy positions as possible. It is positively alarming just how close a reasonably careful group of experienced riflemen can approach at night before the intruders are heard or seen in the blackness. The assault moves through the objective, and at that point (or anywhere en route that the enemy intervenes) parachute flares are normally fired by grenadiers and supporting howitzers and mortars to light up the surprised enemy defenders. A limit of advance is established on a major terrain feature (such as a road) to keep the attacking troops from going too far. It is all very tightly controlled. There are circumstances where the whole thing may be tried without illumination (if the OPFOR is caught asleep, for example, to avoid alerting neighboring adversaries). However, the TOC will always plan to call for light everywhere from the LD to the limit of advance and beyond.

The warning order and the short dialogue between the Team Bravo captain and the operations officer were finished by 1700, and the S-3 went with the colonel back to the TOC. On the way the battalion commander mentioned the brigade commander's advice to attempt a mounted attack. The colonel pointed out that it would not take much work to doctor the movement-to-

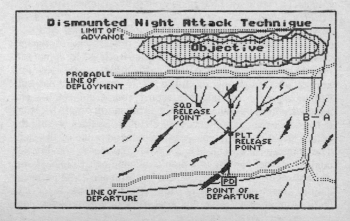

contact OPORD Shelf-attack scheme to create a plan for a
mounted night attack. It would be as easy as driving up the
valley with the lights out, said the colonel. The S-3 could see
the colonel had made up his mind, and by the time they got to
the TOC, the major had shifted his mental gears to calculate the
effects of a vehicular attack. The S-3 had misgivings, which he
would express, but the commander's mind was set.

The Tactical Operations Center was the nerve center of the
task force. Organized around the S-3 section and under his staff
supervision, the TOC was the information-processing nexus
for all data relating to the battlefield performance and readiness
of TF 2-34. Besides gathering reports from the fighting, combat support, and service support elements for brigade, the TOC
also translated the commander's concepts into standard five-
paragraph orders, building these schemes on the basis of the
reports from the units and the notices from higher headquarters. Normally the TOC used FM voice radio to talk to the
companies and brigade, though if stationary for any length of
time, the communications platoon was supposed to lay field
telephone wire. This was rarely done in TF 2-34.

In the TOC one could find three M577s, each belonging to
one of the three major subordinate sections. The Dragons normally connected the command post carriers of the operations
(S-3) and intelligence (S-2) staff crews to facilitate face-to-
face communications and provide an area for order briefings.
The two tracks were linked ramp to ramp by their green canvas
extensions, tentlike shelters on collapsible frames. In the S-2
M577 a single map was maintained, showing the current enemy situation (with friendly-unit graphics included for comparative analysis). The intelligence officers and sergeants
created *drops* (removable clear plastic overlays) to depict terrain characteristics (such as soil trafficability, vegetation, and
key terrain for the ongoing mission), reconnaissance and surveillance plans, and possible enemy courses of action. The
latter was often instrumental in the formulation of OPORDs, as
in the movement to contact on 16 October. Besides writing the
enemy situation paragraph (part of paragraph one of the standard operations order), the S-2 staff monitored the brigade
intelligence net and the battalion command net. S-2 also coordinated recon patrols and ground surveillance radars and requested aerial photography from brigade when necessary.
During the engagements, S-2 kept track of enemy losses, up-

Operations Order Format

Task Organization: S-3
1. Situation
   a. Enemy: S-2
   b. Friendly: S-3
   c. Attachments/Detachments: S-3
2. Mission: S-3
3. Execution: S-3
   a. Concept: Commander/S-3
   b. Subunit missions: S-3
   c. Coordinating Instructions: S-3
4. Service and Support: S-4, S-1
5. Command and Signal
   a. Command: S-3
   b. Signal: Communications Officer

Annexes: (as needed)
      Fire Support: FSO
      Recon/Security: S-2
      Obstacles: Engineer
      Logistics: S-4, S-1, BMO
      March Order: S-3 (to position the force)
      Air Defense: ADA platoon leader
      Air Assault: Aviation element

dated enemy order-of-battle information, and offered educated predictions of enemy activity based on the flow of unit spot reports.

Across the green tarpaulined common space was the S-3 M577. Inside, the section updated a current situation map, based upon radio reports and the operations order graphics for the mission under way. Three FM radios were used, one on battalion command, one on brigade command, and one on administration-logistics frequency. The radios were also remoted to small speaker/transmitters out in the briefing area, so that soldiers working in that space could issue guidance or receive reports while writing at the many small folding desks against the canvas walls. (This was a requirement demanded by the 2-34 battalion commander.) The S-3 section kept two maps outside of their M577 on big easels. One, the briefing map, was a cleaned-up version of the track compartment situation map, with complete logistic, intelligence, and operations graphics. On its peripheral borders were displayed the current task organization and the present unit combat strengths (tanks, TOWs, and infantry squads). This big chart was used to give the commander XO, S-3, or any other visitors a snapshot view of the task force's status without bothering the men inside the two flanking command post carriers. The other map in the extension was marked with the symbology of the operation in process but little else. This was the planning map, used by plan writers, the S-3, and the colonel to cogitate upon their orders. It was often laden with S-2 drop overlays of key terrain or OPFOR intentions.

The S-3 planners usually wrote their orders out under the extension, leaving the track interior to the radio operator and S-3 duty NCO. S-3 had overall responsibility for the operations order production, to include map overlays. The S-3 section also wrote the second paragraph (mission statement) and the third paragraph (execution), the tactical nuts and bolts of any OPORD. Naturally, this scheme of battle was drawn up after consultation with the S-2 and under the guidance of the battalion commander. Some colonels actually provided their own written concept of operations to aid in the preparation of paragraph three, though the TF 2-34 commander preferred to give a detailed explanation to his bright operations officer (or to the equally insightful S-3-Air captain) and allow them to create the graphics and text from that explanation of intent. The operations section also furnished the friendly situation for paragraph one of an order and the "command" information for paragraph five, command and signal. The S-3 coordinated for twelve-hour shifts, furnishing the duty officer for both tours. Of course, during a battle, a displacement, local defense drills, or OPORD preparation, the "off-shift" troops were very much on duty.

The TOC had one other primary component, the M577 run by the fire support officer from 1-35 Field Artillery. This captain's track was parked nearby, though separated to provide some dispersion in the TOC. The FSO and his team planned and coordinated all artillery and mortar fires, gathering input from the company FISTs, culling out duplications, and forwarding the tightened list to the FDCs of the howitzer batteries. The artillerist also sent copies to the elements of the task force, and wrote the fire support annex for every operations order. The FSO track listened to battalion command, the heavy mortar fire frequency, the fire direction net of the artillery, and the artillery fire coordination net. The FSO himself, like the S-2, usually went forward with the colonel in his command track. He left an NCO behind to mind the store.[3]

The engineer, Vulcan, Chaparral, and ground surveillance radar leaders also stopped by the TOC during planning periods to offer advice and information on how to best utilize their assets. Sometimes the scout lieutenant or Antitank Platoon leader would be called in for expert opinions on the use of their units. By doctrine the S-1 and S-4 (and perhaps the motor officer) were required to come up from the combat trains to aid in order preparation, contributing paragraph four and a logistics service overlay to the OPORD. The Dragons had glossed over that fourth paragraph, to their detriment, during the first force-on-force training period. The battalion XO was often forward to consult with the colonel or to get a tactical update. These transients were not permanent members of the command post.

There were two other regular parts of the TOC—a detachment of the communications platoon to run a message center and the headquarters company commander. At NTC the hard-driving motorcycle scouts lent by the 101st Airborne Division (Air Assault) worked here, running written missives to the brigade TOC and trains. The communications officer doubled as the nuclear/biological/chemical officer and provided help to

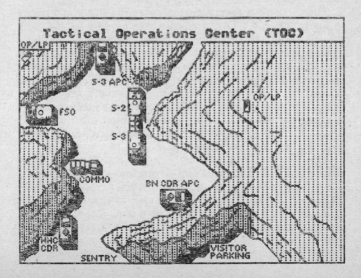

Tactical Operations Center (TOC)

the S-3 in that area, besides repairing and replacing radios with his small team. The communications lieutenant also contributed the last half of paragraph five, the task force signal instructions. The headquarters company commander acted as headquarters commandant, responsible for securing and moving the TOC in accord with the colonel's and S-3's guidance. The HHC captain set up a perimeter security ring around the TOC, using a few listening posts and a sentry at the entrance. Every TOC soldier had a spot on the defensive circle, but they were called to their defensive positions only if the command post came under direct assault.

The headquarters commandant could count on the use of the battalion commander's APC and the S-3's M113 whenever these leaders were not forward. He regularly integrated their crews and weapons into his protection circuit. Additionally, he had his own M113 (which was supposed to belong to the Air Force liaison officer, who obligingly came with his own jeep and his own strange radio configuration). The HHC commander was required to displace the TOC, usually splitting it in half, taking the S-2 track first with representatives from the S-3 and fire support sections to establish the new site. Good communications higher and lower were the priority siting considerations, though cover and concealment were also important.

There was a constant controversy over how often (and when) to move the TOC. Displacement, even by split section, was always very disruptive during a battle. Between fights, there were orders to be produced, and that required a stable environment. Fort Irwin added the unexpected problem of leaders who were driving to meetings after dark and who were unable to find the well-camouflaged TOC, particularly when it had jumped from a familiar spot at dusk. So, even though everybody agreed that the TOC ought to move more often, it tended to get in a hole it could talk from and stay there, SOPs to the contrary and doctrine be damned.

The TOC was kept as orderly as possible. Food and drink were prohibited inside the S-2/S-3 complex in order to preserve the radio logs and operations orders. When an order was completed, an alcohol copy fluid was used to reproduce it, one sheet of orders or map markings at a time. These big white sheets could be seen around the tarpaulin, hanging up like laundry to dry. In daytime the canvas was rolled neatly to permit a breeze in the extension. But at night tight light flaps were lowered all around the dropped canvas walls to prevent leaks from the electrically lighted interior. Day or night, 0200 or 1600, one could find a duty officer from S-3, a shift NCO, an S-2 officer, an FSO officer or NCO, and several clerks and radio-telephone operators busy filling out staff journals, servicing the tracks' engines, posting maps, or talking on the radios. The 34th TOC was run under strict, specific guidelines set down by the colonel. As noted earlier, it usually did a fine job.

It takes only one mistake to lose a battle; the two that lost the 17 October night engagement occurred in the 34th TOC during the composition of the operations order in the early evening of 16 October. The S-2 and S-3 soldiers, concentrating on cranking out orders to meet the 1930 briefing time, were only too happy to avoid the complexities involved in the usual night infiltration. The projected maneuver was quite simple: Team A in the north, Team B in the south, and weak Team C (with its single infantry platoon from Bravo and its sole tank platoon) trailing Bravo to support by fire or to press ahead if needed. For some reason, the planners forgot about hill 692, the small bulb of rocks that jutted off Furlong Ridge dead in the path of Bravo and Charlie and just off Alpha's flank. It was small, and one could drive past it in a minute.

The operation would be mounted all the way, with guide lights on the rear of every track and tank to prevent collisions. Doctrine prescribes a mounted limited-visibility attack when the enemy has been pressed hard all day, to maintain momentum against a weakened foe in a hasty, ill-organized defense. The 34th assumed the motorized rifle company was just a collection of vehicles scattered around the lip of The Shelf. This assumption was questionable, as the task force had not been in contact with the OPFOR since 1100 hours. For some reason (probably the inertia caused by the long AAR and the onset of darkness thereafter), there had been no attempt to keep an eye on The Shelf. The Scout Platoon had lost two of its tracks and most of its men to the OPFOR regiment, which limited its effectiveness until replacements arrived. The companies had taken no steps to fill in for the absent reconnaissance troops. Getting up to the objective to look around was not of much interest to anyone in the TOC either, the second major oversight that sealed the Dragons' fate even before the OPORD was issued.

TASK ORGANIZATION: TF 2-34 INFANTRY
17 OCTOBER 1982

Team A

Company A
3d Platoon, Company C (tanks)
2 AT sections

Team B

Company B (−)
1st Platoon, Company C (tanks)
1 AT section (+ 1 squad)

Team C

Company C (−)
3d Platoon, Company B

TF Control

Scouts (−) (KIAs and WIAs never replaced)
AT Platoon (−) (KIAs and WIAs never replaced)
Heavy Mortars
GSR teams (4), B Company, 124th MI.
Vulcan Platoon, A Battery, 5-52 ADA Battalion
Chaparral Platoon, A Battery, 5-52 ADA Battalion

OPPOSING FORCES (OPFOR) MOTORIZED RIFLE COMPANY

1 Motorized Rifle Company (MRC) (10 BMP infantry vehicles)
1 Tank Platoon (4 T-72 tanks)

It was not the mounted attack that was wrong; no, it could have worked, with provisions for the two factors the 34th colonel, S-2, and S-3 had ignored. The battalion commander and his men got it backward, assuming that since they were operating mounted, the enemy must therefore be weak and conveniently lumped right on The Shelf. Had they led the mounted thrust with a strong patrol to secure the hill 692 and to establish surveillance on The Shelf, the Dragons would have provided for all likely contingencies. Instead, they created a simple plan and trusted the enemy to oblige. A dismounted attack would have forced consideration of hill 692 and the enemy dispositions, or at least the Dragons would have run into him so slowly on foot that reaction would have been easier. By adhering to the brigade commander's recommendation, the battalion colonel might have made a few points in the Great Game, but only if the 34th mission succeeded. The lieutenant colonel was getting a bit careless after the last few days.

The company commanders of Alpha and Bravo were less excited about the form the maneuver had taken. During the 1930 orders group, both captains pleaded with their commander to consider a conventional marching infiltration. Bravo's commander was seriously worried about hill 692, wondering what would be done if the enemy was there in force. The colonel said the task force would react to that situation when it arose. The battalion commander was pleasant, but he refused to alter the plan. Task Force 2-70 had pulled it off, hadn't they? Could the 34th do any less?

The muffled grumble of tank engines and the sharper hum of the M113s filled the middle of the Valley of Death with noise as the Dragons deployed across the line of departure at 0200. Everybody was on time and fully awake, except the scouts and TOW platoon. These vehicles and men had not been replaced and brought back to life because of errors in the ALOC, depriving the task force of its eyes and its main antiarmor punch. The disappointed CSC platoons sat out the attack, betrayed by another foulup in Combat Service Support. Not one patrol had left the TF 2-34 frontlines to check The Shelf. It was too late now, as the dusty columns spread open into their axes of advance, red taillights hooded to allow following tracks to keep up.

Navigation was not a problem this time, and both teams could see each other across the shadowy valley floor. Alpha in the north and Bravo in the south were talking to each other by radio as well, which helped them to keep alignment as they churned slowly up the valley. Both commanders assumed that illumination was on call if needed.

Though no one was aware of it, this trust was unfounded. The fire support teams in the task force were all on the wrong frequency owing to an error made by the battalion fire support officer. This was not known because the last fires on the objective had been shot more than two hours earlier, before the scheduled shift in radio call signs and net frequencies. There had been no other communication traffic, and all was assumed

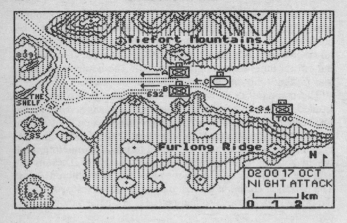

to be well. If the Dragons needed illumination or high explosives, they would have to rely on their mortars. The observer controllers would fire flares if the 34th called properly for light. In the meantime, however, there was no artillery on call, despite a fine, fully disseminated plan.

Throughout the first hour the two lead teams drove through the night, serene and confident that, in fact, the colonel had guessed right again. Like the armor task force, the Dragons would catch the OPFOR napping on their escarpment and overwhelm them. It was getting harder to see or hear with the dust and the track noise, and the laconic radio transmissions lulled everyone into the belief that everything was all right. The colonel was following Team B, and Team C reported it was just behind the battalion commander's dust trail. The S-3 was with Team A to the north.

About 0300 Team B pulled even with the tip of hill 692, and the soldiers were amazed as the sky filled with flares. The Bravo commander received reports that his tanks were taking hits from an unknown direction. The infantrymen and TOWs could not see where the shots were coming from, but the Bravo captain was certain they were coming off of hill 692, hulking just past the left flank of his column. The company could not stay in the open, leaving only two choices. Bravo could turn and assault its tormentors (already a tank and a track were gone), dismounting to clear the hill. The other option was to apply the spurs and try to run out the kill zone, heading for The Shelf. The Team commander wavered momentarily, then ordered his men to drive as fast as they could for the objective. It was the wrong decision, though the 34th commander concurred. Doctrine for a deliberate attack encouraged bypass of enemy outposts and swift movement to the main objective, but the enemy on 692 was no outpost. Team B was heading dead into a firetrap.

So was Team A, also showered with flares and taking losses. It, too, was directed to go for The Shelf, and the colonel called for Team Charlie Tank to come up and clear hill 692. The Charlie captain affirmed that he was almost there, and the colonel watched Team B's column thread ponderously through the well-sited ambush. Nobody could even see where the OPFOR were shooting from in the glare of the illumination rounds and the smoke grenades Bravo had thrown to cover its movement. The OPFOR engaged every vehicle in Team B's column, killing off three of four tanks and all three TOWs. Bravo's commander should have called for illumination on the dark hill 692, but he did not, and his mortars sat idle. In Team A, losses were also mounting, but the Alpha captain exhorted his men to drive for The Shelf. Only three tracks, a tank, and three ITVs made it, saved more by their distance from hill 692 than by sound deployment. The S-3 was "destroyed" in the mad dash. Alpha ran into a fence and mines and stopped to clear it at the bottom of the cliff.

Where was Team C? The colonel called again, since it had been almost ten minutes. The Charlie Tank captain assured his commander that he was just about up to hill 692. But it was five

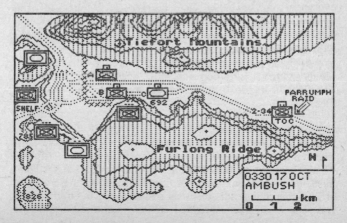

more long minutes before Charlie arrived. The tankers had been dragging very far back indeed. Bravo was on foot, its pitiful remnants of infantry tearing open the south half of the obstacle belt Team A had encountered. Only one tank remained, and it and the two clots of Bravo soldiers killed two BMPs and a tank after breaking through the barrier. Bravo's captain was "dead," and nobody was on the battalion net in Team B. It mattered little; the colonel's track began to flash its kill indicator just as Team C finally arrived, and he also was gone. It was only 0345.

The TOC tried to reestablish communications as the leaders dropped off the net, but the chaos forward was soon exacerbated by a guerrilla raid on the TOC itself.[4] Closely coordinated with the OPFOR ambush, the lightning strike by the Parrumph irregulars was beaten back without loss, but it took valuable time and manpower from the control of the degenerating fight. Alpha's commander went down as his few remaining elements crested The Shelf, and the only leaders forward were the commanders of CSC and Team C. Charlie had stumbled into the 692 ambush, and only the commander (for some reason in the very trail APC) had survived. The debacle was complete. The OCs allowed the infantry in Alpha and Bravo to struggle up The Shelf before stopping the conflict, resulting in the destruction of two T-72 tanks and three BMPs over in Alpha's zone. Bravo's lone tank got the last OPFOR T-72 just before 0530 as the OCs mercifully called a halt to the disastrous proceedings.

Task force losses had been horrendous. Alpha had been reduced to a tank, three M113s, and three ITVs. Bravo consisted of a few foot troops, a backpack radio, and a single tank. Charlie had only the commander's track. The CSC commander's APC and two scout tracks had survived, and the rest of the scouts and the AT Platoon were still "dead" from 16 October. The OPFOR had lost four tanks and five BMPs for their troubles.

What had gone wrong? The company After Action Reviews stressed failures to dismount promptly under effective anti-armor fire and poor use of supporting indirect fires. Alpha's 81-mm section and the battalion 107-mm tubes each fired two missions, and Bravo's did not fire. Considering there was no artillery support at all, this was pathetic. All three maneuver companies had been shredded so fast in the initial OPFOR firing that their subsequent performance barely merited discussion.

The task force AAR was as tough and cold as the previous day's had been encouraging. The loss figures alone were sobering, but the obvious questions were all raised. Why had a mounted attack been tried? Why was no recon effort directed at The Shelf? Why was the 692 knob ignored until it was too late? The colonel sat with his eyes lowered, lacking excuses. He had permitted his pleasure with the Dragons' recent performance to shadow his usual good sense. Task Force 2-70's attack had succeeded because it was launched across open ground with heavy smoke support, not in a constricted valley with clear night skies and a dead artillery net.

Other issues surfaced. The colonel and all of the commanders and platoon leaders except Team Alpha's captain were surprised to hear of a prisoner of war captured at 1700 the previous day. The S-2 said little when he was asked why the prisoner was not searched thoroughly. When the intelligence officer said that he thought the enemy had been examined, the senior controller pointed out that the prisoner had a map of the enemy defenses and a knife in his uniform, neither of which had been confiscated. In fact, the PW had "wounded" two inattentive Alpha guards en route to brigade. Evacuation of the captured soldier to brigade took well over four hours, a gross violation of the usual procedures. The map would have greatly eased the Dragons' many troubles after midnight, as it clearly depicted the fire sack.

The colonel's humiliation was complete, and he dutifully assumed the blame for the miscarried mission. The 34th would shake it off, he assured his leaders. The battalion commander promised his subordinates that he would trust his own judgment and theirs, not the well-intentioned suggestions of people taking showers every night.

LOSSES: 17 OCTOBER 1982

	Tanks		APCs		TOW/Sagger	
	Start	Lost	Start	Lost	Start	Lost
Team A	4	3	8	5	4	1
Team B	4	3	5	5	3	3
Team C	5	5	4	3	0	0
CSC	0	0	5	2	0	0
Bn. TF	13	11	22	15	7	4
OPFOR	4	4	10	5	0	0

Source: *Take-Home Package, Task Force 2-34 Infantry*, pp. IV-I-1-1 and III-A-1-1.

TIMELINE: DELIBERATE ATTACK
17 OCTOBER 1982

16 OCT 82-1700:	Warning order
16 OCT 82-1930:	Battalion OPORD
16 OCT 82-2100:	Company OPORD (B Company typical)
17 OCT 82-0200:	Line of departure/Time of attack
17 OCT 82-0300:	Contact made by Team B; mounted bypass attempted
17 OCT 82-0400:	Team A reaches The Shelf; Team B remnants reach The Shelf
17 OCT 82-0530:	TF remnants assume hasty defense
17 OCT 82-0630:	Company After Action Reviews
17 OCT 82-0830:	TF After Action Review

Notes

1. Bruce Catton, *A Stillness at Appomattox* (1953; reprint, New York: Washington Square Press, 1958), 134.

2. To refresh memories, previous night marches, on 6, 12, and 13 October, had been very mixed up. The 13 October night defense was poor.

3. Besides the FSO, the colonel's track included the S-2 and an NCO from the S-3 section to post maps. The S-3 usually used his own track in a different, secondary sector or zone.

4. Norman interview; *Take-Home Package, Task Force 2-34 Infantry*, IV-I-2. There is some disagreement over how many times Parrumph guerrillas raided the TOC. Captain Norman recalls two unsuccessful raids and the last, successful attack. As the NTC controllers note poor TOC security on 17 October, this author has gone with Captain Norman and recorded the third, initial Parrumph assault.

Note: Other sources for material in this chapter include: interviews; *Take-Home Package, Task Force 2-34 Infantry*; relevant doctrinal manuals.

Chapter Fourteen

Delay in Sector

"General, if you put every man on the other side of the Potomac on that field to approach me over the same line, and give me plenty of ammunition, I will kill them all before they reach my line."

James Longstreet to Robert E. Lee, Fredericksburg, 1862[1]

For the second time during NTC Rotation I-83, the 34th had suffered such extensive losses that observer controllers allowed unit replacement.[2] This method simulated the way in which a severely weakened battalion would be supplanted by a different, fresh unit in an actual conflict. It was the final slap in the face, crowning the humiliating reverse on the night attack of 17 October, yet it was also a relief to the battalion's haphazard logistics system, freeing the combat trains from the dreary business of sorting casualties and requesting replacements for men and armored vehicles. The battered supply sections could concentrate on the more immediate problem of bringing up truckloads of wire and land mines for the next mission: delay in sector.

It was 1030 on 17 October when the battalion staff and commanders received the definite word from brigade. The repulse of the limited-visibility assault on The Shelf left the Dragons in control of the valley basin, with the remnants of the OPFOR motorized rifle company having withdrawn off The Shelf. Brigade's concept assigned the 34th a sector stretching from The Shelf all the way east to Red Pass Lake. The given lateral boundaries anchored on Tiefort and its eastern foothills to the north. To the south the border ran across Furlong Ridge, then north of The Whale, and across the top of the Bitter Springs wadi bowl. In essence, the Dragons' delay could run all the way back across the same turf covered on the 16 October movement to contact. Brigade issued a few caveats in its plan. The task force would have to stop the enemy west of Red Pass Lake, preventing OPFOR penetration of Red Pass. A notional southern task force was blocking Furlong/Whale Pass, so that would not be a problem for TF 2-34. Brigade would not permit a force stronger than a platoon forward of the bottom of The Shelf, reflecting the unsettled aftermath of the Dragons' failure to seize the clifftop. Finally, the 34th must by ready to delay as of 1000 hours on 18 October 1982.

The colonel and his S-3 heard these brigade directives, marking a few salient points on the dirty map sheets plastered onto the battalion commander's jeep hood. Motioning his curious company commanders and special platoon leaders to him, the lieutenant colonel began to consider the best way to go about winning this delay action. It was not the colonel's nature to hold councils of war, though he would listen to suggestions now and then. Shaken by his mistakes on the night mission, the battalion commander sought comfort and reassurance in the company of his subordinate leaders. The colonel wanted to be certain that he did not overlook anything in analyzing the mission.

The S-2 started talking first, used to opening the formal OPORDs and, with his knowledge of terrain and enemy, a logical lead-off man. The intelligence staffer started with the ground, noting that the most defensible terrain was in the western half of the battalion sector. The stretch from The Shelf to the slight rollover six and one-half kilometers east of that cliff was the best place to hold tight, said the S-2. Once one passed that fold in the valley floor, Tiefort's slab sides slipped farther and farther north and Furlong's rocky slopes tapered gradually to the south, opening an ever-wider funnel. While there were decent positions near The Whale, it was out of sector, and the enemy could easily skirt it in the wide flats to the north by staying just out of range. The only positions in the spreading, creosote-crusted plain were a few rocky lumps along the main east-west tank trail, again easily bypassed. It would take extensive engineer work to use this big region to slow the OPFOR. As for the area around Red Pass, it offered good possibilities as a bastion. It would be quite risky, however, to bank one's fortunes on action at that distant, last-ditch location.

With more than half of the 34th's sector a baked, gently sloping creosote-bush field well suited to an OPFOR regimental formation, the S-2 turned his remarks to the six and one-half kilometers at the west end of the Valley of Death and the adjoining Shelf. If the enemy attacked in regimental strength (and that would have to be assumed, given the minimum three-to-one ratio of strength needed to beat a defender), the OPFOR

TASK ORGANIZATION: TF 2-34 INFANTRY
18 OCTOBER 1982

Team A

Company A
3d Platoon, Company C (tanks)
2 AT sections
1 engineer squad

Team B

Company B(−)
1st Platoon, Company C (tanks)
1 AT section (+ 1 squad)

Team C

Company C (−)
3d Platoon, Company B

TF Control

Scouts
AT Platoon (−)
Heavy Mortars
DS Engineer Platoon (−)
GS Engineer Platoon
GSR teams (4), B Company, 124th MI.
Vulcan Platoon, A Battery, 5-52 ADA Battalion
Chaparral Platoon, A Battery, 5-52 ADA Battalion

OPPOSING FORCES (OPFOR) MOTORIZED RIFLE REGIMENT

3 Motorized Rifle Battalions (MRB) (31 BMPs each, plus 2 in HQ—95 total)
1 Tank Battalion (Reinforced) (53 T-72 tanks)
1 SP Artillery Battalion (18 x 122-mm SP howitzers)
1 Recon Company (3 BMPs, 9 BRDM2s, 5 motorcycles)
1 Antitank Battery (9 BRDM2s)
1 Antiaircraft Battery (4 x ZSU-23-4s, 4 x SA-9s)

would have to squeeze their march columns into the Valley of
Death along three well-defined entrance corridors. One motorized rifle battalion, with an attached T-72 tank company leading, could be expected to debouch to the north between Tiefort

and ridge 839. Another MRB with tanks leading would emerge in the center, pushing through the gap between 839 and hill 785. The final OPFOR battalion would squirm up from the south, between the west corner of Furlong Ridge and the north-south 826 feature. With the Furlong/Whale Pass out of bounds, these were the only vehicular routes into the valley floor. The S-2 confirmed the obvious when he stated that both ranges, the soaring Tiefort and the jumbled Furlong, were impassable to vehicular traffic.

The S-3 had listened thoughtfully to these points, then brought up some tactical factors to complement the S-2's incisive comments. The brigade had authorized up to a platoon atop the escarpment; why not station the scouts' usual three observation teams on the north face of 839, in the rock clutter of 785 and on the east side of hill 826? In that way the Dragons could survey each of the three inlets. The S-3 recommended getting the scout sections in position immediately after the breakup of the ongoing consultations.

Based on the width of the western part of the valley, units on Tiefort and Furlong could mutually support across the central floor, as it was between 1,500 and 2,000 meters from side to side. TOWs could be placed in the forbidding crags on either side of the sector, dismounted and dug in. Bravo Company's three antitank missile squads had enjoyed great success on 9 October with similar techniques. Tank 105-mm main guns would also be effective throughout the west part of the canyon. This close concentration of weapons would grow increasingly harder to achieve as the battalion moved back into the expansive open ground east of the Valley of Death. The narrow end of the valley was tailor-made for barrier construction, and the engineer platoon leader (back with the 34th but still short some heavy equipment)[3] agreed that he could block the valley with successive engineer constructions.

The fire support officer added that he had authority to plan and execute three long antiarmor FASCAM fire missions. FAS-CAM is an acronym for Family of SCAtterable Mines. Artillery FASCAM consisted of a carefully spaced barrage of special 155-mm rounds that released numerous small minelets just before the casing struck the ground. FASCAM comes in both antitank and antipersonnel varieties, usually mixed in the volleys just to keep the enemy honest and to force him to breach the instant obstacles. The little mines had automatic self-destructor mechanisms, so that after a specified time, the

U.S. units could drive through them with relative safety. FAS-CAM was good for reseeding broken barricades, covering open flanks, or choking defiles. It was best fired atop an enemy already struggling in a constricted area. The FSO recommended allowing the scouts to direct all three FASCAM minefields, dropping them on the middle of the advancing MRBs in the narrow gorges. The scout lieutenant nodded with agreement, imagining the damage that would occur when the OPFOR's lead units reached the valley only to find their following columns all mired in howitzer-fired mines.

The colonel was warming to these ideas, excited by the possibilities inherent in the tight landforms. The S-4 and battalion XO convinced their commander that the necessary materials to build a solid defense were already on the way. The Antitank Platoon leader commented that he was certain even a few decent obstacles would turn the area just east of The Shelf into a Valley of Death indeed. Even the engineer lieutenant, rarely a contributor to the battalion's planning processes, gestured with excitement at the valley floor near little 692, vowing that his dozer blades and soldiers could shut off the valley as cleanly as a series of concrete dams. Yet the colonel wondered a little. After all, his mission was delay, not defend a battle position.

The substance of a delay mission is to fight the attacker hard enough to force the adversary to deploy for assault time after time, killing OPFOR vehicles in the process. Wearing down the enemy through attrition without losing one's own force is the key. Sometimes, the mission is a "low-risk" delay, allowing the U.S. commander to do what he can to stop and destroy the enemy columns without sacrificing his own force. More typically, the U.S. commander is given a "high-risk" delay, such as the one the 34th had gotten on 17 October. Here, the American units must hold the enemy for a certain time and/or in front of a specific landmark. When the delaying elements run out of space and time, they are expected to trade blood and bodies. The enemy must not get by.

Delay tactics differ from defense tactics in that units avoid the close-in battle (under 1,000 meters), working the enemy with indirect fires, tanks, and TOWs. Delaying forces in a high-risk situation will fight the close battle to accomplish their assigned tasks, but the delay positions are often poorly prepared for a short-range slugfest because of the short time given to prepare for most delays and the long distance of the average delay sector. Delays are what divisions do when they are too weak to defend themselves or to attack the enemy facing them.

Battalions don't usually fight delays on their own. They usually operate as part of a brigade or division delay, which at battalion level turns into a succession of defenses, withdrawals, and counterattacks. But battalion task forces might delay on their own if a heavier enemy attack was striking elsewhere in the brigade, the situation posited in the 34th's orders from 1st Brigade.[4] The things the Dragon commander was hearing from his subordinates sounded like recommendations for a static defense.

The Team Bravo commander was often a source of advice. He spoke up forthrightly at this time, referring to his company's good fortunes in the Central Corridor. Without real artillery to scare the OPFOR, real dead men to upset their clockwork formations, heavy smoke to cover the 34th withdrawals, layer upon layer of mines and tank ditches, and tremendous gunnery by the 34th tanks and TOWs, the Dragons had little chance of successfully disengaging from the rampaging OPFOR regiment. Even if the battalion's companies managed it once, where were they to go on the broad expanse of plain that adjoined the Valley of Death? If they ran for Red Pass, they might not get there in strength before the racing OPFOR. Had not the Dragons pointedly avoided a mobile gunfight with a big OPFOR regiment on the 16 October movement to contact? Why try one now?

However, suppose the Dragons didn't try to bound back to Red Pass? Everybody agreed that the first six or seven kilometers of valley were the only place besides Red Pass proper to hold the OPFOR. The Bravo captain concluded that there was a high-risk intent in the mission, so the Dragons should take it literally. Put the whole battalion in the valley, wired and mined in tight, without withdrawal lanes or fallback battle positions that would never work anyway. Use the available time to dig ditches and bunkers, suggested the captain, and forget about running. The position would be so strong that as long as the Dragons had ammunition, no ground assault down the canyon floor would break it.

The colonel asked the Alpha captain for his opinion, and he agreed with the Bravo commander. The S-3 also thought the battalion should hold in the Valley of Death. The colonel thought a minute or two then began folding up his map. The operations order would be issued at 1200 at the TOC. The 2d

Battalion (Mechanized), 34th Infantry, and its attachments would stand.

There was much to do after the operations order, but the 34th had time to accomplish most of its tasks for a change. Scout Platoon deployed forward onto The Shelf, hiding watchful OPs above each of the three entrance lanes. Team Alpha, still with all three infantry platoons and its attached tanks and TOWs, went forward to emplace around hill 692. Team Bravo, minus its third rifle platoon and with its customary tank and TOW attachments, arrayed east of Alpha, facing north into the basin bottom. Team Charlie, still truncated with a tank platoon and Bravo's third infantry platoon, spread out across the valley floor just west of the critical foldover where the Valley of Death opened out to the east. Charlie would benefit from a major tank wall to its immediate front that the engineers were building, allowing it to fight effectively in the clear ground. The vitally important Antitank Platoon was fifty feet up on Tiefort's side, strung in ground-mount bunkers from Team C's northern corner west to hill 692. The engineers were charged with creating two major obstacles: a minefield with wire fence stretching from hill 692 to Tiefort Mountain and a yawning tank ditch/tank wall/mine barrier furrowing from wall to wall just in front of Charlie Tank. The air defense platoons spread across the sector to provide overlapping Vulcan cannon and Chaparral missile coverage to the whole task force.

A defending company team has many competing tasks that must be done in a short period of time, so doctrine establishes priorities of work to aid the building efforts.[5] These priorities change slightly with the unique requirements of each different mission. Battalion task force priorities of work are more flexible, with the quick commencement of engineer reinforcement of terrain quite high on every list. In general, however, the priorities of work are fairly similar from squad through company level on every defensive assignment.

Following a leader's reconnaissance and delineation of platoon sectors, the company team begins to work on its defensive area. The first priority is local security, achieved in daylight by the occupation of observation posts and in darkness by close-in listening posts. These security emplacements are manned continuously to provide early warning to the working soldiers on the battle position. The OP/LPs may be augmented by patrols and are augmented by the detection capacities of task force-controlled assets such as the scouts or ground surveillance radars. Security spans the entire period of defensive preparation. It is a vigilance that can never safely be relaxed.

The second priority of work is the positioning of weapons and soldiers to bring fire into the designated engagement areas. Before Fort Irwin it was not uncommon for company commanders in the 34th to give their platoon leaders a general chunk of ground to prepare and leave it at that. The Bravo commander, while still a company executive officer, had been taught by a Vietnam veteran to use a more effective method: personally emplacing TOWs, tanks (in close consultation with their crews and leaders), and company-designated obstacles, then aligning his infantry platoons to guard the big guns and the barriers. By 17 October 1982 Bravo Company had refined its standard operating procedures. The captain sited tanks, TOWs, obstacles, infantry platoons, and infantry platoon engagement areas. Platoon leaders positioned their APCs, squads, machine guns, and Dragon missile launchers to sweep their near-battle engagement areas. Squad sergeants set in the riflemen, grenadiers, and Viper rocket-launcher men. The siting leader made sure he got on the ground, not just airily pointing here and there as he walked about the area. Alpha still used the old, more general, technique. Charlie Tank used only its limited variety of order and map directions.

Once everything was put where it belonged (and after the usual shifts back and forth to tie in flanks), fields of fire were marked and cleared, and range cards were prepared. Machine gunners would have their assistants walk their final protective lines, watching over their gunsights to see if their partners dropped out of sight in any dead space, then mark the covered

Priorities of Work

Following leaders' reconnaissance:
1. Provide security
2. Position key weapons
3. Clear and mark fields of fire
4. Prepare fighting positions
5. Emplace obstacles
6. Prepare alternate/supplementary positions
7. Lay communications wire

"Improve positions"

ground on t...
adjusted to allow ...
men and checked by the
whether Viper, Dragon, TOW; ...ghting positions had to ...
maximum range and erected maximu... it was done by the ...ntiarmor gunners,
was especially important for the missile crew... out to their ...kers. This
farther through their sights than they could reliably ...ld see
Squad sketches summarized the interlocking lattice of gunfire,
and platoon sector diagrams took the squad sketches and added
indirect fire targets. All of this went to the company commander, who with his FIST officer and mortar leader completed the fire support plan and a detailed company defensive
drawing. Battalion S-3 got a copy of the company layout, and
the FSO got the target overlay and list.

While the leaders consolidated the many range cards into
sector sketches, the soldiers moved on to their fourth priority of
work: digging in. This was the big one, because a failure to
fully complete a good examination of fields of fire before turning dirt could result in (at best) a changed emplacement site
and more digging or (at worst) an unintended gap in the crossfire frontage. Soldiers naturally wanted to dig first, then fit their
weapons' directions to whatever hole they hacked out. This
backwards method was likely if leaders did not enthusiastically
keep the men on the scheduled priorities. Once he was allowed
to start shoveling, the average regular Army infantryman would
have a good hold in a few hours (even in the hard, basaltic
rocks in the California high desert). Left alone for a day with
sandbags, lumber, and steel plates, he would create a stout
bunker.

The fifth priority was the construction of obstacles. Mines
were the easiest to use, and the fastest. Concertina wire rolls
were also employed, usually along the final machine-gun protective lines. The 34th had learned at Irwin that relying on a
single engineer platoon (or even two, as occasionally showed
up) was no guarantee of a sound barrier plan. Infantry units did
most of their engineer work in the under-1,000-meter area.

The sixth priority was the choice of alternate and supplementary positions. Like "aggressive patrolling" and "frequent
TOC displacement," these positions were always mentioned
and rarely designated. The idea was that each tank, TOW, or
troop had at least one other spot (alternate) from which to fir
into his main target area, and another place (supplementar
from which to shoot into an unexpected direction, such as fl

...ued these alternate locations,
or rear. Tanks and ... ...uid soon blanket any source of
since enemy ...tected rush to their next positions (let alone
rounds dama... ...ofi to really try it under intense artillery bombard-
to survive ...ade alternate positions moot without trenches to reach
their i... ...Use of supplementary emplacements meant that the sit-
...efi. uation was already getting out of hand (the enemy was on an
unanticipated flank), and the ground troops would have to be
moved, hazardous though it would be. This choice of alternate
and supplementary positions also referred to examination of
subsequent BPs and the evaluation and rehearsal of movements
to reach these rear locations. The 34th plan for its delay in
sector had a few "goose-egg" BPs drawn in depth, but the
colonel and S-3 told the commanders not to worry much about
them. They seemed to be on the overlay for the sake of form.

The seventh and final formal priority of work was the provision of communications wire from the company command
post forward to the platoons. Platoon leaders would have wire
run to their squads. OP/LPs carried field phones and backpack
radios linking them directly to the platoon and company headquarters.

There was an eighth step, and it never changed and was not
usually on the doctrinal lists, though it was always mentioned
in the adjacent texts. This measure was to "improve positions," and a defensive position was never beyond improvement. There was no such thing as a completed field fortification
by the exacting standards of professional officers or sergeants.

There were really only four priorities of work that had to be
done in order. Security, siting weapons, clearing/marking
fields of fire, and digging had to be done in that order to permit
a coherent defense. There was no problem with having some
people work on laying commo wire or fusing land mines, as
long as no rifleman broke ground on his hole before the firing
lanes had been thoroughly walked, cleared, marked, and inspected. In TF 2-34 the strictest adherence to these defense
rules could be seen in Team B, with the AT Platoon and,
surprisingly, Charlie Tank also close to the mark. The TOW
and tank gunners have a trained knowledge about the impor-
ance of range cards and maximum engagement lines, and
...harlie had Bravo's equally indoctrinated 3d Platoon. In Alpha
... situation was not as cohesive, but that was balanced by the
...that Alpha would be fighting a close-in battle at hill 629 the

whole way. The Team A ~~mactor~~ or without set trajectory paths.

As the riflemen chipped into the ~~ot lack for targets, with~~ trudged out to plant their range stakes (~~b~~th and the tankers strips that could be seen after sundown), th~~e~~ little luminous was chugging along on the tank ditch and tank ~~weer platoon~~ Charlie. Parts of the DS platoon were still way up no~~for Team~~ TF 2-70 in its live-fire training, but the GS platoon w~~as~~ ~~lping~~ hand, as well as two blades, a D-7 bulldozer, and a combat engineer vehicle. The engineers got involved in hauling mines and wire for some reason (probably because, in the world of peacetime property accountability, their company commander had signed for those controlled materials). Blade time was also used to dig tank positions for Team C, stuck as it was out in the flats. Nevertheless, major progress was being made, and a single lane in each of the two main belts was to be closed at 0900 the next morning.

The S-2 and S-3 collaborated on a set of combat patrols to protect the building effort and blind the enemy reconnaissance teams. Unwilling to expose the well-hidden scout OPs to tangle with OPFOR recon, the TOC sections devised a schedule of protective maneuvers that included all three companies. Charlie Tank would sweep from its tank ditch to the Alpha minefield and back, staying north of the northernmost tank trail on the valley bottom. Bravo was to watch the area between Team A's position and its own, sticking to the turf south of the northern tank trace. Alpha would run a guard force up and

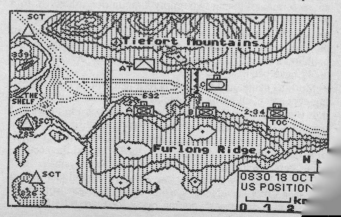

...field to intercept OPFOR infiltra-
down the outside o... to begin its squad moves at 2100 and
tors. Each comp..., well after dawn. Contact points were
to end them ...northernmost and southernmost ends of the
designated ...fence to allow the three patrols to coordinate.
Team A... were encouraged to rotate squads to allow for rest,
Comp...yes, and continued work in the main emplacements.
fres,

There were some nagging weaknesses afflicting the Dragons as the bulldozers scraped and the infantry patrols crossed the dark valley. The ground surveillance radar teams, burdened with finicky equipment and riding in excess M577 double-decker command post carriers, had become a liability over the last few missions. Repeatedly, their complex scanners had either broken down when needed or been unable to "see" OPFOR vehicles crawling through the waist-high scrubs. The clear desert air allowed alert soldiers to outperform the sophisticated electronic systems, even at night. Exasperated with the balky devices, the S-2 took a half-serious suggestion by the Team B captain and used the GSR M577s to create a false TOC, leaving them in the old command post location to await repairs and, it was hoped, to draw off the Parrumph guerrillas. The ruse worked, but the observer controllers with the Parrumphs noted the misuse of a potentially valuable asset.

The Parrumphs were active across the task force rear, though the toiling frontline infantry and tankers were undisturbed. The TOC was struck again as the sun set, though it managed to chase off the irregulars without loss. The combat trains were not so fortunate, losing two empty ammunition trucks, all four fuel tankers (also empty), the ALOC M577, and several soldiers. This disruption was embarrassing to the S-4, but most of the task force had refueled already, and the damage to the battalion's service support network was less serious than it could have been.

Morning came, and the patrols returned with stories of fleeting encounters all along the Alpha barrier. The OPFOR recon unit was unable to cut open the wire or breach the mines and never got to the B or C positions. Two enemy BMPs made it to the front row of mines after midnight, but the usual night-time dearth of switched-on MILES, the OCs, and the accurate ring kept the brushes "bloodless." The enemy surveillance ...ort had been thwarted. For the Dragons, the hidden scouts ... seen OPFOR vehicles starting up in their garrison motor ... back on main post, getting ready for their activities.

a f[...]
with the [...]
Then 0900 came and [...] ~~in Sector~~
ricades, starting out near Team[...]
were not coming back. The bulldozers [...]
troops moved slowly back past Furlong Ridge to maint[...]ing
tracks, clean up, and sleep. They had been digging, stringing
wire, or pulling dozer laterals since 1300 the previous day,
fueling on the run from a rotation of diesel trucks and five-
gallon cans.

The infantrymen fussed like grandmothers over their positions, shoring up overhead cover or walking firing alleys for
the hundredth time. MILES was zeroed on tracks sent down
into the killing zones on the valley bottom. The S-4 had more
barrier material to bring up, and only about half of the ground
holes had overhead protection, but the colonel refused to permit the barriers to reopen until after the attack. The TOC
laconically relayed reports from the scouts, who still reported
bustle in the OPFOR motor parks but no movement yet. So the
time droned on, with minor foxhole alterations, leader inspections in all the companies, eating, shaving, and watching and
waiting. This time the 34th was ready, keyed up, and convinced that it was all going to come together. They waited with
the anticipation of a master hunter watching for the big game
to enter his baited ambush.

High noon, and now there was motion from the direction of
main post as huge dust clouds billowed up, rising in thin gray
pillars hundreds of feet straight up. The scout OPs were all on
the battalion command net, tracking the incoming motorized
rifle battalions the way NASA radars follow an orbiting space
shuttle. The commanders and TOC could visualize the proud
OPFOR columns, rolling in to avenge the accidental mishap of
16 October. Alpha reported that OCs were allowing jeeps with
smoke generators to park along their barrier, no doubt to represent the heavy smokescreen the enemy was sure to call for as
his tracks approached the 34th.

By 1230 all the shovels had been stowed, and the dusty
chemical suits zipped up. Helmets were on, eyes were peeled,
and most of the machine gunners, tankers, and antitank missilemen had already loaded and were searching their assigned
sectors. Riflemen banged blanks into place and neatly stacked

"banana clip" ... on the rims of their
fighting parape... ...ated, their tubes cranked
onto their fir... ...Drata, tied by radio to the platoon
forward... ...th... then it came, confirmed by the scouts.
The M... ...entering the three twisting approach corridors.
...counseled the fire support officer, eagerly watch-
...the telltale dust rising all around the west edge of the
valley. The scout lieutenant, his slow drawl creeping across the
radio with practiced calm, told Alpha and the TOWs to watch,
for the lead tanks were about to nose onto the visible part of
The Shelf and head downward. In the basin the smoke jeeps
began spewing forth gray clouds, and the scouts called in to
report that the OPFOR were increasing speed. The leading
vehicles appeared on The Shelf, green dots with high, straight
dirt smudges behind them.

Now came the hard part, the necessary risk. Alpha and the
TOWs had to wait; they had to keep their eyes squinting and
fingers tense, but they must not fire until the enemy filled the
bowl between cliff and minefield. Then, with the OPFOR driving for the fenceline and their following BMPs crowding into
the defiles, the scouts would unload the FASCAM that even
now (simulated, of course) waited in the tubes of the supporting big guns. The OPFOR came forward smartly, spreading
out as they came off the escarpment, waiting for their smoke to
cover them. But the Dragon colonel clapped his hands with
glee, because the smoke climbing from the churning generator
jeeps was drifting skyward in stringy, dark, beautiful, utterly

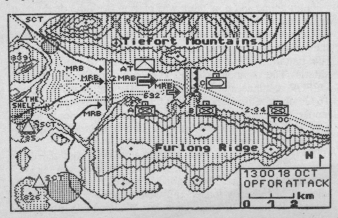

useless wisps.[6] The OPFOR came on, exposed, ranks thick in the tight confines of the valley. They approached the land mines.

The FSO was screaming now, the scout lieutenant calling for the FASCAM, calling in the patches of sky mines on the unsuspecting, shoving clusters of BMPs. The colonel stared out at the worthless, twisting smoke streams and ordered Alpha and antitank to engage. The north lower face of Tiefort erupted in white smoke, and hill 692 was swathed in clouds of backblast. By the time the sound rolled back to the colonel and the operations officer, the gunsmoke was lifting, and many yellow lights were spinning in the milling mass of enemy tanks and BMPs.

The idea was for Alpha and TOW to fight the battle at the front obstacle, then for Bravo's TOWs and tanks and Charlie's tanks to join in once the enemy breasted the minefield. It would be critical for the tanks to wait until the OPFOR had come in a third of the way past the Alpha barricade, as enemy Saggers could hit the tanks the whole way, but the M60 main guns were effective only out to two kilometers.

The information from the scouts revealed that the enemy had lost several vehicles in each of the attack lanes and that the tail end of all three columns had been cut off and stranded by the minefields since all the OPFOR assault engineers were well forward and unavailable to help clear the scatterable mines. What the enemy had in the valley was all he was going to get.

This good news was balanced by the report from Team A that it was under heavy assault all along its front but that the minefield was holding. Team A's positions around hill 692 were popping with smoke and clattering with all varieties of weapon sounds. Artillery missions were constantly being fired. Even the long-neglected heavy mortars and Alpha and Bravo 81s were deluged with fire requests from ecstatic forward observers. This, truly, was a "target-rich environment."

It was the battlefield the TOW was built for, and the ground-mounted systems of Antitank Platoon were tearing whole strips out of the OPFOR array. As the enemy sat in the bowl suffering, three MTLB open-topped armored carriers (actual Soviet artillery ammunition tracks sent by the Israelis) with OPFOR engineers were straining to break through the belts of antitank and antipersonnel mines. It was 1330 before the OPFOR soldiers got two lanes through, but by then the force on the valley floor (less destroyed comrades across The Shelf in the FAS-

CAM or walled off behind the artillery mines) had been trimmed by half. The enemy rolled through, however, picking up speed.

Alpha continued to shoot, as did the TOWs, shifting to follow the decaying OPFOR battalion. An armored vehicle launched bridge (U.S. type) was in the southernmost battalion, following the shrunken engineer squads toward the tank ditch. Bravo's TOWs began execution at their typically effective long distance, and so, remarkably, did every M60 in Charlie Tank. The colonel raged as the badly out-ranged American tanks tried to shoot at BMPs 3,000 meters away. The Charlie Tank captain blissfully reported, "Am engaging T-72s and BMPs at maximum range and achieving multiple hits," confidently crediting his men for kills made by TOW and Alpha. The colonel's frustration was increased as the OPFOR BMPs coolly slowed to a halt and picked off the Charlie Tank M60s, one after another. Within five minutes six M60s were gone.

And the OPFOR came on, littering their path with blinking carcasses, thrusting in three truncated masses for the big tank ditch. The TOW crews were running out of ammunition, and in the AT Platoon, a pre-positioned trailer was dragged up the rocks by hand to reload the key weapons. Bravo's tanks joined in, stripping off BMPs and T-72s. The enemy slowed as he reached the second major barrier, firing back with the precision for which he was famous. Bravo lost a track and two tanks, but the infantry of Bravo's 2d Platoon down near the ditch joined with its cross-attached 3d Platoon friends in Team C's sector to pummel the enemy engineers with rasping machine guns. A Bravo TOW got the AVLB a scant hundred meters from the ditch, and the Team B 81-mm section fired by direct lay from its location to blast the OPFOR engineer MTLB. Artillery bursts peppered the valley floor, the little simulators flowering among the halted, flashing OPFOR vehicle casualties.

The pounding continued, and it was evident that there were problems controlling the meager remnants of the OPFOR. One MTLB ran headlong to discharge its men near the TOW platoon's emplacements, where they were beaten off by rifle fire from the determined missile squads. Alpha, still very much in action on hill 692, sniped against OPFOR stragglers wandering in the boneyard that was the valley bottom. The OPFOR had failed utterly, and the only thing to do now was to pull back the shattered wreckage of the great motorized rifle regiment. Scuttling around their scattered, mute fellows, the last half-dozen

LOSSES: 18 OCTOBER 1982

	Tanks		APCs		TOW/Sagger	
	Start	Lost	Start	Lost	Start	Lost
Team A	2	2	12	12	4	3
Team B	3	2	8	1	3	0
Team C	6	6	4	1	0	0
CSC	0	0	5	2	9	0
Bn. TF	11	10	29	16	16	3
OPFOR	53	46	98	52	18	0

Source: *Take-Home Package, Task Force 2-34 Infantry*, pp. IV–J–11 and III–B–1–1.

TIMELINE: DELAY IN SECTOR
18 OCTOBER 1982

17 OCT 82-1030:	Warning order
17 OCT 82-1200:	Battalion OPORD
17 OCT 82-1330:	Company OPORD/Leader recon (B Company typical)
17 OCT 82-1600:	Units in position
17 OCT 82-2100:	Early patrols out
18 OCT 82-0300:	Late patrols out
18 OCT 82-0830:	Main obstacle belts complete
18 OCT 82-1230:	Scouts engage
18 OCT 82-1300:	Enemy main body appears/Enemy smoke ineffective/FASCAM strikes
18 OCT 82-1330:	Enemy breaches Team A obstacle
18 OCT 82-1430:	Enemy attempts to breach tank ditch; repulsed by Team B and Team C infantry
18 OCT 82-1500:	Enemy survivors withdraw
18 OCT 82-1530:	Company After Action Reviews
18 OCT 82-2000:	TF After Action Review (Star Wars trailer)

BMPs and a few tanks withdrew as fast as they could, spitting a few random shots without effect. A TOW got one of the BMPs as the pitiful column passed.

Alpha was nearly out of ammunition, and the six American tanks blipped out in the basin, the sole serious Dragon foolishness in an otherwise sterling performance. The colonel could see blinking BMPs and T-72s carpeting the engagement areas, and the scouts assured him more enemy tanks squatted ''dead'' in the three tight crevasses. The battalion commander was surprised to hear loud, raucous shouting drifting from Alpha on 692, rising from Bravo around and above him, rolling across the ridges from the TOW bunkers and echoing back, swelling with the fullness of pride. And then the colonel knew and climbed atop his track with the jubilant S-3 major. The colonel joined his soldiers, all of them cheering wildly like little children in the bright desert sun. The Dragons had destroyed the OPFOR regiment.

Notes

1. Douglas Southall Freeman, *Lee's Lieutenants, Volume II* (New York: Charles Scribner's Sons, 1943), 364.

2. The first such unit replacement occurred after the 9 October defense in sector.

3. Some of the engineer equipment was up north, aiding TF 2-70. Remember that the engineer platoon consists of the three squads, M561 1¼-ton truck, and a dump truck. All other items were attached by C Company, 3d Engineer Battalion.

4. Department of the Army, *FM 71-2 The Tank and Mechanized Infantry Battalion Task Force* (Washington, D.C.: Headquarters, Department of the Army, 30 June 1977), 5-2. Delay is usually a cavalry mission, but there is only one cavalry squadron in a division.

5. Department of the Army, *FM 7-7 The Mechanized Infantry Platoon and Squad* (Washington, D.C.: Headquarters, Department of the Army, 30 September 1977), 5-36. This manual was the current (1982) doctrine for H Series rifle platoons and squads. It was the source for NTC controller inspection of priorities of work.

6. The ineffectiveness of the enemy smoke was probably caused by the early afternoon prevailing winds and the temperatures in the open ground. Smoke is more effective at dawn, since it hugs the warm ground the way fog does.

Note. Other sources for this chapter include: interviews; *Take-Home Package, Task Force 2-34 Infantry;* relevant doctrinal literature.

Chapter Fifteen

Defend in Sector (II)

"But really I think one shouldn't leave a man too long in a position of such heavy responsibility. Gradually, he loses his nerve. It's different if one's in the rear. There, of course, one keeps one's head."

Adolf Hitler[1]

The After Action Review at 2000 was eagerly awaited by the jubilant Dragon leaders, anxious to relive their smashing triumph. The convocation would occur in the brightly lighted, air-conditioned Star Wars trailer where the 34th commanders had been so soundly rebuked on the evening of 9 October. Now the task force had crushed the OPFOR, crushed them by a risky interpretation of mission, crushed them by bold use of mines and large-scale ambush, crushed them by teamwork from private to colonel, and absolutely crushed the motorized rifle regiment in full view of the observer controllers and report keepers. It was a victory of record, and a quantum success in the Great Game. The colonel could coast for a long time on this one.

The actual substance of the AAR was less dramatic than the expectant commanders and staff had hoped. The senior controller was congratulatory, but he also ticked off the usual array of sins on his little placards. The colonel was taken aback when he was chided for being unable to observe Team Alpha's sector. Combat trains losses from the Parrumph raid were covered, with the standard comments about weak security. The GSR role as a "false TOC" was decried as an indefensible wastage of the radar tracks. Finally, the senior OC denigrated the engineer effort. He pointed out that the obstacles were not out at maximum standoff range (though the front mines were backed off from Teams B, C, and part of the AT Platoon). The controller went on to annotate shortcuts in construction techniques on both obstacles, quoting engineer field manuals to back up his contentions that the tank ditch was too shallow and that the Team C tank hull-down spots were dug in backwards. (The spoil on a tank emplacement should be spread out to the rear, not lumped in front like a loose parapet.) The senior OC also blamed poor Combat Service Support supervision for the fact that the engineer troops spent an inordinate amount of time hauling barrier materials instead of installing them.

Much of the criticism centered on the colonel's rigid decision to stand in place. Alpha and the scouts should have had withdrawal routes, said the senior controller. There should have been subsequent battle positions. Still, as the controller's chart stated, "The TF rendered an OPFOR motorized rifle regiment combat ineffective."

More positive remarks came out too, though not in the glowing words the Dragon leaders wanted to hear. TOW fire coordination slowed and destroyed the OPFOR, making use of all systems and flank shots. TOW and tank gunnery and positioning rated as "good," and fire support complemented the battle plan. Mortars and artillery, especially FASCAM, were found to be "effective." Air defense platoons stationed themselves efficiently. The final kill statistics were one-sided, even allowing for the OC inclusion of Alpha and some scouts just because they had been "overrun." The enemy had lost forty-six of fifty-three tanks and fifty-two of ninety-eight BMPs in the slaughter pen. The meeting ended with congratulations from the 1st Brigade commander, the 24th Infantry Division commanding general, and the brilliant, moody assistant division commander for training.

The battalion colonel and his subordinates crowded around their brigade commander, who smiled and said that the mission they were about to get was their last one. The Dragons had delayed so well that they would shift to an actual defense. The full colonel said the 34th should be ready to defend by 0500 on 20 October, building up their current lines and reinforcing their obstacles. The brigade commander cautioned the Dragon colonel to plan positions in depth and leave gaps for the withdrawal of forward units; after all, that was doctrinal. (The OCs had mentioned as much in the AAR.) Based on the 34th's great victory, the Dragons would be permitted to occupy The Shelf with as much force as the lieutenant colonel chose to employ. The brigade commander then stepped back, allowing his operations officer to issue the details for the Dragons' last task of the NTC rotation.

As the 34th S-3 copied down the new mission information, the ADC-T motioned to the Dragon battalion commander. This senior colonel could not be ignored, as he was third in rank in the division. Aside from the normal, proper deference to experience and rank, there were possible implications for the Great Game. True, this assistant division commander did not write major portions of maneuver battalion commander officer efficiency reports (OERs). The division commander wrote the most important remarks on the OER of each of his battalion commanders.[2] At NTC the commanding general could judge the Dragons' performance for himself. But the NTC exercise was nearing completion, and back in the Fort Stewart garrison, things might become clouded. There the views of the ADC-T might influence the Dragon commander's reputation. Cognizant of that senior officer's biting "hey girls" speech of 13 October, the 34th colonel listened carefully to the assistant division commander. The Dragon leader was leery of unsolicited "advice" after the night-attack debacle, but this full colonel was not a man to be taken lightly.

The ADC-T emphasized something the brigade commander had suggested. Get a force upon The Shelf, he told the battalion commander in no uncertain terms. Stop the OPFOR early; do not let them deploy. If the task force could get a strong outfit up there, TF 2-34 could start killing OPFOR earlier at very extended ranges. The ADC-T recommended liberal use of night-vision goggles and ground surveillance radars to extend the vision of the forward team. The battalion commander nodded as he heard the ADC-T's thoughts.

The lieutenant colonel returned to the tail end of the brigade S-3's briefing and told his operations officer that the Dragons would sleep that night. He told the small assembly that they would have to get a force up on The Shelf but took no steps to do so at that time. By ones and twos the 34th leadership went into the cool desert night, looking forward to some solid rest. Security that night across the task force was almost nonexistent. The OPORD was set for 0800 the next day.

The skies were uncharacteristically overcast as the standard group of commanders, staff, and special platoon leaders gathered under the canvas extension spanning the S-2 and S-3 M577s. Speculation about rain alternated with exciting stories of the previous day's tremendous success. The captains and lieutenants joked and relaxed, pleased by the fact that tomorrow the NTC engagements would be over. The Bravo captain remarked that he had heard wars were like this, and the battalion XO, a Vietnam veteran, said that combat was easier, with a few important, hair-raising exceptions.

It was 0800 on the nose, 19 October 1982, when the colonel took his central seat and the S-2 cleared his throat to begin. The intelligence officer ran through a quick analysis of the now-familiar Valley of Death, then turned to the OPFOR. He ventured that the enemy would try a dawn attack, using the three entrance channels. The OPFOR would try to make better use of its smoke, which tended to hang right over the ground just before sunrise. The S-2 lieutenant anticipated a stronger, more persistent OPFOR recon effort, with definite attempts to open the forward minefield under cover of darkness. When the attack came, it would be a repeat of the day before, a full regimental array.

The S-2 had concluded his factual summation of the situation, but he did not move off to the side just yet. He offered some opinion statements, reaching into his own undergraduate and graduate schooling in psychology at Temple University. Had anyone watched the OPFOR commander at the AAR? The intelligence officer had seen some unusual actions. The OPFOR leader usually lounged in AARs, coming forward to brief his plan then retiring calmly to the rear of the group. This time the OPFOR boss seemed intent, taking numerous notes. His briefing had been curt and bitter. He had made none of his customary jokes.

The S-2 explained what he thought these changed activities augured. The OPFOR was accustomed to winning with their standard game plans, which had worked time and time again during the first year of NTC rotations. The regiment had been chagrined on 18 October; its lieutenant colonel had a big reputation to protect. The S-2 lieutenant guessed that the OPFOR would try something unorthodox to regain their status, though beyond better use of smoke, a dawn assault, and a beefed-up reconnaissance threat, the S-2 could see no other likely means of altering the basic OPFOR tactics. The ground simply did not permit it.

Then the S-3 came forward to brief the Dragons' program for 20 October. Discounting any strange aberrations the OPFOR could apply, the operations officer and his men had developed a scheme that compromised the need to hold the strong lines the battalion occupied with the colonel's insistence that an element occupy The Shelf. The task organization had some changes. Alpha remained intact with its usual reinforcing

TASK ORGANIZATION: TF 2-34 INFANTRY
20 OCTOBER 1982

Team A

Company A
3d Platoon, Company C (tanks)
2 AT sections
1 engineer squad

Team B

Company B(−)
1st Platoon, Company C (tanks)
1 AT section (+ 1 squad)

Team C

Company C (−)
3d Platoon, Company B

Team Satyr

2d Platoon, Company B
Command vehicle section, HHC 2-34 INF.

TF Control

Scouts
AT Platoon (−)
Heavy Mortars
DS Engineer Platoon (−)
GS Engineer Platoon
GSR Teams (4), B Company, 124th MI
Vulcan Platoon, A Battery, 5-52 ADA Battalion
Chaparral Platoon, A Battery, 5-52 ADA Battalion

OPPOSING FORCES (OPFOR) MOTORIZED RIFLE REGIMENT

3 Motorized Rifle Battalions (MRB) (31 BMPs each, plus 2 in HQ—95 total)
1 Tank Battalion (Reinforced) (53 T-72 tanks)
1 SP Artillery Battalion (18 x 122-mm SP howitzers)
1 Recon Company (3 BMPs, 9 BRDM2s, 5 motorcycles)
1 Antitank Battery (9 BRDM2s)
1 Antiaircraft Battery (4 x ZSU-23-4s, 4 x SA-9s)
(1 MRB was dismounted for this operation)

tanks and TOWs, dug in out on knob 692. Charlie Tank stayed as before. Team Bravo surrendered its second rifle platoon, the one near the big antitank ditch, to a new element created to go up on the escarpment. It was designated Team Satyr.

Satyr was under the command of the Headquarters Company commander, who had been pleading for a more active role in the fighting. The code name referred to the HHC captain's (and to some extent, the battalion commander's) alleged barroom escapades. Besides Bravo's two-track 2d Platoon, it included the S-3 APC and the HHC's captain's M113. Satyr's mission was to get up on the west edge of The Shelf as soon as possible to destroy the expected enemy recon attempts. In the morning Satyr was to call in artillery high explosives and FASCAM on the approaching regiment. The command vehicle section was told to strip the TOC of its M60 machine guns, Vipers, and Dragons, which up until that time had been helpful in staving off Parrumph incursions. Satyr would also establish an infantry antiarmor ambush in the southernmost inlet gorge, optimizing the shock effects of close engagements by the infantry AT weapons. Team Satyr's return was not fixed, though the colonel pointed out that Bravo would regain control of its 2d Platoon prior to the arrival of the OPFOR main body.

The rest of the plan was the same as the setup for 18 October, though lanes were to be created in both obstacles to allow the return of the scouts, Satyr, and even Team A, if necessary. The commander of Company C, 3d Engineers, was on hand to supervise the refinement of the task force barrier diagram. Nevertheless, the S-3 prudently placed the CSC commander and the alternate CP at the tank ditch to supervise the blocking of that crucial gap. Alpha retained an engineer squad, as it had the day before. This squad was to close the opening on order, whereas the day before, it had been on hand to help with local mining operations. The basic construction duties prescribed by the OPORD were more in the line of shoring up present barricades than building new ones.

Fire support again relied on the full spectrum of delivery means and rounds, with a major use of FASCAM. Five FASCAM missions were allotted, and the two new ones were zeroed in on the intentional lanes in the major obstacles, just in case the enemy prevented closure. Airstrikes were available and were integrated into the target overlay. The indirect fire system had been a big killer on 18 October, and the plan required only minor adjustments to meet the needs of Team Satyr.

Some new players available for the battle (leaden skies permitting) were the speedy, lethal AH-1S Cobra attack helicopters. A platoon of five would be sent by brigade, though they would have no direct command relation to TF 2-34. A battle position was set aside for the powerful attack "birds," and their aviator captain platoon leader had come to the TOC to coordinate and exchange radio information. The Army aviation would hide in the rocky jumble on the eastern tail of Furlong Ridge, popping up to clean away any enemy vehicles that made it through. If the OPFOR did not breach the ditch (as all hoped they would not), the attack choppers would be called up to join in the carnage in the bowl.

In the world of administration and logistics, the combat trains had gotten back the fuel trucks, ammo trucks, and M577 lost in the Parrumph raid. Ammunition was available in the trains, and had been stockpiled forward in each company battle position. Fuel had been replenished, and casualty evacuation on 18 October, employing UH-60 Blackhawk helicopters, had been outstanding and swift. The only real problem was that the Dragons had shipped forward all available barrier materials and mines, and there was still some excess up in the battle area. No new obstacles were designated, as noted earlier. Rather than go back to brigade to get more materials, the logistics officer recommended making do with what was on hand. This was fine as far as the colonel was concerned, but it was a violation of the defensive maxim that positions (and barrier plans) could always be improved. The knowledge that the NTC "war" was ending the next day was causing the service support leaders to cut corners. Considering how costly the S-4's previous shortcuts and omissions had been, it was not wise for the colonel to assent to any intentional logistics shortfalls.

One voice dissented in the TOC, cutting through the general air of optimism. It was the Team B commander, worried about the fact that his 2d Platoon was being pulled for the Satyr mission. The Bravo captain explained that this left no Bravo infantry to cover the big lane the engineers were to doze through the ditch. The captain stated that if his 2d Platoon went forward, he would never see it again. Far worse, holes would be left in the obstacles, waiting for the return of units that would never come back. The OPFOR would come, however, and they would come in force.

The colonel dismissed the Bravo captain kindly but without wavering in his conviction. It was critical to get a unit out to punch out the OPFOR recon BMPs. It was a great opportunity to rack up the score in the narrow canyons. Team Satyr was going to The Shelf.

The S-2's speculations about OPFOR unorthodoxy proved to be all too true. While the Dragon leaders met in the TOC under the scudding clouds of 19 October, the OPFOR's heavily re-inforced surveillance teams were already hidden across The Shelf and a kilometer down Furlong Ridge. The 34th might be wrapping up its war on 20 October, but the OPFOR troops did this for two weeks every month. Fighting, and winning, in the desert was a day-to-day job for them, and they returned to the valley stealthily, hungry for revenge.

The enemy observers squatted in the big rocks, scanning the lethargic Dragons throughout the day on 19 October. A sprinkle of rain drifted over just after noon, but it did not stop the secretive collection effort. Full drawings were made, pinpointing TOW locations, tanks, and the unchanged minefields. The 34th's soldiers dug nonchalantly as the afternoon wore on and the sun and blue sky reappeared. There were no evident alterations from the day before, except where a bulldozer was opening gaps at the south end of both barriers. Those could prove useful. An accurate picture would be returned to OPFOR headquarters.

Two BMPs appeared about 1600 along the crest of Furlong Ridge, just beyond Team A's south flank infantry platoon. The Alpha antitank teams set out in a fruitless chase, clambering up to the razorback ridgeline as the BMPs pulled back. It was a curious incident in that the enemy tracks could barely negotiate the steep, rock-crusted skyline of Furlong Ridge. Alpha called back to the TOC and was told to shift a platoon off the slope and up the ridge line for the night.

The BMP probe was a diversion, covering a small group of skillful OPFOR soldiers who skirted around Alpha and headed slowly east, picking out a path in the big boulders, sticking to the shadows. The Bravo soldiers did not notice the enemy up and behind them. The OPFOR patrol was finding a route for a movement planned early the next morning, in the wee hours. The OPFOR commander had elected to dismount a motorized rifle battalion (an American infantry company filled that role at NTC), giving up a third of his BMPs to put a hundred infantry

on the ground. The OPFOR ground force was to infiltrate down
Furlong Ridge, splitting into three platoons en route. Two
platoons would sneak into Team Alpha, with one proceeding
on to tear open the wire fence, clear mines, and set out smoke
pots. The second platoon would remain hidden, emerging at
first light to snipe apart Alpha's TOWs and tanks from the rear.
The third group would move into Bravo to destroy its TOWs
and tanks as well.

With the infiltration having disrupted and cleared Alpha and
Bravo of their long-range antitank systems, the smoke would
be lighted in the valley and the rest of the regiment would roll.
The OPFOR colonel insisted that his leaders personally survey
and walk their approaches. The BMP probe near Team A was
part of this. Additionally, the OPFOR commander demanded
that his forces occupy The Shelf with strong security units. He
hoped to ferret out the artillery observers who had rained mines
on his OPFOR BMPs.

The 34th obliged its enemies. The OPFOR had been allowed
uninterrupted visual observation of the Dragons' positions
throughout 19 October. The scouts had not shifted position and
were stalked by the OPFOR and marked for later destruction.
Alpha's commander told his flank platoon to put a squad on the
ridge, though he had been told by the TOC to move a platoon
up there. The platoon leader responded by sending up two men
with a TA-1 field phone. This dilution was not reported to the
TOC, and Alpha's commander did not check his high platoon.
So a flank was open.

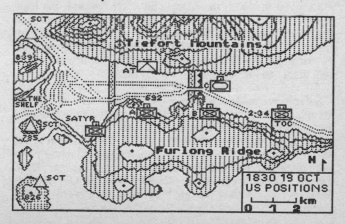

On the valley floor the engineers had puttered about most of the day without doing much more than patching up the concertina wire and replacing mines. The GS platoon was released to move to the north and begin cleaning up TF 2-70's live fire. The DS platoon, less its forward squad, was deployed around the hole in the AT ditch, its D-7 dozer ready to push the ditch shut on order of the CSC commander. The engineer company commander parked near the AT furrow, consulting with the CSC captain. Both commanders stayed the night at the lane in the big trench.

At 1700 the first lieutenant assistant S-3 climbed into a little OH-58 with the aviation platoon leader for a last light recon. The agile scout copter spun around the valley, noting that The Shelf was thick with BMPs wedged into cracks and hollows. The assistant S-3 briefed the Team Satyr commander after he landed in the twilight, and the tall HHC captain marked his map.

The Satyr force had delayed its departure again and again, allowing the Bravo platoon to finish its bunkers during the dull afternoon. The NCO leader of 2d Platoon, Company B, trusted he would return to use the fighting positions. It took awhile to brief and issue ammunition, and all four tracks (2 HHC, 2 Bravo) were laden with blue ceramic land-mine simulators and checked again and again. Finally, at 1830 Team Satyr chugged off on its ill-defined, open-ended mission.

The task force settled down to an unearned good rest that night. Security was marginal in the maneuver teams, and the local patrols of 17/18 October were not utilized. The S-2 and S-3 figured that with the scouts and Satyr forward, the local sweeps were not needed. Alpha ran a patrol down its wire fence before midnight, but the attempt was desultory and unsupervised. In fact, both Alpha and Charlie Tank dropped off the battalion command net just after midnight. It was a clear, cool night, and it belonged to the OPFOR.

Satyr never made it to The Shelf. After a series of random firefights with roving BMPs, the little ambush team holed up in the southern approach canyon. The team found OPFOR columns parked in orderly rows of locked T-72s and BMPs, but the OCs would not allow these administrative field motor parks to be disturbed. It was only fair; the enemy tracks were placed there for the convenience of the hard-working OPFOR soldiers, not by tactical design.[3] Besides, they were heavily guarded.

The TOC had its own problems. With the headquarters commandant and the antiarmor weapons gone with Satyr, the command post suffered heavily in a Parrumph raid just after midnight. The artillery M577 was destroyed in the quick scuffle, along with the commo platoon's M561 1¼-ton truck. Friendly return fire was limited to three rifles aimed wildly at the retreating enemy. As a result, the TOC lost almost an hour between 2400 and 0100, allowing Alpha and Charlie to drift unbothered into slumbering radio silence in the process.

The trickle of infiltrators down Furlong Ridge began at 0200, unopposed by anyone in the 34th. The TOC could talk to Team Satyr, the scouts, and Team B. The forward elements' reports convinced the S-2 BICC officer on duty in the TOC that the dawn attack would be tried for sure. The 34th's stand-to was slated for 0430, so alertness should not be a problem; however, 0430 came and went, with only Team B calling in to report stand-to complete. Bravo would not be caught sleeping again after the embarrassment of 16 October. Charlie Tank and Alpha sent no reports.

Only one-third of the Dragon battalion was awake, and that in the weakened Team B. Bravo's 1st Platoon had already been bypassed by the enemy RPG gunners, who lay curled up, waiting to blast away when the sky grayed. Alpha's little ridgetop listening post had not heard or observed the two enemy units slipping through the Alpha BP. The left flank Alpha platoon's lieutenant woke up about 0500 and went to check his forward team; it was awake but had not noticed any activity. The platoon leader returned to his track, unaware that he was thirty minutes late for the task force stand-to. Alpha stand-to had been set for 0530.

The infiltration had been undetected, and as the eastern sky slowly lighted up into another clear blue day, the OPFOR struck. Alpha's newly awakened soldiers were amazed at 0615 when dark-clad men with Dragons (standing in for Soviet rocket-propelled grenades, which do not come in MILES as yet) rose like wraiths in their midst, killing two tanks and three APCs with the laser shots. Enemy machine guns killed two TOW crews in their emplacements, even as other dark figures ignited many smoke devices along the obstacle belt. This time the smoke flattened ten feet up, spreading like a gray wool blanket in the half-light.

Bravo was no better, losing a tank and a TOW bunker to the OPFOR infantry. Bravo's earlier stand-to helped a little. The

1st Platoon quickly hunted down and "killed" the intruders, but not before another tank and the FIST APC were destroyed. As the reports from Team B came in to the TOC and smoke expanded in the Valley of Death, the colonel tried to raise the scouts. There was no answer.

The scouts were gone, finished off in a quick swath of tank and machine-gun fires. The battalion commander abandoned any attempt to go forward and remained in the bustling TOC. Alpha was as silent as a tomb, and the tip of hill 692 was all that poked through the blanket of smoke. One of the lieutenants ran to the command track, which was closed up tight. He pounded and pounded, but he was cursed away, unable to awaken the irritated commander. Alpha went down easily, its firing disjointed, its radio voice quiet.

Satyr reported that the enemy was on the move, and this puny force got two BMPs before the colonel ordered it to release Bravo's 2d Platoon. The colonel was pleased to hear Team C come on the net, and he ordered the Charlie commander to rush men down to the tank ditch lane. Unable to contact Alpha and concerned that the enemy was through the forward barrier, the colonel directed the FSO to fire all FASCAM. The assistant S-3 first lieutenant went outside the TOC to board an OH-58 scout helicopter, as the TOC waited for word that the Cobras were on hand.

The smoke was thick, and the infiltrators effective. By 0700 the colonel had definite confirmation from the Antitank Platoon on the Tiefort wall that the OPFOR lead units had breached the minefield easily and were heading east. Bravo and Charlie reported that the smoke at Alpha's end of the valley was so thick that nothing could be seen, and OPFOR infantrymen had started smoke canisters in front of the antitank ditch. The CSC commander requested permission to close the wide trench, as he knew the enemy was closing in.

Reporting was fragmentary and disjointed, but the extremely thick smoke was delaying the MRR as well as hiding it. The assistant S-3 notified the colonel that the Cobras would be on station by 0800. The sharp-eyed lieutenant's report from the little scout helicopter shed little light, since all he could see was a grayish white soup from Team C forward to The Shelf. The FSO tugged at the colonel and told him that all the FASCAM except the last target had been fired. This action sealed the dim chances of Bravo's 2d Platoon, creeping toward destruction in a friendly minefield.

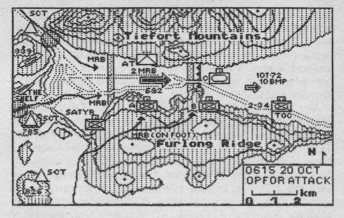

The colonel wanted to pull Alpha back, a pointless move in light of the heavy OPFOR concentration east of the mute forward team. The task force would have to fight where it stood. CSC's captain came on the net to request again that the ditch be closed, but the colonel said "not yet," wavering as Alpha suddenly came up on the command frequency. Should Satyr and Alpha be withdrawn? The colonel gave the order to both, and the HHC commander began bounding his two remaining tracks to the rear. Alpha's captain affirmed the order, but a quick survey of the forward BP convinced the Team A leader that the OPFOR were not through with him yet. So Alpha stayed on 692, trapped by the OPFOR regiment and blinded by the smoke.

The CSC captain disappeared from the radio about 0730. His APC had been eliminated by a lead MRR T-72 tank. The enemy main body was taking losses through shreds in the smoke concealment, with the Antitank Platoon firing down into the boiling stew of tracks and curling obscurants. It would take a short time, but the enemy was approaching the big antitank trench, and the gap still yawned unattended.

The confirmation that Bravo's 2d Platoon was destroyed came in at 0745, and the S-3 instantly ordered the engineer captain to block the gap with his bulldozer. But the engineer captain was not on the radio, and the word from Bravo and Charlie Tank was that the enemy was swarming near the tank ditch. Two BMPs slipped through the lane; then the lieutenant company commander shrieked onto the battalion net. "They're comin' through the gap! They're comin' through the gap! One guy with a Dragon could kill 'em all!''[4] But there were no guys with Dragons nearby, though the tank company infantry was running along the back wall of the tank ditch laden with Dragons and Vipers. The guys with Dragons that belonged in the gap were stalled and blinking six kilometers east, victims of friendly FASCAM.

The Bravo TOWs picked off the two fast BMPs. But the breach was made. The Bravo captain was uncertain about pulling his 1st Platoon down to the ditch, still thick with OPFOR T-72s and BMPs trading shots with the Americans through the drifting smoke. Bravo's 1st Platoon was already farther west on the valley floor, firing into the stalled adversary columns. The colonel said to forget about that and get infantry to the ditch, so the Team B commander turned in his cluttered command APC. His XO was with him, forward to see this last NTC battle. The first lieutenant was ordered to run to the 81-mm mortar section, busy firing simulated missions in a neighboring gully. The instructions were succinct: gather up a few men and the Vipers and get down to the ditch. It was 0750, and Bravo's XO sprinted off, heading into the smoky maelstrom.

The colonel knew the ditch was split and useless, especially with reports that Team C was down to one tank. Bravo's tanks were all gone, and two Team B TOWs were straining to kill the surging enemy forces. Team Charlie's infantry were in the ditch itself, trading rifle and machine-gun fire with OPFOR engineers who were trying to effect another breach. The smoke was clearing a little now, and the Anti-tank Platoon reported it could engage the OPFOR trail elements effectively. The S-3-Air told them to get to work. The colonel wanted to use his FASCAM, but with friendly infantry all over the ditch, it was not possible. About 0750 the colonel ordered Teams B and C back from the ditch, an order easier to give than to implement. It took time the Dragons did not have to lose.[5]

Not surprisingly, the flow and ebb of infantry at the ditch eased the OPFOR breaching effort, which succeeded in pressing vehicles quickly through the hole. OPFOR T-72s and BMPs poured across, though the battalion FSO was cleared to shoot a few minutes later and cut the OPFOR flood about 0805 with a clot of sky mines. The biggest delay to the foe had been the small width of the gap, the only limit on the breakthrough elements. Ten BMPs and ten T-72s were on the loose in the rear, two more tanks having been cut down by Team B TOWs.

But the Dragons had a new trick up their sleeve, and as the penetrating element pushed east, they came under the hovering TOW launchers on five AH-1S Cobras. By 0810 the heavily armed choppers had whittled the enemy unit down to nothing, ducking and bobbing up from south of Furlong Ridge. Of course, it was an observer controller judgment call, since the Cobras had no MILES,[6] but it helped assuage the Dragons' guilt about their sloppy execution. The Valley of Death was sprinkled with many dead OPFOR BMPs and T-72s; however, today there was no cheering. The 34th's NTC battles were over; they had ended with a taste of bile.

The gathering of leaders for the After Action Review occurred in a valley buzzing with activity. Soldiers were busy in their battle positions, picking up construction lumber and training-aid mines, uprooting concertina wire stakes and folding the sharp-edged rolls. Tracks rumbled by, en route to turn in ammunition or to guide the ungainly fuel trucks. The soldiers of the 34th were leaving the Southern Corridor, and in a week's time, all of them would be back in Georgia. For the moment, however, the commanders, staff, and special platoon leaders sat in the open valley just north of the TOC, discussing what had transpired.

It had been an odd battle in that the Dragons had managed a lopsided, "excuse-me" win that they did not deserve. The 34th had lost the reconnaissance struggle, slept through a large infiltration, and been rendered sightless by thick clouds of hanging smoke. The battalion commander and his staff had let their self-assurance get the better of them. In many ways it was similar to the terrible night attack on 17 October, when the Dragons had gotten a bit too impressed with themselves and had tried to play games with tactical basics. There are no immutable laws of war, but combat is a science as well as an art. The Dragons had played fast and loose with the requirements of security, enjoying an easy pace of work on 19 October. They paid for their restful tempo in the mindless confusion on 20 October. Fortunately for the men of the 34th, their terrain location was so innately strong that even serious oversights and mistakes could not tip the scale in the balance of the skillful OPFOR. The casualty statistics reflected the Dragon's narrow success.

The AAR was unusually merciful, though the battalion commander continued to eye his brigade commander, the assistant division commander for training, and the calm division commanding general. How would they react to the comments? The senior battalion OC found fault with the poor security effort, noting the dearth of patrols and lack of leader involvement. The scouts had gotten careless and had been blotted away. The TOC had been raided. Finally, the stand-to was weak again, which doubled the effects of the fine enemy infiltration plan. The biggest errors were the failure to anticipate the thick obscuration (though the S-2 had warned them all) and the late closure of the tank ditch that allowed twenty OPFOR tracks to rush through. The removal of a key infantry platoon from the ditch for the "marginally effective" Satyr patrol contributed to the problems at the gap.

But the battalion commander was not left in the lurch. The commanding general interrupted to defend the 34th, remarking that seeing through smoke so thick was humanly impossible. The OC did not blink in replying that it was a contingency to prepare for, and the general backed off a bit with the remark that he did not see how anyone could have done any better in the turgid fog.[7] It was a significant exchange, and it assured the battalion commander that his unit's performance to date had been considered "good." The senior OC went on to discuss air defense and fire support effectiveness, but the engagement had been ruled a "win" as soon as the general had made his contribution.

The AAR closed as they all had, with the casualty board. On 20 October it showed twenty-seven OPFOR tanks and thirty-two BMPs destroyed, against nine American tanks, eighteen APCs, and four TOW squads. It was a confirmation that, as usual, the privates with the Dragon launchers, the grimy TOW gunners, and the determined riflemen had supplied what was lacking in their leaders' concepts. The average soldiers did not play the Great Game, but they liked to do well at what they did. They did the dirty work for their officers, who sometimes seemed preoccupied with the whims of distant superiors. It is said that a real war can be like that.

This was the NTC, not a real conflict. The "war" ended with handshakes and an exchange of little keepsake awards between OCs and player units. The OPFOR colonel said he would be glad when the Dragons left. TF 2-34 had fought to win and did not quit, the OPFOR leader stated. The 34th battalion commander swelled with pride for his men. With that, the leaders of Task Force 2-34 Infantry concluded their field operations at the Fort Irwin National Training Center.

LOSSES: 20 OCTOBER 1982

	Tanks		APCs		TOW/Sagger	
	Start	Lost	Start	Lost	Start	Lost
Team A	3	2	12	6	4	2
Team B	3	3	8	3	3	1
Team C	5	4	4	2	0	0
Team Satyr	0	0	4	2	0	0
CSC	0	0	5	5	8	1
Battalion TF	11	9	33	18	15	4
OPFOR	53	27	98	32	18	0

Source: *Take-Home Package, Task Force 2-34 Infantry*, pp. III–B–1–1 and III–K–1–1.

TIMELINE: DEFEND IN SECTOR
20 OCTOBER 1982

19 OCT 82-0800: Battalion OPORD
19 OCT 82-0900: Company OPORD (B Company typical)
19 OCT 82-1700: Last-light helicopter recon
19 OCT 82-1830: Team Satyr departs
20 OCT 82-0200: Enemy dismounted MRB begins infiltrating A and B companies
20 OCT 82-0615: Dawn; enemy MRR attacks
20 OCT 82-0700: Smoke screens entire valley; A Company bypassed
20 OCT 82-0730: CSC CO killed trying to close tank ditch
20 OCT 82-0745: Satyr elements eliminated by A Company mines and FASCAM; enemy breaches the main tank ditch
20 OCT 82-0750: Infantry redeploys into smoke at valley floor
20 OCT 82-0805: FASCAM closes breach after ten BMPs and twelve T-72s penetrate; two tanks destroyed by Bravo TOWs
20 OCT 82-0810: Cobras under TF 2-34 Infantry direction destroy penetration forces
20 OCT 82-0915: Company After Action Reviews
20 OCT 82-1130: TF After Action Review

Notes

1. Matthew Cooper, *The German Army 1933–1945* (New York: Stein and Day, 1978), 387. The Hitler quote was recorded by Gen. Walter Warlimont. Hitler was discussing Erwin Rommel in North Africa.

2. The division commander was the senior rater for maneuver battalion commanders in October 1982. Senior rater rankings and comments are generally considered the key blocks of an OER.

3. The OPFOR use these field motor parks to reduce wear and tear on their tracks. The OPFOR troops not involved in night operations are allowed to go to the barracks to sleep now and then.

4. *Take-Home Package, Task Force 2-34 Infantry,* IV-K-2, IV-K-5, IV-K-6, Norman interview.

5. Norman interview. This order caused much confusion, since it was unexplained during the swift flow of events. Just as Team B infantry was heading down for the ditch, it had to be recalled.

6. Norman interview. The Cobra "kills" were not averaged into the final kill results, but the term "overrun" was changed in the formal AAR.

7. The commanding general's intervention was quite unusual, since he usually listened at AARs and did not contribute comments.

Note. Other sources for this chapter include: interviews; *Take-Home Package, Task Force 2-34 Infantry;* relevant doctrinal literature.

Chapter Sixteen

Winners and Losers

"Because such a general regards his men as infants they will march with him into the deepest valleys. He treats them as his own beloved sons and they will die with him.

"During the warring states, when Wu Ch'i was a general he took the same food and wore the same clothes as the lowliest of his troops. On his bed there was no mat; on the march he did not mount his horse; he himself carried his reserve rations. He shared exhaustion and bitter toil with his troops.

"Therefore the Military Code says: 'The general must be the first in the toils and fatigues of the army. In the heat of summer he does not spread his parasol nor in the cold of winter don thick clothing. In dangerous places he must dismount and walk. He waits until the army's wells have been dug and only then drinks; until the army's food is cooked before he eats; until the army's fortifications have been completed, to shelter himself.' "

Sun Tzu, The Art of War[1]

There was a last, supersize, After Action Review held on the morning of 21 October 1982 in an auditorium in the operations group control building. The soldiers of 1st Brigade were back in their orderly little tent city, beginning the unpleasant task of returning their battered tanks and tracks to the Boeing Services Equipment Yard. There would be abusive engagements aplenty over the next few days, rivaling any contention in the Central Corridor, but the battle of the Boeing yard is beyond the purview of this study. Suffice to say that the troops were gainfully employed while the brigade leadership gathered for the final outbriefing.

The Dragons were joined by the officers and senior sergeants of the 2d Battalion, 70th Armor, and by the captains, lieutenants, and sergeants of the 1st Battalion, 35th Field Artillery (155-mm, Self-Propelled). The engineer leaders from Charlie Company, 3d Engineers, took seats, as did the air defense officers from 5th Battalion, 52d Air Defense Artillery. The entire brigade staff crowded into the back of the room, jostling for space with the many service support officers from the medical battalion, the 24th Supply and Transport Battalion, and the 724th Maintenance Battalion. A few confident pilots from 24th Combat Aviation Battalion sauntered in, wearing their flight coveralls. Observer controllers lined the side walls.

The room quieted, and the men came to attention as the commanding generals of the National Training Center and 24th Infantry Division (Mechanized) strode through the door together. The command "take seats" was issued, and the room darkened. An unidentified officer announced that the outbrief would cover both task forces simultaneously and would examine each of the seven systems in detail. Click, and two screens came alive with the activities of 2-70 Armor in tanker yellow to the left and those of the Dragons on infantry blue background to the right.

It was an impressive show, demonstrating that the 70th had suffered most of the same travails that had afflicted the Dragons. Statistical summaries showed surprised Dragon officers that the tank battalion task force had fought only seven force-on-force tangles with the OPFOR. The Dragons had fought eight. Both battalions ran through an identical live-fire scenario. The tank battalion had acquitted itself well, with a string of marginal wins. The armor unit did not have big successes similar to the 18 October Dragon delay mission. On the other hand, the 70th did not have glaring failures in its later operations like the 34th's sorry night attack.

The slide show flashed along, pointing up the weaknesses in each task force. The Dragons on the whole seemed to have shown more tactical prowess than the tank unit, but the armor task force had been blessed with a smooth-running logistics system from the very first battle. The 34th, hamstrung by CSS foulups, had no such advantage. One other thing came through loud and clear. The 70th had used an informal means of generating plans and orders, relying on discussion among maneuver commanders to determine the course of operations. The 34th had used a more conventional series of troop-leading procedures and order formulation. Both ways appeared to have worked.

As the last slides winked out, the lights came on. The commanding general of the National Training Center took center stage and began speaking in his rolling, even tones. This is just a building block, said the brigadier general. Take home the lessons learned and work on them. By all means, cautioned the commander, do not allow the experience of NTC to be forgotten once you are back at Fort Stewart. He looked sternly at the seated men, exhorting them not to lapse into old, bad habits in the less demanding atmosphere of home station, but the brigadier general was lecturing students who felt they had already passed the final exam. The grades, in combat readiness and the Great Game, were already known. For most of the audience, this test was over and already half-forgotten. The "real" Army waited for these men in the garrison and meeting rooms, the officers' clubs and motor pools.

It was not that the leaders wanted to discard their hard-won knowledge; it was, instead, that the daily demands of unit activity at Fort Stewart did not allow for much calm contemplation of the NTC experience. Indeed, it became more typical to hear the Fort Irwin "lessons learned" discussed in the officers' club.[2] Still, the trip to Fort Irwin became the measuring stick, the threat, and the mark of "veteran" soldiers in the battalion. NTC equals war, said the division commander, and the Dragons were true believers now.[3] "That wouldn't work at NTC" was heard many times after the October rotation, from the colonel's training meetings to squad patrol operations orders. As soldiers began to leave the 34th and replacements came in, the men with NTC experience, regardless of rank, became sources of how things should be done.

It would be gratifying to tell how the Dragons returned from the desert and went to the woods, polishing their techniques and refining the rough edges of their organization. It would be great to picture the 34th, desert-trained, united by the hardening communal experience of Fort Irwin, as being fully ready to move for Rapid Deployment Force contingency duties. The Army, however, does not work that way, at least not yet. By bits and pieces, almost as soon as the aircraft carrying the battalion back to Georgia touched down, the teams and squads and crews began to fragment as soldiers, and sergeants left for Germany, Korea, Panama, other stateside units, or civilian life. The departing men carried the NTC training with them and were, no doubt, better soldiers for having been there. Still, the Dragons a year after Irwin were a totally different unit. The only traces of Irwin were written reports, word of mouth, and fading memories of the few officers, sergeants, and troops who had participated in NTC Rotation 1-83. The stories remained, passed along like Norse sagas, and the incremental changes in use of dismounted infantry and logistics push packages testified to Irwin's influence.

Exaggeration and embellishment abound in the Army, and those unable to seek the "bubble reputation" at the "cannon's mouth" willingly settle for a good kill ratio in a MILES engagement and a few favorable comments at the AAR. Ask any old soldier about his battles and he will say he won them all, and NTC soldiers are not an exception to the rule. The NTC cadre does not worry about victories or defeats, but it does not take a Clausewitz to interpret the engagement results and quantify the Dragons' performance.

Task Force 2-34 Infantry participated in eight force-on-force clashes and three live-fire missions. Of those eleven missions, the 34th had accomplished its assigned task five times: the 13 October day defense live fire, the 14 October movement-to contact live fire, the 16 October movement to contact, the 18 October delay, and the 20 October defend in sector. The Dragons had failed in five missions: the 7 October movement to contact, the 9 October defend in sector, the 10 October counterattack, the 13 October night defense, and the 17 October night attack. The deliberate attack on 8 October was a draw, since the 34th had been winning (albeit at cost) when it was mistakenly ordered to halt by brigade. The overall 34th record was five wins, five losses, and one tie.

In terms of real combat, the Dragons' fumbles on 9 October and 13 October (night) were the most serious, since in each case an effective OPFOR regiment sliced through the lines and into the rear area. The heavy TF 2-34 casualties in the 17 October night attack were also quite bad, though the small size of the OPFOR unit precluded any dangerous exploitation by the enemy. It would be fallacious to think that a real American unit could sustain repeated heavy carnage like those defeats without a morale collapse. But, as pointed out earlier, the fear factor simply cannot be re-created at Fort Irwin. Consequently, units fight to the last man and last weapon.

Aside from two weeks of time and energy spent at Fort Irwin (not to mention the MOJAVE VICTORY II deployment and redeployment periods and the DESERT FORGE preparatory training), the cost (to the American taxpayers) of 1st Brigade's desert exercise was just over three million dollars. For the money, the average citizen got a better trained brigade. Even by inflated Pentagon prices, it was definitely a bargain. How much is a two-week preview of modern warfare worth? Let the American Army lose in a real war and we'll find out.

All the units of the task force had contributed to the Dragon record, though as expected, some had contributed more than others. In the general afterglow of a decent task force perfor-

Final Battle Record
Task Force 2-34 Infantry
NTC Rotation 1-83

Wins: Five

    13 October 82 LFT, Defend a battle position (day)
    14 October 82 LFT, Movement to contact
    16 October 82 FFT, Movement to contact
    18 October 82 FFT, Delay in sector
    20 October 82 FFT, Defend in sector

Losses: Five

    7 October 82 FFT, Movement to contact
    9 October 82 FFT, Defend in sector
    10 October 82 FFT, Counterattack
    13 October 82 LFT, Defend a battle position (night)
    17 October 82 FFT, Deliberate attack (night)

No Decision: One

    8 October 82 FFT, Deliberate attack

---

mance, the colonel was rightfully reluctant to criticize the weak. Praising the strong is all right, but Great Game etiquette is gentlemanly in the extreme when it comes to handling ineffective leader actions. Like any bureaucracy, the Army prefers to damn with faint praise. Regardless of one's social skills or political instincts, the Great Game demands the same exhibition of leadership accomplishment required to train and command men in combat. Perhaps this is why the Army allows the Game to continue; it gets things done in a back-door, corkscrew sort of way.

In the 2d Battalion, 34th Infantry, the colonel could well appreciate the assistance of his Tactical Operations Center. The S-3 had provided good plans on time, and his men had monitored the battles with skill. S-2 section had risen to the occasion, quite often giving lucid analyses of terrain and enemy, which was doubly impressive in light of the S-2's lack of military intelligence training. Communications from the TOC had been dependable, though listening at the other end had sometimes dwindled.

The S-1 and S-4, along with the battalion XO, garnered few laurels for the disappointing combat service support chain. This was predictable; the 34th colonel had ignored supply matters, and they had brought him to a halt more than once out at

Fort Irwin. The 34th logisticians overhauled their standard operating procedures after the rotation ended, but the horses were out of the barn by then. It was too bad, because there had been a lot of work in the CSS areas. The outstanding execution of the rail and air movement to California and back was eclipsed by the missed refuels, the short ammo stocks, and the maintenance slowdowns. Hard work without proper direction is wasted, and the dejected CSS supervisors were forced to accept their shortcomings. They had tried, but there was just too much ground to make up in altering lax Fort Stewart habits.

Combat Support Company's special platoons had all done well. The scouts' overall successes were not marred by their quick exit on 20 October. Scout Platoon saw the battlefield and let the colonel visualize things through their accurate reports. The heavy mortars had done well, improving as the fire support plan got sorted out. The Antitank Platoon had made the biggest turnaround of the rotation, switching from a liability to a devastatingly effective force between 10 and 13 October. This was a tribute to the antitank lieutenant's relentless commitment to sort things out, keep his men informed, and apply DESERT FORGE training to the reformed platoon. CSC's commander had steadied things upon his return from emergency leave, and the CSC executive officer had proven he could tolerate stress.

Of the maneuver units, Company A had recovered well, despite a lapse on 20 October. Alpha sometimes did things the hard way, it seemed, but it did things, and the colonel was grateful for that. The company was at its best in conditions requiring tight control. The colonel thought he could count on Company A. As a result, he did not begrudge the company commander's methodology. Alpha had persevered despite a poor start.

Bravo had been the rock of the battalion. Company B's infantry had been aggressive throughout. The company learned the NTC ropes faster than the others, and Bravo's troops applied their skills in defensive positions and obstacle breaching with practiced professionalism. Perhaps having two NCO-led rifle platoons made the difference. In any case, Bravo had made fewer mistakes than Alpha.

Charlie Tank's role at Irwin had been strangely schizoid. Tank fires usually accounted for about half of the battalion's kills (with TOWs getting a quarter and infantry weapons, mines, air, and artillery splitting the rest), demonstrating that C Company's gunners and tank sergeants knew their trade.

Getting positive action out of the company itself, as a head-quarters or as an entity, however, was an uncertain proposition. It was hard to even contact C Company regularly on the radio. That weakness deprived the task force of its armored punch and altered the tempo of operations. C Company's reduction to two platoons in the last force-on-force period was no accident. The colonel was ready to reduce it to one, but terrain stayed his hand.

The fire support officer recovered from his early errors, galvanizing his FIST soldiers to produce some truly outstanding fire plans. The artillery observers contributed mightily to the 34th victory on 18 October and had done much to salvage a win from the smoke on 20 October. How much can one tell about artillery without really firing it (done only during the live-fire maneuvers)? The observer controllers had been stringent in demanding proper planning techniques, and the FSO had responded. The FSO had not seemed to be a strong link before the rotation began, but he had grown in his duties to become a valuable member of the task force.

The air defense platoons had done their tasks well, and both the Vulcans and Chaparrals endeared themselves to the TOC by staying on the radio net. The ground surveillance radar sections remained on the radio as well. The mechanically unreliable radars provided no support to the battalion commander, who was only too happy to disregard them. That was not smart, since the radar teams could have done much to alleviate the infiltration on 20 October. These attachments sometimes seemed like a couple of balls too many in the TOC's juggling act, but by the second week the 34th could at least keep track of, if not fully employ, them.

The hapless engineers were the true sad sacks of Irwin, edging out even the tank company headquarters and the logistics organization for dead last in performance. In all fairness the responsibilities of building barriers and blowing them open were so crucial to every mission that few men could have pulled it off with style. The colonel had to admit that his supply system had not helped the engineers much; the S-4 rarely brought up materials in a timely fashion. Nevertheless, the engineer image at Irwin would be frozen forever in the colonel's mind: a little row of vehicles at a diesel pumper while Bravo's infantry picked through the big minefield at Objective GO. The timing was always off.

*   *   *

This examination of Task Force 2-34 Infantry concentrated on leaders and their actions. In the final view that is where a conflict will be won or lost. The best troops, the best rifles, the fastest tanks, and the most sophisticated missilery are all just means to an end. The linkage of all the disparate units and terrain—the seven systems, if you prefer—is the responsibility of the officers assigned to command. The Army offers a dedicated man the latitude to make decisions that will result in life or death, victory or defeat. The U.S. Army sends battalions to NTC so leaders can learn how to make and carry out those decisions.

Commanding a mechanized infantry task force is a complex, demanding job. As the Dragons' operations make clear, it is not just a matter of issuing a few directives then sitting back and putting pins in the map. Command takes a mixture of imagination and experience, tempered with enough humanity to remember that soldiers are men, not "assets." But of all the things that make a good commander, force of personal example is the most important. "Follow me" is not just a nice thought for the orderly room wall.

The soldiers watch their leaders at all times, and the privates judge their activities by what the commander does or does not do. Does the platoon leader check range cards; more important, does he check them by walking the sector and getting down in the fighting position? Has the company commander looked at the breaching drill in 2d Platoon—can the "old man" demonstrate and explain how to do it if the troops do not know? Will the battalion commander check the minefield the engineers put in? Is the captain in his sleeping bag at midnight or out crawling from hole to hole, checking his men? And probably the most critical question when the battle starts: Is the commander buried in his radios, "managing," or is he forward, on the ground, with his privates, sergeants, and lieutenants, pulling them onward? Every professional soldier knows the "right" answers, but it is so easy to be lazy, especially in training. "I'll change when the war starts," say the bad commanders.

But they will not, because units fight the way they train, and so will leaders. By giving a glimpse of what a fight with the ruthless Soviets could be like, the National Training Center should be a kick in the head to the slothful and an iron goad to the ignorant. NTC allots complacent American leaders a few Kasserine Passes[4] with only yellow MILES lights and embarrassment to pay. With the OPFOR tearing at them and the observer controllers noting every failing in front of respected superiors, commanders get the urge to change before the war. The blood they save may be their own.

Notes

1. Sun Tzu, *The Art of War*, translated by Samuel B. Griffith (New York: Oxford University Press, 1982), 128–129.

2. There was also a conscious effort to share the knowledge of NTC with fellow battalions as they prepared to deploy to Irwin. The 34th had benefited from the 3-19 Infantry and 5-32 Armor debriefings. Each unit from Fort Stewart that went to Irwin after the Dragons did better than its predecessors.

3. Col. Taft C. Ring, "The Evolution of Training Strategy in the 24th Infantry Mech" (Fort Stewart, Ga.: 24th Infantry Division [Mechanized], 27 May 1983), 1.

4. Kasserine Pass was an American defeat in Tunisia in February 1943. It is examined and discussed at Army schools as an example of what can befall poorly led, poorly employed units in their first battle.

Appendix 1

Order of Battle—NTC Rotation 1-83 (October 1982)

Positions and ranks as of October 1982.

24th Infantry Division (Mechanized)
Commanding General: Major General
Assistant Division Commander–Support (ADC-S): Brigadier General
Assistant Division Commander–Training (ADC-T): Colonel

1st Brigade, 24th Infantry Division (Mechanized)
Commander: Colonel
Executive Officer: Lieutenant Colonel

The Brigade Staff
S-1 (Adjutant/Personnel): Major
S-2 (Intelligence): Captain*
S-3 (Operations): Major
S-4 (Logistics): Major
Fire Support: Major

2d Battalion (Mechanized), 34th Infantry, plus attachments (Task Force 2-34 Infantry)
Commander: Lieutenant Colonel
Executive Officer: Major

The Battalion/Task Force Staff
S-1 (Adjutant/Personnel): Captain
S-2 (Intelligence): 1st Lieutenant*
  Assistant: 1st Lieutenant (BICC)
S-3 (Operations): Major
  S-3-Air: Captain

S-3 Assistant: 1st Lieutenant
S-3 Assistant: 2d Lieutenant**
S-4 (Logistics): Captain
Fire Support: Captain
Chaplain: 1st Lieutenant

HHC (Headquarters and Headquarters Company)
Commander: Captain
Executive Officer: 1st Lieutenant
First Sergeant: First Sergeant
Medical Platoon: 2d Lieutenant
Communications Platoon: 1st Lieutenant
Maintenance Platoon/Battalion Motor Officer: Captain
Support Platoon: 1st Lieutenant

A Company
Commander: Captain/FIST: 1st Lieutenant
Executive Officer: 1st Lieutenant
First Sergeant: First Sergeant
1st Platoon: 2d Lieutenant
2d Platoon: 1st Lieutenant
3d Platoon: 1st Lieutenant
Mortars: 1st Lieutenant

B Company
Commander: Captain/FIST: 2d Lieutenant
Executive Officer: 1st Lieutenant
First Sergeant: First Sergeant
1st Platoon: Staff Sergeant*
2d Platoon: Sergeant First Class*
3d Platoon: 2d Lieutenant
Mortars: Sergeant*

C Company, 2d Battalion, 70th Armor, (attached)
Commander: Captain/FIST: 2d Lieutenant
Executive Officer: 1st Lieutenant
First Sergeant: First Sergeant
1st Platoon: 2d Lieutenant
2d Platoon: 2d Lieutenant
3d Platoon: 2d Lieutenant

CSC (Combat Support Company)
Commander: Captain
Executive Officer: 1st Lieutenant

First Sergeant: First Sergeant
Scouts: 1st Lieutenant
Heavy Mortars: 1st Lieutenant
Antitank (TOW): 1st Lieutenant

C Company, 3d Engineers (elements attached)
Commander: Captain
Platoon (DS): 2d Lieutenant
Platoon (GS): 1st Lieutenant (attached for defense missions only)

A Battery, 5th Battalion, 52d Air Defense Artillery (elements attached)
Platoon (Vulcan cannon): 2d Lieutenant (12–20 Oct 82)
Platoon (Chaparral surface-to-air missile): 2d Lieutenant (12–20 Oct 82)

B Company, 124th Military Intelligence Battalion
GSR Teams

Fort Irwin Cadre
Commander, National Training Center: Brigadier General
Chief, Operations Group (COG) ("2d Brigade Commander"): Colonel
Team Chief, "Blue Team": Lieutenant Colonel

OPPOSING FORCES (OPFOR) (elements 6-31 Infantry and 1-73 Armor)
Commander, OPFOR: Lieutenant Colonel (commands 6-31 Infantry)
Operations: Major
1st Motorized Rifle Battalion Commander: Captain
2d Motorized Rifle Battalion Commander: Captain
3d Motorized Rifle Battalion Commander: Captain
Tank Battalion Commander: Captain
Reconnaissance Company: 1st Lieutenant

*These slots were held by soldiers junior to the ranks authorized.
**This position was in augmentation to the standard Table of Organization.

Appendix 2

Schedule, Task Force 2-34 Infantry, NTC Rotation 1-83, October 1982

6 October 1982: Move to Central Corridor
7 October 1982: Force on force, movement to contact
8 October 1982: Force on force, deliberate attack (day)
9 October 1982: Force on force, defend in sector
10 October 1982: Force on force, counterattack
11 October 1982: Live fire, preparation, zero weapons
12 October 1982: Live fire, move to Northern Corridor
13 October 1982: Live fire, defend a battle position (day and night)
14 October 1982: Live fire, movement to contact
15 October 1982: Move to Southern Corridor
16 October 1982: Force on force, movement to contact
17 October 1982: Force on force, deliberate attack (night)
18 October 1982: Force on force, delay in sector
19 October 1982: Force on force, prepare for defense
20 October 1982: Force on force, defend in sector

Bibliography

Books

Bonds, Ray, ed. *The U.S. War Machine (Updated Edition)*. New York: Crown Publishers, 1983.

Cockburn, Andrew. *The Threat: Inside the Soviet Military Machine*. New York: Random House, 1983.

Defense Intelligence Agency. *Warsaw Pact Ground Forces Equipment Identification Guide*. Washington, D.C.: Defense Intelligence Agency, August 1980.

Dunnigan, James F. *How to Make War*. New York: William Morrow, 1982.

Fallows, James. *National Defense*. New York: Random House, 1981.

Hay, Lt. Gen. John H., Jr. *Vietnam Studies: Tactical and Material Innovations*. Washington, D.C.: U.S. Government Printing Office, 1973.

Maclear, Michael. *The Ten Thousand Day War*. New York: St. Martin's Press, 1981.

Sawicki, James A. *Infantry Regiments of the U.S. Army*. Dumfries, Va.: Wyvern Publications, 1981.

Sun Tzu. *The Art of War*. Translated by Samuel B. Griffith. New York: Oxford University Press, 1982.

Suvorov, Viktor [pseud.]. *Inside the Soviet Army*. New York: Macmillan Publishing, 1982.

Suvorov, Viktor [pseud.]. *The Liberators*. New York: W.W. Norton, 1981.

Westmoreland, Gen. William C. *A Soldier Reports*. Garden City, N.Y.: Doubleday, 1976.

Army Publications

Department of the Army. *Armor Reference Data, Volume I*. Fort Knox, Ky.: U.S. Army Armor School, 1979.

Department of the Army. *FM 6-20 Fire Support in Combined Arms Operations*. Fort Sill, Okla.: U.S. Army Field Artillery School, 28 January 1982.

Department of the Army. *FM 6-40-5 Modern Battlefield Cannon Gunnery*. Washington, D.C.: Headquarters, Department of the Army, 1 July 1976.

Department of the Army. *FM 7-7 The Mechanized Infantry Platoon and*

Squad. Washington, D.C.: Headquarters, Department of the Army, 30 September 1977.

Department of the Army. *FM 7-10 The Rifle Company, Platoons, and Squads*. Washington, D.C.: Headquarters, Department of the Army, April 1970.

Department of the Army. *FM 23-1 (Test) Bradley Infantry Fighting Vehicle*. Fort Benning, Ga.: U.S. Army Infantry School, 8 December 1983.

Department of the Army. *FM 71-1 The Tank and Mechanized Infantry Company Team, Coordinating Draft*. Fort Benning, Ga. and Fort Knox, Ky.: U.S. Army Infantry School and U.S. Armor School, April 1982.

Department of the Army. *FM 71-2 The Tank and Mechanized Infantry Battalion Task Force*. Washington, D.C.: Headquarters, Department of the Army, 30 June 1977.

Department of the Army. *FM 71-2 The Tank and Mechanized Infantry Battalion Task Force, Final Draft*. Fort Benning, Ga. and Fort Knox, Ky.: U.S. Army Infantry School and U.S. Army Armor School, June 1982.

Department of the Army. *FM 71-100 Brigade and Division Operations (Armor/Mechanized)*. Fort Leavenworth, Kan.: Combined Arms Center, May 1977.

Department of the Army. *FM 100-5 Operations*. Washington, D.C.: Headquarters, Department of the Army, 1 July 1976.

Department of the Army. *FM 101-5-1 Operational Terms and Graphics*. Washington, D.C.: Headquarters, Department of the Army, 31 March 1980.

Department of the Army. *FM 105-5 Maneuver Control*. Washington, D.C.: Headquarters, Department of the Army, December 1967.

Department of the Army. *Soviet Army Operations*. Arlington Hall Station, Va.: U.S. Army Intelligence Threat Analysis Center, April 1978.

Department of the Army. *ST 7-170 Fire Support Handbook, United States Army Infantry School*. Fort Benning, Ga.: U.S. Army Infantry School, 1983.

Department of the Army. *ST 7-176 Infantry Reference Tactics Data Book*. Fort Benning, Ga.: U.S. Army Infantry School, 1983.

Department of the Army. *TB 9-1200-209-10 MILES, Multiple Integrated Laser Engagement System*. Rock Island Arsenal, Ill.: U.S. Army Armament Materiel Readiness Command, February 1981.

Department of the Army. *TC 7-1 The Rifle Squad (Mechanized and Light Infantry)*. Fort Benning, Ga.: U.S. Army Infantry School, 31 December 1976.

Department of the Army. *TT 71-2J The Mechanized Infantry Battalion Task Force*. Fort Benning, Ga.: U.S. Army Infantry School, 1983.

Documents

Carter, President James Earl. "The State of the Union Address," 20 January 1980.

Daniel, Col. E. L. *After Action Report, Mojave Victory II*. Fort Stewart,

Ga.: 1st Brigade, 24th Infantry Division (Mechanized), 23 November 1982.

Department of the Army. *FORSCOM Circular 350-83-10 Rotational Unit Training at the National Training Center*. Fort McPherson, Ga.: U.S. Army Forces Command, 15 March 1983.

Department of the Army. "Information Paper Live Fire Training (LFT)." Fort Irwin, Calif.: National Training Center Operations Group, 1 September 1982.

Department of the Army. *Take-Home Package, Task Force 2-34 Infantry*. Fort Irwin, California: National Training Center, Training Analysis and Feedback Division, 22 October 1982.

Department of the Army. *Take-Home Package, Task Force 3-19 Infantry*. Fort Irwin, Calif.: National Training Center, Training Analysis and Feedback Division, 20 August 1982.

Leland, Col. E. S., Jr. "Mojave Victory Dependent Information." Fort Stewart, Ga.: 1st Brigade, 24th Infantry Division (Mechanized). October 1980.

Leland, Brig. Gen. E. S., Jr. "NTC Training Observations." Fort McPherson, Ga.: U.S. Army Forces Command, 18 November 1982.

Meyer, Gen. E. C. "The Role of the National Training Center." Washington, D.C.: Headquarters, Department of the Army, 10 March 1980.

Prillaman, Maj. Gen. Richard L. "Career Development, or Stairway to the Stars." Fort Ord, Calif.: 2d Training Brigade (Provisional), 21 March 1972. (Reprinted with cover letter, Fort Hood, Tex., 4 December 1980.)

Ring, Col. Taft C. "The Evolution of Training Strategy in the 24th Mech." Fort Stewart, Ga.: 24th Infantry Division (Mechanized), 27 May 1983.

7th Infantry Division. "Terrain Analysis: Fort Irwin, Brave Shield XVII." Fort Ord, Calif.: 7th Infantry Division, 1 January 1978.

Periodicals

Binder, L. James. "The War Is Never Over at Fort in the Mojave." *Army*, April 1983, 30–35.

Bolger, Capt. Daniel P. "Dragon Team 3-82; Trial Swing of the RDF's Heavy Punch." *Army*, September 1982, 14–20.

Brown, Sfc. Michael. "The Eyes of Battle." *Soldiers*, February 1984, 24–25.

———. "Learning the Hard Way." *Soldiers*, February 1984, 14–19.

———. "Live from NTC—It's the War." *Soldiers*, February 1984, 26–28.

Cavazos, Gen. Richard E. "Readiness Goal Is Ability to Deploy on Short Notice." *Army*, October 1983, 40–48.

Chadwick, Frank A. "Designer's Notes." *Assault*. Bloomington, Ill.: Game Designers' Workshop, 1983.

———. "Soviet Organization." *Assault*. Bloomington, Ill.: Game Designers' Workshop, 1983.

Department of the Army. "Command and Staff." *Army*, October 1985, 329–42.

Gourley, Capt. Scott R., and Capt. David F. McDermott. "Evolution of the BMP." *Infantry*, November/December 1983, 19–22.

House, Maj. Randolph W. "NTC Live Fire: One Step Closer to Battlefield Realism." *Military Review*, March 1980, 68–70.

International Institute for Strategic Studies. "The Military Balance 1983/84." *Air Force*, December 1983, 69–139.

Johnston, Staff Sgt. Rico. "MILES." *Army Trainer*, Winter 81/82, 26–28.

Keays, Staff Sgt. Ann. "National Training Center." *Army Trainer*, Winter 81/82, 5–9.

Keays, Staff Sgt. Ann, and Staff Sgt. Rico Johnston. "REFORGER." *Army Trainer*, Winter 81/82, 34–39.

Meyer, Gen. Edward C. "Time of Transition; Focus on Quality." *Army*, October 1982, 18–24.

Otis, Gen. Glenn K. "The Enormous Responsibility of Preventing World War III." *Army*, October 1983, 80–90.

Rodriguez, Capt. Frank E. "Continued Observations on the National Training Center (NTC)." *Red Thrust Star*, April/June 1983, 5–12.

Simpkin, Brig. Richard E. "When the Squad Dismounts." *Infantry*, November/December 1983, 15–18.

Steiner, Maj. Charles R. "Thunder in the Desert." *Armor*, May/June 1982, 12–18.

Train, John. "With Our Forces in West Germany." *The American Spectator*, vol. 16, no. 2 (February 1983): 16–18.

Interviews

Clarahan, 1st Lt. James P., interview, 18 November 1982.

Finley, Capt. Jack, interview, 20 October 1982.

Morin, 1st Lt. Frank, interview, 4 June 1983.

Mornston, 1st Lt. Harry E., interview, 8 April 1983.

Newton, 1st Lt. Ralph G., interview, 16 July 1983.

Norman, Capt. Raymond K., interview, 11 April 1983.

Ramsey, 1st Lt. John A., interview, 20 January 1984.

Sayers, 1st Lt. Timothy, interview, 14 November 1982.

Schwendeman, 1st Lt. Kenneth, interview, 13 February 1984.

Index

295

About The Author

Daniel Bolger is a Regular Army officer, currently stationed in Korea. A graduate of the army's prestigious Command and General Staff College, he holds an M.A. in Russian History and a Ph.D. in International Military History from the University of Chicago and was previously on the faculty of the United States Military Academy at West Point. In addition to *Dragons at War*, Bolger is the author of *Americans at War 1975–1986: An Era of Violent Peace* and of the novel *A Feast of Bones*.